D1218531

# THE WAR ON TERROR
# AND THE LAWS OF WAR

# THE WAR ON TERROR AND THE LAWS OF WAR

## A MILTARY PERSPECTIVE

Michael W. Lewis

OXFORD

UNIVERSITY PRESS

# OXFORD
## UNIVERSITY PRESS

*Oxford University Press, Inc., publishes works that further Oxford University's
objective of excellence in research, scholarship, and education.*

### Note to Readers:

This publication is designed to provide accurate and authoritative information in regard to the
subject matter covered. It is based upon sources believed to be accurate and reliable and is intended
to be current as of the time it was written. It is sold with the understanding that the publisher is not
engaged in rendering legal, accounting, or other professional services. If legal advice or other expert
assistance is required, the services of a competent professional person should be sought. Also, to
confirm that the information has not been affected or changed by recent developments, traditional
legal research techniques should be used, including checking primary sources where appropriate.

*(Based on the Declaration of Principles jointly adopted by a Committee of the
American Bar Association and a Committee of Publishers and Associations.)*

You may order this or any other Oxford University Press publication
by visiting the Oxford University Press website at www.oup.com

# TABLE OF CONTENTS

# FOREWORD

Major General Charles J. Dunlap, Jr.
United States Air Force
April 2009
Washington, DC

Historians like to speak of revolutions in military affairs to describe the dramatic evolutions in warfare that technology and other developments produce at various points in warfare. While the remarkable rise in the prominence of law in war in recent years might not be quite as impressive as, say, the invention of gunpowder on armed conflict, the effect of law in twenty-first century conflicts is nevertheless quite extraordinary, a reality understood by the military profession. An iconic example of this recognition came from General James L. Jones, USMC, then the commander of NATO, and now in retirement heading the U.S.'s National Security Council. In 2003, he remarked that going to war was once a task focused on leading combat forces, but now "you have to have a lawyer or a dozen. It's become very legalistic and very complex."[1]

Why is this? As I have noted for many years, the reasons are manifold. The rise of globalized commerce with its insistence on legally binding arrangements—not to mention an ever-expanding number of international legal forums to resolve disputes—all serve to normalize law as a feature in international affairs to an unprecedented degree. Add to this the emergence of information technologies that enable the near instantaneous communication around the world of incidents that raise legal issues and it is readily apparent how law gets the attention it does these days. Indeed, that such developments infuse law into almost every aspect of modern war, much as it has penetrated virtually every other aspect of contemporary life, is hardly surprising.

Clearly, evaluating the propriety of twenty-first century military operations requires a sophisticated understanding of the law of war, an understanding made all the more complicated by the rise of non-state actors who operate transnationally and use terrorism as their principal weapon. Of course, there are a significant number of experts skilled in the history

---

1    Lyric Wallwork Winik, *A Marine's Toughest Mission (Gen. James L. Jones)*, PARADE MAG., Jan. 19, 2003, *available at* http://www.parade.com/articles/editions/2003/edition_01-19-2003/General_Jones.

of the development and delineation of the meaning of the law of war. Moreover, a growing body of scholarship seeks to discuss the conceptual application of the law of war to terrorists in various situations.

However, in practice, the law of war—like other legal disciplines—much depends upon the ability to appreciate the factual context in which the law must operate. For the practitioner, understanding the "facts" of military operations can be quite daunting. The military "client" is engaged in a "business," so to speak, that is fundamentally unlike most human endeavors. It involves extraordinarily intricate and unique technologies, as well as complex psychological interactions all designed, in the final analysis, to facilitate—when necessary and unavoidable—the melancholy task of killing other human beings.

The volume you are holding aims to bring to the discussion the perspective of lawyers who have served in what the Supreme Court in *Parker v. Levy*[2] calls the "specialized society separate from civilian society" which is the armed forces. By virtue of their military service in this "specialized society," these attorneys bring a unique perspective to the law of war, questions that bedevil decision-makers at every level attempting to deal with the threat of terrorism. This mindset is derived not only from the academic exploration of the law, but perhaps more importantly from years spent developing expertise in the context in which the law is intended to apply. This context, I submit, is an essential component in developing a genuine appreciation for the purpose and objectives of the law, which in turn is essential to critically analyzing the role of this law in the emerging realities of warfare. In short, the collective experience of these authors in the art of war—understanding the weapons, tactics, and, especially, the psychology of warriors on a non-traditional battlefield—enables the authors to provide an often overlooked perspective on these increasingly complex and important legal issues.

The linkage of a technical understanding of the law of war with the actual practice of war is vital. I can well recall a symposium of highly regarded civilian international lawyers convened in the aftermath of the Kosovo conflict. Almost to a person, these law-of-war experts were critical of what they understood to be the American practice of conducting air operations at altitudes no lower than 15,000 feet. They were convinced that what they thought was "high-altitude" bombing was the cause of what they took to be excessive civilian casualties.

---

2    Parker v. Levy, 417 U.S. 733, 744 (1974).

What is striking is that for all their legal erudition, virtually none of these lawyers had a real understanding of the technology of modern warplanes. They simply did not comprehend that lower altitude strikes were typically less precise than those conducted at altitudes that optimized sophisticated targeting equipment. In addition, they did not appreciate that lower altitudes not only unnecessarily increased risk to the pilot, but also to those on the ground who could find themselves in the path of a 20-ton fuel and weapons-laden aircraft shot out of the air to tumble out of control into whatever happened to be in its way.

This is not to suggest that only those with military service should advise the military and the civilian authorities on law of war matters. On the contrary, the explosion of interest in this field has produced a rich landscape of critically important scholarship, debate, and commentary. However, it has and will remain critically important that those who wade into these murky waters remain cognizant of the reality that their conclusions will ultimately inform the development of law that must be applied by belligerents. Because of this, a keen understanding of how the law of war is implemented by warfighters in today's battles against terrorists and extremists, a heretofore underrepresented viewpoint in the contemporary scholarly landscape, can only contribute to the advancement of the law. This book seeks to provide a military perspective on the difficult task of ensuring adherence to the law under circumstances hardly imaginable only a decade ago.

The practical impact of law on the war on terror is also well understood today. No observer of the post-9/11 era fails to recognize that the most serious setbacks for the American military involve not an adversary's battlefield successes, but rather alleged violations of the law by the U.S.'s own forces. But this was no revelation for the profession of arms. For members of the American military profession who came of age in the era between Vietnam and September 11, the significance of legal legitimacy at the strategic, operational, and tactical levels had become virtually axiomatic. These professionals understood what Professors Michael Reisman and Chris T. Antoniou rightly pointed out in their 1994 book, *Law of War*—that popular modern democracies will not support military operations "no matter how worthy the political objective, if people believe that the war is being conducted in an unfair, inhumane, or iniquitous way."[3] Professor William G. Eckhardt articulated a similar view in terms

---

3    W. Michael Reisman and Chris T. Antoniou, THE LAWS OF WAR xxiv (1994) (emphasis added).

intuitive to the military professional: The legality and morality of military operations are, in strategic terms, a "center of gravity" for the U.S. and other nations who embrace the rule of law.

The first line of defense of such a center of gravity is to ensure that one's own forces follow the law, and to be able to prove such observance. And the first "fighting position" in that line of defense is to ensure that a pragmatic understanding of when, why, and how the law applies to combat operations—an understanding informed by the realities of military operations—drives the evolution of the law.

*The War on Terror and the Laws of War: A Military Perspective* is especially timely and apt because it squarely addresses some of the thorniest issues of recent years. While it will be a prized refresher for many military practitioners, its greatest value may be as a source for those without a military background who may nevertheless wish to inform their analysis with a complete range of views. Because it does not shrink from tackling the toughest topics, some assertions in this book may generate strong dissents from the reader (including the reader in uniform). Yet as everyone steeped in the advocacy system appreciates, truth emerges from the reasoned analysis of conflicting views well presented and skillfully articulated. This book gives you just such a presentation of the military perspective.

# ACKNOWLEDGMENT

The authors would like to first collectively acknowledge all the great leaders who mentored and shaped them as officers and legal professionals. Our collective experiences serving the United States as members of the armed forces—although in often divergent circumstances—provided a common bond that made working together on this project a genuine pleasure. Our service has also offered us the opportunity to consider these complex issues through an important and in many ways unique lens.

We would each also like to thank our research assistants. Without these devoted and exceptional students, this project could never have come to fruition as efficiently as it did. These students are: from South Texas College of Law, Sarah Khalifa and Lindsay Kauffman, from New England School of Law, Jillian Cavanaugh and from Ohio Northern College of Law, Kyle Bickford.

We would also like to thank Col. Gary Brown, USAF and Capt. Jesse Greene, USA for their comments on the Battlefield Perspectives chapter.

Finally, we would like to thank the editors at Oxford University Press. The polish they put on our work will undoubtedly make the experience of reading these pages much more pleasant.

# INTRODUCTION

By Geoffrey S. Corn

This book is about commitment, commitment to a tenet that has animated the development of the laws and customs of war since their inception centuries ago. That tenet is that the authority of war must be tempered by limitations that mitigate the suffering inevitably caused by war. Many might consider this premise intuitive. Certainly from the warrior perspective—the original source of the laws of war—conflict without regulation is almost oxymoronic, for it is through regulation that the moral legitimacy of that endeavor is preserved. But as will be revealed in the chapters that follow, the intersection of a post September 11 decision to characterize the struggle against transnational terrorism as "armed conflict" with the law-triggering paradigm that evolved from the ashes of the Second World War challenged this tenet as never before.

On September 10, 2001, virtually every law of war expert in the world, including the members of the U.S. military legal profession—a profession that had grown to unprecedented strength and had made expertise in the law related to the planning and execution of military operations a core competency—assumed that the laws of war could apply only in two distinct situations. The first was inter-state warfare, where the armed forces of two opposing states engaged with each other to accomplish a national purpose. The second was intra-state conflict, in which the armed forces of a state battled against an internal opposition group that had attained military-type capabilities. These two law-triggering situations were understood through the ubiquitous characterization derived from common articles 2 and 3 of the four Geneva Conventions of 1949: the common article 2, international (inter-state) armed conflict; and the common article 3, non-international (intra-sate) armed conflict. This two-part paradigm was so pervasive that it formed the foundation of law-of-war education for an entire generation of military lawyers.

But these lawyers had also learned first-hand the operational limits of this paradigm. This education began well before the events of September 11, originating with the Vietnam conflict. In response to the uncertainty associated with determining the locus within this law-triggering spectrum of operational decisions related to that conflict, the Department of Defense adopted what became its bedrock law of war mandate: that U.S. forces would comply with the principles of the law of war during any military operation no matter how that operation was legally characterized. This policy was intended to ensure that operational planning and execution would be based on the well-established principles of the law most suited for such a purpose: the laws of war. The policy was also intended to provide military commanders and the staffs that advised them essential predictability by providing a consistent standard of operational regulation, and by ensuring that every soldier, marine, sailor, and airman was trained to one standard of operational conduct.

This policy "gap filler" proved remarkably effective during the years between Vietnam and September 11 and was particularly essential during the era of "peace operations" that dominated the 1990s. During that era, U.S. armed forces conducted countless military operations that by definition failed to trigger the laws of war, by then referred to as the law of armed conflict (LOAC). Yet these operations nonetheless necessitated an operational, regulatory framework. Thus, LOAC principles guided operational decision-making for detention in Kosovo, medical treatment obligations in Haiti, the use of combat power in Bosnia, and detainee interrogations in Somalia.

A somewhat ironic, second-order consequence of this policy extension of the law was that it inhibited any consideration of whether these principles should be applicable in such third-category situations not just as a matter of policy, but as a matter of law. When the U.S. initiated military action against al Qaeda in response to the terror attacks of September 11, the limits of this policy mandate were quickly exposed, and military lawyers throughout the Department of Defense were finally forced to contemplate this long-overlooked issue. This was the result of a simple reality: the United States government had invoked the power of war to address the challenge of transnational terrorism. Thus, the United States has and continues to consider the military component of the struggle against transnational terrorism as an "armed conflict." While all the authors acknowledge that this determination was and remains controversial, it is also indisputable. As a result, U.S. military combat power was unleashed against this non-state transnational enemy. Thus, military legal advisors confronted a genuine anomaly: military operations designated by the nation as "war" or "armed conflict" that failed to fit neatly within the accepted common article 2 or 3 law-triggering paradigm.

The initial response to this anomaly seemed logical: apply LOAC principles in accordance with Department of Defense policy. This method had provided an effective response to similar uncertainty in the past, and rendered the uncertainty as to whether the LOAC was applicable as a matter of law essentially transparent at the operational level. However, almost as soon as these military operations began, another reality entered into the equation that exposed the limits of policy: new directives and orders from the Department of Defense that essentially contradicted this "principled" approach to operational regulation. The most notorious example of this impacted the status and treatment of individuals captured during this struggle. The operational assumption that all such individuals would be treated "as if" they were prisoners of war was quickly overridden by senior Executive branch policy makers who imposed a new category of status and treatment: the unlawful enemy combatant.

As the full impact of this GWOT legal paradigm slowly emerged in the weeks and months following September 11, it became increasingly clear that the U.S. was essentially exploiting the common article 2/3 law-triggering paradigm to expose a gap in LOAC application. This gap existed in the interstitial realm between inter-state conflict and "internationalized" conflict between a state and a non-state entity, what we will refer to in the following chapters as "transnational" armed conflict. Relying on the inter-state/internal interpretation of the common article 2/3 law-triggering paradigm, high-level legal advisors in the Bush administration asserted (not illegitimately) that these treaties had never been intended to apply to extraterritorial armed conflict against a non-state enemy. However, what these advisors failed to consider was the critical subsequent level of analysis for operational legal advisors: does this interpretation of treaty-based obligations necessitate and justify the conclusion that no law applies to regulate this armed conflict?

How this issue was ultimately tackled will be addressed in subsequent chapters. These chapters will illustrate how military legal advisors realized from the very outset of this process that such a premise is ultimately incompatible with the historic purpose of the law of war: the balance of power and restraint. This realization, coupled with the reality that they could no longer avail themselves of the longstanding practice of policy-based LOAC compliance, forced them to finally address the question of whether the common article 2/3 law-triggering paradigm was exclusive, or whether an underlying core of customary principles applies to any military operation characterized by the nation as armed conflict.

The United States Supreme Court mooted the need to analyze this question as it relates to the treatment of detainees when it ruled in *Hamdan v. Rumsfeld* that common article 3 applied in "contradistinction" to common article 2. While the treaty interpretation element of this ruling is certainly susceptible to criticism, it nonetheless constitutes a profound rejection of the "authority without obligation" theory that gripped the Bush administration. *Hamdan* is also an equally profound endorsement of the logic that drove Department of Defense policy for decades: that the invocation of LOAC authority requires acknowledgment of the balancing obligations derived from the same source of law.

How this core logic and spirit of the law of war have influenced operational decisions related to all aspects of the military response to the threat of transnational terror is ultimately the story that will play out in the following chapters. Each chapter will address a specific operational issue and illustrate how resolution of that issue will serve a commitment to preserving this balance between authority and obligation. Some chapters will go further, explaining why the legal principles alone are insufficient to address the challenges of this conflict, or how the law needs to be advanced to deal with continuing uncertainty. But all the book's chapters share a common thread: That legitimate, disciplined, and credible military operations cannot occur in the absence of an operational regulatory framework derived from the laws of war. This premise is not only central to the book itself, but is also the common perspective of each of the authors, all of whom share experience as both scholars and warriors.

A brief note on what this book is not about is in order. This book is not a critique of the theory that a nation can be engaged in an armed conflict with a transnational non-state enemy. All of the authors recognize the controversy associated with this proposition, and many scholars and legal experts reject the premise outright. However, because this book is focused on the operational resolution of issues related to the application of military power by the United States, it begins with the premise that because the United States has characterized the struggle against terror as an armed conflict—a characterization reflected in the decisions of all three branches of our government—there is no doubt that the United States has and will continue to invoke the law of war as a source of authority for military operations to destroy, disable, capture, and incapacitate terrorist enemies. As a result, the book's focus will be on how operational decisions ensure that the balance referred to above is preserved in this tremendously complex operational and legal environment.

# CHAPTER 1

# WHAT LAW APPLIES TO THE WAR ON TERROR?

By Geoffrey S. Corn[†]

On September 11, 2001, the legal framework for the regulation of armed conflict, the framework that guided military lawyers and that influenced decisions made in reliance on their advice, was thrown into disarray.[1] Until that day of infamy, these lawyers applied an "either/or" law-triggering paradigm that dictated when the law of armed conflict (LOAC)[2] applied

---

[†] Associate Professor of Law at South Texas College of Law in Houston Texas, where he has been on the faculty since 2005. He is a graduate of Hartwick College and the U.S. Army Command and General Staff College, and the U.S. Army Officer Candidate School. He earned his J.D., *highest honors* at George Washington University and his LL.M., *distinguished graduate*, at the Judge Advocate General's School. Prior to joining the faculty, Professor Corn served in the U.S. Army for 21 years, retiring as a Lieutenant Colonel in the Judge Advocate General's Corps. He earned his commission in 1984 from Officer Candidate School and served five years as a tactical intelligence officer before attending law school and joining the JAG Corps. As a Judge Advocate, Professor Corn's experience focused primarily on criminal and international law, including service as a supervisory defense counsel for the Western United States; Chief of International Law for U.S. Army Europe; and Professor of International and National Security Law at the U.S. Army Judge Advocate General's School, and Chief Prosecutor for the 101st Airborne Division.

[1] Adam Roberts, *Counter-Terrorism, Armed Force and the Laws of War,* Survival (quarterly journal of IISS, London), vol. 44, no. 1, (Spring 2002), at 7.

[2] The term "law of armed conflict," "laws of war," or "law of war" will be used throughout the book to refer to the law governing the conduct of belligerents engaged in armed conflict. This term, while certainly less in favor than "humanitarian law," is the term used in official Department of Defense Doctrine. *See* U.S. Dep't of Defense, Dir. 2311.01 E, DoD Law of War Program, (9 May 2006); *see also* Chairman, Joint Chiefs of Staff, Instr. 5810.01 B, Implementation of the DOD Laws of War Program (25 Mar. 2002). The following excerpt demonstrates the continuing significance of retaining this characterization in lieu of the more popular "humanitarian" law:

> In this Article, I have used the term "laws of war" referring to those streams of international law, especially the various Hague and Geneva Conventions, intended to apply in armed conflicts. To some, the term "laws of war" is old-fashioned. However, its continued use has merits. It accurately reflects the well-established Latin phrase for the subject of this inquiry, *jus in bello,* and it is brief and easily understood. It has two modern equivalents, both of which are longer. One of these, the "law applicable in armed conflicts" is unexceptionable,

to U.S. operations: either those operations involved hostilities against the armed forces of another State so as to qualify as international armed conflicts; or they involved hostilities against insurgent forces within a State on whose behalf the United States had intervened, thereby falling into the alternative category of internal armed conflict.[3] Derived from Common Articles 2 and 3 of the Fourth Geneva Convention (1949), this law-triggering paradigm was a genuine article of faith for U.S. military lawyers trained in the LOAC at their respective introductory and advanced military law courses.

These lawyers and the forces they supported were not, however, unfamiliar with military operations that fell outside inter/intra-state armed conflict paradigms. Such operations, they were taught, were regulated by U.S. military policy that dictated compliance with LOAC principles even if those principles did not apply as a matter of law.[4] These principles

---

but adds little. The other, "international humanitarian law" (IHL), often with the suffix "applicable in armed conflicts," has become the accepted term in most diplomatic and UN frameworks. *However, it has the defect that it seems to suggest that humanitarianism rather than professional standards is the main foundation on which the law is built, and thus invites to a degree of criticism from academics, warriors, and others who subscribe to a realist view of international relations.*

*Adam, Roberts, The Laws of War: Problems of Implementation in Contemporary Conflicts,* 6 Duke J. Comp. & Int'l. L. 11,14 (1995) (emphasis added).

3    *See* Int'l & Operational Law Dept, The Judge Advocate General's Legal Center & School, The Law of War Deskbook, at Chapter 3 (2000); *see also* International Committee of the Red Cross, *What is International Humanitarian Law,* Advisory Service on International Humanitarian Law, (07/2004), *available at* http://www.icrc. orO/web/enz./siteenzO.nsf/iwpList104/707D6551B17F0910C1256B66005B30B3. This fact sheet clearly reflects the international/internal evolution of the triggering paradigm:

   International humanitarian law distinguishes between international and non-international armed conflict.

   **International armed conflicts** are those in which at least two States are involved. They are subject to a wide range of rules, including those set out in the four Geneva Conventions and Additional Protocol I.

   **Non-international armed conflicts** are those restricted to the territory of a single State, involving either regular armed forces fighting groups of armed dissidents, or armed groups fighting each other. A more limited range of rules apply to internal armed conflicts and are laid down in Article 3 common to the four Geneva Conventions as well as in Additional Protocol II.

   *Id.*

4    *See* Geoffrey S. Corn, *Snipers in the Minaret—What is the Rule? The Law of War and the Protection of Cultural Property: A Complex Equation,* The Army Lawyer,

---

**THE WAR ON TERROR AND THE LAWS OF WAR**

included, at a minimum, military necessity, distinction, proportionality, and humanity. From Panama in 1989 to Kosovo in 2000, this policy-based LOAC application proved remarkably effective. As a result, U.S. forces operated under the policy-driven assumption that they would follow these fundamental LOAC principles during all their operational missions, regardless of technical legal characterization. Because of this, the operational impact of technical LOAC applicability was minimal because commanders at that level were expected to comply with the LOAC as the "default" standard.[5] Based on this methodology, when U.S. forces first "hit the ground" in Afghanistan, operational legal advisors, like their predecessors in places like Panama and Somalia, followed this "default" approach and advised their commanders to comply with the LOAC as if they were involved in an international armed conflict.[6]

Unlike prior operations, however, the limits of this policy-based LOAC application were quickly exposed when U.S. forces began to capture and detain opposition fighters. Almost immediately, commanders were directed to halt the practice of treating captured personnel "as if" they were prisoners of war because a new "status" had been adopted for these detainees: "unlawful enemy combatant."[7] This characterization was created to denote a detained enemy operative who did not qualify for status as a prisoner of war, and who would therefore not be entitled to claim the benefit of LOAC protections. Relocation to a newly established high

---

28 (July 2005) (discussing policy-based application of law of armed conflict principles in accordance with Department of Defense Directives).

5    Chairman, Joint Chiefs of Staff Instruction 3121.01B, Standing Rules of Engagement/ Standing Rules for the Use of Force for U.S. Forces, encl. A, para. 1d (13 June 2005); *see also* Corn, *Snipers in the Minaret—What is the Rule?*

6    Center for Law and Military Operations After Action Review of Operation Enduring Freedom (from 2005); *see generally* CRS Report for Congress, *Terrorism and the Laws of War: Trying Terrorists as War Criminals before War Commissions*, Order Code RL31191, (December 11, 2001) (analyzing whether the attacks of September 11, 2001 triggered the law of war).

7    *See* Convention (III) Relative to the Treatment of Prisoners of War, Aug. 12, 1949, 6 U.S.T. 3316, 75 U.N.T.S. 135, *reprinted in* Dietrich Schindler & Jiri Toman, The Laws of Armed Conflicts, 430–31 (2d ed. 1981) which outlines the requirements to be considered a prisoner of war a status reserved for lawful combatants. *See also* Geoffrey S. Corn and Eric Talbot Jensen, *Untying the Gordian Knot: A Proposal for Determining Applicability of the Laws of War to the War on Terror*, (*available at* http://ssrn.com/abstract=1083849), at 16 (Sept. 7, 2008).

security detention facility in Guantanamo Bay, Cuba thus became a permissible option.[8]

In the months and years to follow its first utilization, this term became a lightning rod for U.S. policies related to the war on terror. However, for purposes of this chapter, the significance of this new detainee characterization is the legal theory upon which it was founded. A new legal position began to emerge: the authority of the LOAC would be asserted to provide the legal basis for the execution of military operations against al Qaeda—an entity considered to be engaged in an armed conflict with the United States; however, unlike their Taliban counterparts who could at least in theory claim the protections of the LOAC (because they were captured in the context of what the United States ultimately conceded was an inter-state armed conflict), al Qaeda captives were afforded no such claim to LOAC protections because the conflict they engaged in defied classification under either Common Article 2 or 3.[9]

The incongruity of this theory was readily apparent: the United States was engaged in an armed conflict that provided the authority to engage, destroy, capture, and detain the newly defined enemy; however, it was an armed conflict that did not fit into the traditional Common Article 2/3 "either/or" law-triggering paradigm, the LOAC did not apply to constrain or regulate U.S. operations. With regard to execution of combat operations, this incongruity had little impact due to the military practice of following LOAC principles during all operations as a matter of policy. However, as the U.S. began to capture and detain alleged terrorist operatives, it became quickly apparent that the inapplicability of LOAC

---

8   *See* Human Rights Watch, United Nations Finds that U.S. Has Failed to Comply with International Obligations at Guantanamo Detention Center, *available at* http://hrw.or.eienglish/docs/2006/02/16lusdorn12833.htni (last accessed August 30, 2006).

9   Geoffrey S. Corn and Eric Talbot Jensen, *Untying the Gordian Knot: A Proposal for Determining Applicability of the Laws of War to the War on Terror*, (*available at* http://ssrn.com/abstract=1083849), at 17 (Sept. 7, 2008); *see* Alberto R. Gonzales, Memorandum for the President, Subject: Decision re Application of the Geneva Convention on Prisoners of War to the Conflict with Al Qaeda and the Taliban (Jan. 25, 2002), *available at* http://www.msnbc.msn.com/id/4999148/site/newsweek/ (articulating the basis for the conclusion that al Qaeda detainees did not fall under either law triggered by Common Article 2 nor the humane treatment obligation of Common Article 3).

obligations would be a key component to the development of detainee treatment and interrogation policies.[10]

The law-triggering paradigm relied upon by the United States to assert the inapplicability of LOAC obligations to captured and detained al Qaeda operatives was based on an interpretation of Common Articles 2 and 3 of the Geneva Conventions. Based on these law-triggering provisions, President Bush determined that the LOAC applied to two, and only two, situations. The first, based on Common Article 2's language that "the present Convention shall apply to all cases of declared war or of any other armed conflict which may arise between two or more of the High Contracting Parties, even if the state of war is not recognized by one of them,"[11] required hostilities between the armed forces of two States (High Contracting Parties). The second, based on Common Article 3's language "armed conflict not of an international character occurring in the territory of one of the High Contracting Parties"[12], while encompassing armed conflict with non-state entities was limited to conflicts contained within the territory of a State, or intra-state armed conflicts. Based on this interpretation of these law-triggering provisions, this enemy could not claim the protective benefit of the LOAC to constrain U.S. conduct.[13] Exacerbating the impact of this incongruity was that, unlike prior operations, this "seam" in LOAC coverage would no longer be filled by a policy-based application of LOAC principles. Instead, that seam would be exploited to deny application of those principles. Thus, this first salvo in the legal drama that would define the

---

10    See Jay S. Bybee, Memorandum for Alberto Gonzales, Counsel to the President, and William J. Haynes II, General Counsel of the DoD (Jan. 22, 2002), *available at* http://news.findlaw.com/hdocs/-docs/doj/bybee I2202mem.pdf.

11    Geneva Convention for the Amelioration of the Condition of the Wounded and Sick in Armed Forces in the Field, August 12, 1949, T.I.A.S. 3362, at art. 2.

12    Geneva Convention for the Amelioration of the Condition of the Wounded and Sick in Armed Forces in the Field, August 12, 1949, T.I.A.S. 3362, at art. 3.

13    See Jay S. Bybee, Memorandum for Alberto R. Gonzales, Counsel to the President, and William J. Haynes II, General Counsel of the DoD (Jan. 22, 2002), *available at* http://news.findlaw.com/hdocs/-docs/doj/bybee12202mem.pdf; *see also* Alberto R. Gonzales, Memorandum for the President, Subject: Decision re Application of the Geneva Convention on Prisoners of War to the Conflict with Al Qaeda and the Taliban (Jan. 25, 2002), *available at* http://www.msnbc.msn.com/id/4999148/site/newsweek/; Donald Rumsfeld, Memorandum for the Chairman of the Joint Chiefs of Staff, Subject: Status of the Taliban and Al Qaida, [sic] (Jan. 19, 2002), *available at* http://news.findlaw.com/hdocs/docs/dod/11902mem.pdf.

GWOT (Global War on Terrorism) revealed a simple truth: *what national policy makers giveth, national policy makers can taketh away.*

The first component of this emerging equation of inconsistency was quickly revealed. President Bush characterized the terror strike against the United States as an "armed attack,"[14] and he and the Congress of the United States almost immediately invoked the war powers of the nation to respond to the threat presented by al Qaeda, a non-state entity operating throughout the world.[15] This characterization was embraced not only by the United Nations Security Council,[16] but by the North Atlantic Treaty Organization[17] and others.[18] Since that time, the executive branch has struggled to articulate, and in many judicial challenges defend, how it could invoke the authorities of war without accepting the obligations of the law regulating war.[19] While judicial challenges would ultimately

---

14    *See* Mil. Or., Detention, Treatment, and Trial of Certain Non-Citizens in the War against Terrorism, 66 Fed. Reg. 57833 (Nov. 13, 2001).

15    *See* Council on Foreign Relations, *Backgrounder* (discussing origins, structure, and goals of al Qaeda), *available at* http://www.cfr.org/publication/9126/ (last visited December 5, 2007).

16    *See* UNSCR 1368, 1373.

17    *See* Press Release, NATO, Statement by the North Atlantic Council (Sept. 12, 2001) *available at* www.nato.int/docu/pr/2003/p01–124e.htm.

18    *See* 96 AJIL 905, 909 (2002).

19    *See* Jay S. Bybee, Memorandum for Alberto R. Gonzales, Counsel to the President, and William J. Haynes II, General Counsel of the DoD (Jan. 22, 2002), *available at* http://news.findlaw.com/hdocs/-docs/doj/bybee12202mem.pdf; *see also* Alberto R. Gonzales, Memorandum for the President, Subject: Decision re Application of the Geneva Convention on Prisoners of War to the Conflict with Al Qaeda and the Taliban (Jan. 25, 2002), *available at* http://www.msnbc.msn.com/id/4999148/site/newsweek/; Donald Rumsfeld, Memorandum for the Chairman of the Joint Chiefs of Staff, Subject: Status of the Taliban and Al Qaida, [sic] (Jan. 19, 2002), *available at* http://news.findlaw.com/hdocs/docs/dod/11902mem.pdf. In a message dated January 21, 2002, the Chairman notified combatant commanders of the Secretary of Defense's determination. Message from the Chairman of the Joint Chiefs of Staff, Subject: SECDEF Memo to CJCS Regarding the Status of Taliban and Al Qaida [sic] (Jan. 22, 2002), *available at* http://news.findlaw.com/hdocs/docs/dod/12202mem.pdf; President Bush Memorandum of February 7, 2002, Subject: Humane Treatment of al Qaeda and Taliban Detainees, http://www.justicescholars.org/pegc/archive/White_House/bush_memo_20020207_ed.pdf#search=%22bush%20february%207%20memo%20on%20humane%20treatment%20of%20al%20qaeda%22 (announcing the President's determination that although the conflict against Afghanistan triggered the Geneva Conventions, captured Taliban forces were not entitled to prisoner of war status because they

---

mitigate the extremity of this incongruity, the basic premise of an extra-territorial armed conflict against a non-state enemy, or "transnational" armed conflict, remains as robust today as it was when it first emerged.

The second component of this incongruity gradually exposed by U.S. legal decisions related to the treatment of al Qaeda operatives captured in Afghanistan and later in other locations. By exploiting an asserted seam created by the Common Article 2/3 law-triggering paradigm, the Bush Administration developed what can only be understood as a legal black hole. While captured al Qaeda operatives would be treated humanely as a matter of policy, they could claim no such protection as a matter of law.[20]

The ultimate irony inherent in this invocation of the proverbial "sweet without the bitter" is how its architects relied on the Geneva Conventions—treaties intended to maximize applicability of the LOAC and eliminate the definitional manipulation that creates an "authority without obligation" paradigm. By focusing on the traditionally under-stood scope of LOAC derived from the law-triggering provisions of those treaties, Common Article 2 for inter-state armed conflicts[21] and

---

failed to meet the implied requirements imposed by the Convention on members of the regular armed forces). This determination endorsed the analysis provided by the Office of Legal Counsel of the Department of Justice to the General Counsel of the Department of Defense that reflected a restrictive interpretation of legal applicability of the laws of war. *See* Department of Justice Office of Legal Counsel to the President and the General Counsel for the Department of Defense on the applicability of the Geneva Conventions to individuals detained by U.S. forces during military operations. *See* United States Department of Justice Office of Legal Counsel Memorandum of January 22, 2002, Memorandum for Alberto R. Gonzales, Counsel to the President, and William J. Haynes II, General Counsel for the Department of Defense, *Re: Application of Treaties and Laws to al Qaeda and Taliban Detainees.*

20   *See* President Bush Memorandum of February 7, 2002, Subject: Humane Treatment of Al Qaeda and Taliban Detainees, http://www.justicescholars.org/eegc/archivefWhiteHouse/bush memo 20020207 ed.pdf#search%22bush%20february%207%20memo%20on%20humane%20treatment%20of%20al%20qaeda%22.

21   Geoffrey S. Corn, *Hamdan, Lebanon, and the Need to Recognize a Hybrid Category of Armed Conflict*, 40 Vand. J. Transnat'l L. 295 (2007) (Because there is no defined meaning of "international" or "non-international" in Common Articles 2 or 3, uncertainty has developed in relation to application of this prong of the legal trigger. As a result, reliance on the ICRC Commentary has resulted in operative definition of these terms. With regard to international armed conflict, the Commentary makes the existence of a "dispute between states" the dispositive consideration);

Common Article 3 for non-state armed conflicts,[22] the legal advisors for the Department of Justice charged with the responsibility to interpret the LOAC on behalf of the President exploited this "either/or" law-triggering paradigm: either the conflict was inter-state, thereby triggering the full

---

> Geneva Convention for the Amelioration of the Condition of the Wounded and Sick in Armed Forces in the Field, August 12, 1949, T.I.A.S. 3362, at art. 2 [hereinafter GWS]; Geneva Convention for the Amelioration of the Condition of the Wounded, Sick, and Shipwrecked Members at Sea, August 12, 1949, T.I.A.S. 3363, at art. 2 [hereinafter GWS Sea]; Geneva Convention Relative to the Treatment of Prisoners of War, August 12, 1949, T.I.A.S. 3364, at art. 2 [hereinafter GPW]; Geneva Convention Relative to the Treatment of Civilians in Time of War, August 12, 1949, T.I.A.S. 3365, at art. 2 [hereinafter GC]. Each of these Conventions includes the following identical article:
>
>> In addition to the provisions which shall be implemented in peacetime, the present Convention shall apply to all cases of declared war or of any other armed conflict which may arise between two or more of the High Contracting Parties, even if the state of war is not recognized by one of them. The Convention shall also apply to all cases of partial or total occupation of the territory of a High Contracting Party, even if the said occupation meets with no armed resistance.
>
> *Id.*
>
> *See* Commentary, Convention (I) for the Amelioration of the Condition of the Wounded and Sick in Armed Forces in the Field. Geneva, 12 August 1949 (Jean S. Pictet ed., 1960), at 19–23 [hereinafter the ICRC Commentary]. A similar Commentary was published for each of the four Geneva Conventions. However, because Articles 2 and 3 are identical—or common—to each Convention, the Commentary for these articles is also identical in each of the four Commentaries.
>
> 22   *See* GWS *supra* note 17, at Art. 3; UK Ministry of Defense, *The Manual for the Law of Armed Conflict*, Oxford University Press (2004), at Para. 2.1; Geoffrey S. Corn, *Hamdan, Lebanon, and the Need to Recognize a Hybrid Category of Armed Conflict*, 40 Vand. J. Transnat'l L. 295 (2007) (However, because Article 3 responded primarily to the brutal civil wars that ravaged Spain, Russia, and other states during the years between the two world wars, the trigger for the for this baseline humanitarian provision came to be understood as conflicts that were primarily intra-state, or "internal armed conflicts." However irrespective of this historical context for the creation of Common Article 3, nowhere does the article expressly use "internal" as the indication of the type of armed conflict triggering its humanitarian mandate. Instead, Common Article 3 expressly indicates that its substantive protections are applicable to all "non-international" armed conflicts. Nonetheless, during the five-plus decades between 1949 and 2001, the term "non-international" evolved to become synonymous with internal. This most likely can be attributed to . . . the qualifying language of Common Article 3 indicating that it applies only to non-international armed conflicts occurring within the territory of a High Contracting Party. Although this "within the territory" qualifier became increasingly less meaningful . . . it is difficult to ignore the logical impact of this term in the context of 1949: that it limited the scope of application . . . to true intra-state conflicts).

         THE WAR ON TERROR AND THE LAWS OF WAR

corpus of the LOAC, or the conflict was non-international and confined to the territory of the responding State, thereby triggering the limited humanitarian protections of Common Article 3.[23]

The "war on terror"—or more precisely, the military component of the struggle against transnational terrorism—revealed the need to ensure a balance between LOAC authority invoked for the purpose of engaging and destroying transnational non-state enemies and baseline LOAC humanitarian obligations. Perhaps more importantly, military operations conducted against these non-state enemies exposed not only the limitations of the traditional "either/or" law-triggering paradigm, but also the risk associated with an inflexible adherence to this paradigm. By strictly limiting LOAC applicability to this paradigm, the underlying purpose of the law—ensuring regulation of hostilities—was undermined. The initial U.S. legal response to this struggle demonstrates that this purpose must not be subverted by a narrow focus on the geographic nature of a non-international armed conflict. In operational terms, the more pragmatic focus on the mere existence of armed conflict is essential to ensure that the implicit invocation of fundamental authorities derived from the LOAC—primarily the authority to kill an opponent as a measure of first resort and the authority to preventively detain a captured opponent—are balanced by legally mandated compliance with humanitarian principles of the law.[24]

## UNDERSTANDING THE STATUS QUO ANTE

This inter/intra-state law-triggering interpretation of Common Articles 2 and 3 was not novel. Indeed, at the time of the September 11 attacks, it was almost universally regarded as the exclusive paradigm for determining LOAC applicability, a reality reflected in the following excerpt

---

23    *See* Jay S. Bybee, Memorandum for Alberto Gonzales, Counsel to the President, and William J. Haynes II, General Counsel of the DoD (Jan. 22, 2002), *available at* http://news.findlaw.com/hdocs/-docs/doj/bybee I2202mem.pdf.

24    Corn and Jensen, *Untying the Gordian Knot: A Proposal for Determining Applicability of the Laws of War to the War on Terror,* where authors hold that

> If . . . the ultimate purpose of the drafters of the Geneva Conventions was to prevent "law avoidance" by developing *de facto* law triggers—a purpose consistent with the humanitarian foundation of the treaties—the myopic focus on the geographical nature of an armed conflict in the context of transnational counter-terror combat operations serves to frustrate that purpose.

*Id.*

from a 2004 presentation by the ICRC (International Committee of the Red Cross) Legal Advisor:

> Humanitarian law recognizes two categories of armed conflict—international and non-international. Generally, when a State resorts to force against another State (for example, when the "war on terror" involves such use-of-force, as in the recent U.S. and allied invasion of Afghanistan), the international law of international armed conflict applies. When the "war on terror" amounts to the use of armed force within a State, between that State and a rebel group, or between rebel groups within the State, the situation may amount to non-international armed conflict.... This excerpt is illustrative of the accepted interpretation of the situations that trigger application of the laws of war. According to this interpretation, there are only two possible characterizations for military activities conducted against transnational terrorist groups: international armed conflict (when the operations are conducted outside the territory of the State) or non-international armed conflict (limited to operations conducted within the territory of the State).

Unfortunately, this law-triggering paradigm did not account for the possibility that an extraterritorial combat operation launched by a State using regular armed forces against a non-state enemy could qualify as a law-triggering event. It is therefore apparent why this traditional understanding of LOAC applicability was thrown into disarray when the United States characterized its response to the 9/11 attacks as an "armed conflict" and employed the nation's combat capability to destroy or disable transnational terrorist operatives. The non-state character of the enemy nullified the requisite "dispute between states" element of international armed conflict within the meaning of Common Article 2; and the accepted "internal" understanding of non-international armed conflict—an understanding shared by virtually all scholars and practitioners prior to 9/11—nullified the non-international armed conflict trigger. Accordingly, this "transnational armed conflict"[25] fell into a regulatory gap produced ironically by LOAC provisions developed for the specific purpose of eliminating such definitional law-avoidance. Nonetheless, legal advisors in the Bush administration relied on the transnational scope of these operations and the nature of the enemy to assert that they fall outside the definition scope of Common Article 3.

---

25   *See* Geoffrey S. Corn, *Hamdan, Lebanon, and the Need to Recognize a Hybrid Category of Armed Conflict,* 40 Vand. J. Transnat'l L. 295 (2007) (defining transnational armed conflict as a term used to represent the extraterritorial application of military combat power by the regular armed forces of a state against a transnational non-state armed enemy).

Because the military response to transnational terrorism exposed how strict adherence to this "either/or" LOAC triggering paradigm generated an incongruity between authority and obligation, experts began to reconsider the long-held assumption that this inter/intra-state armed conflict paradigm sufficiently provided for LOAC applicability. As a result, a number of alternative theories began to emerge. These fell into four primary categories. The first was a stoic adherence to the existing interpretation of Common Articles 2 and 3, with an effort to fit transnational counter-terror combat operations into one of those categories (reflected in the ICRC excerpt above and by assertions that the 2006 Israeli operations against Hezbollah qualified as an international armed conflict between Israel and Lebanon[26]). The second theory was the "internationalized" Common Article 3 theory. This theory emphasized Common Article 3's plain language indicating that the article applied to "armed conflict not of an international character occurring in the territory of one of the High Contracting Parties." By emphasizing the "not of an international character" prong of this applicability language, proponents of this theory asserted that Common Article 3 should be interpreted to apply to any armed conflict that fell outside the scope of Common Article 2's inter-state law triggering requirement (an interpretation adopted by the Supreme Court in *Hamdan v. Rumsfeld*[27]). However, this theory ignored the "occurring in the territory of one of the High Contracting Parties" prong of Common Article 3. While it is true that as the result of the universal ratification of the Geneva Conventions the territory of any nation satisfies this qualifier, it seems clear that at the time of Common Article 3's adoption, this qualifier was intended to indicate that the article applied to armed conflicts between a State and *internal* dissident forces, not an armed conflict between States and non-state enemies operating internationally.

The third theory was the concept of "militarized" extraterritorial law enforcement, treating such operations not as armed conflicts but as law enforcement operations ostensibly regulated by the law of human rights. Finally, some parties asserted that a core of LOAC principles apply to all armed conflicts as a matter of custom, and that the law-triggering provisions of the Geneva Conventions operate to bring into force an additional layer of treaty-based regulation for certain types of armed

---

26  *See generally* Geoffrey S. Corn, *Hamdan, Lebanon, and the Need to Recognize a Hybrid Category of Armed Conflict*, 40 Vand. J. Transnat'l L. 295 (2007).

27  126 S. Ct. 2749, 2795–7 (2006).

conflicts.[28] Unlike the "internationalized" Common Article 3 theory, this latter theory (what I have labeled elsewhere as transnational armed conflict) requires that in addition to the humane treatment mandate of Common Article 3, other LOAC principles related to the execution of combat operations also apply to these armed conflicts.

While these theories of law applicability differ on the periphery, what they all share is a common appreciation that armed conflict must be regulated by more than just policy: it must be regulated by law. In this regard, each proposed theory represents a rebuke to the Bush administration's selective invocation of LOAC authority, a rebuke that was central to the opinion by the Supreme Court of the United States in *Hamdan v. Rumsfeld*.[29] In that decision, the Supreme Court held that the procedures created for the trial of detainees before a military commission violated the humane treatment mandate of Common Article 3.[30] In support of its holding, the Court concluded that Common Article 3 operates in "contradistinction" to Common Article 2. This interpretation effectively closed the regulatory gap exploited by Bush administration lawyers and was therefore a profound rejection of the Bush administration's LOAC interpretation that the U.S. could be engaged in an armed conflict *not* triggering any LOAC obligations. Thus, the Court's opinion established an interpretation of treaty obligation that required humane treatment for any operation determined by the U.S. to be an armed conflict.[31]

---

28  *See* U.S. Dep't of Defense, Dir. 2311.01E, DoD Law of War Program, (9 May 2006). The exact language is:

> 5.3.1 Ensure that the members of their DoD Components comply with the law of war during all armed conflicts, however such conflicts are characterized, and with the principles and spirit of the law of war during all other operations.

> *Id.* at par 5.3.1; *see also* Major Timothy E. Bullman, *A Dangerous Guessing Game Disguised as an Enlightened Policy: United States Laws of War Obligations During Military Operations Other Than War,* 159 Mil. L. Rev. 152 (1999) (analyzing the potential that the U.S. law of war policy could be asserted as evidence of a customary norm of international law).

29  Hamdan v. Rumsfeld,126 S. Ct. 2749 (2006).

30  *Id.*

31  *Id.* at 2798 (2006). According to Justice Stevens' majority opinion:

> The Court of Appeals thought, and the Government asserts, that Common Article 3 does not apply to Hamdan because the conflict with al Qaeda, being "international in scope," does not qualify as a "conflict not of an international character." That reasoning is erroneous. The term "conflict not of an international character" is used here in contradistinction to a conflict between nations.

This ruling, however, was only the tip of an analytical iceberg. From the outset of the "war on terror," the legal incongruity that compelled the Court to adopt an interpretation of Common Article 3 that defied its drafting history[32] had also driven many U.S. military lawyers to reconsider the entire either/or law-triggering paradigm, and to ultimately embrace a revised theory of LOAC applicability. Unlike the Supreme Court, the focus of these lawyers was not restricted to the treatment standards for detainees. Instead, every aspect of planning and executing military operations against transnational terrorists was implicated by the uncertainty created by the designation of these operations as an armed conflict against a non-state enemy who operated trans-nationally. While the basic premise of policy-based LOAC application remained intact—that LOAC principles provide the logical regulatory framework for all military operations—the real question was whether LOAC application to these operations was required merely as a matter of policy, or whether the characterization of these operations as "armed conflict" triggered an underlying core of customary LOAC principles applicable as a matter of law.

Revised is the operative term, for the LOAC application paradigm that is arguably emerging from the ashes of September 11 must ultimately be understood as implementing the historic purpose of the LOAC itself: to ensure that legal authority related to armed conflict operates in unison with legal obligations intended to mitigate the suffering associated with armed conflict.[33] The stakes related to determining the applicable legal regime to regulate counter-terror military operations are enormous.

---

*Id.*

*See also* Sanches-Llamas v. Oregon, 126 S. Ct. 2669 (2006) (holding that if treaties are to be given effect as federal law, then it is "emphatically the duty and province of the judicial department" to determine their meanings as a matter of law).

32    *See* Michael W. Lewis, *International Myopia: Hamdan's Shortcut to "Victory,"* 42 U. Rich. L. Rev. 687, 701 (2008) ("... acknowledging that the discussion of Common Article 3 in the Commentaries to the Geneva Conventions focuses primarily on the protection of rebels in internal conflicts and civil wars ...").

33    *See* U.S. DEPT OF ARMY, FIELD MANUAL 27–10, THE LAW OF LAND WARFARE (July 1956), par. 3 [hereinafter FM 27–10]. According to this authoritative Department of the Army Statement:

The conduct of armed hostilities on land is regulated by the law of land warfare which is both written and unwritten. It is inspired by the desire to diminish the evils of war by:

a. Protecting both combatants and noncombatants from unnecessary suffering;

Not only do they have profound impact on the rights and liberties of individuals captured and detained in the course of such operations, but whether operations are conducted under the LOAC legal framework or under the alternate law enforcement/human rights framework fundamentally impacts the authority of State forces to employ combat power. Nor will pigeonholing every operation under the inter-state conflict framework always produce a logical result. While offering the benefit of LOAC applicability, such an approach—for example treating the 2006 conflict between Israel and Hezbollah as a subset of an armed conflict between Israel and Lebanon—results in what many view as an unjustified windfall for non-state forces, namely the opportunity to qualify for the privilege of combatant immunity.[34]

What this ultimately reveals is that determining the *nature* of an armed conflict is secondary to determining the very existence of armed conflict. It is this issue—whether an armed conflict can even exist outside the inter-state/intra-state paradigm—that generates the most fundamental debate related to the military component of the fight against international terror groups. For the United States, the answer is an unequivocal "yes."[35] Assuming this interpretation of international law is legitimate (which is certainly debatable), what becomes essential is identification of a *de facto* law trigger sufficient to ensure LOAC applicability to *any* armed conflict. Failure to identify and embrace such a trigger will perpetuate the risk of selective LOAC invocation exemplified by the legal interpretations adopted by President Bush in the opening months of the U.S. response to the post-9/11 transnational terror threat.

## THE LIMITS OF THE TRADITIONAL COMMON ARTICLE 2/3 LAW-TRIGGERING PARADIGM

Understanding the limitations inherent in the traditional Geneva Convention-based law-triggering paradigm is essential to assess the

---

b. Safeguarding certain fundamental human rights of persons who fall into the hands of the enemy, particularly prisoners of war, the wounded and sick, and civilians; and

c. Facilitating the restoration of peace.

*Id.*

34  *See* Geoffrey S. Corn, *Hamdan, Lebanon, and the Need to Recognize a Hybrid Category of Armed Conflict*, 40 Vand. J. Transnat'l L. 295 (2007).

35  *Authorization for the Use of Military Force*, 107th Congress, Pub. L. 107–40, 115 Stat. 224 (2001).

necessity and validity of characterizing the struggle against transnational terrorism as an "armed conflict." This paradigm evolved from the efforts of the drafters of the 1949 Convention to provide a genuine *de facto* law-applicability criterion.[36] Accordingly, Common Article 2 defined application of the full corpus of the laws of war: international armed conflict'[37] while Common Article 3 required that the basic principle of humane treatment be respected in non-international armed conflicts occurring in the territory of a signatory State.[38] Although neither of these treaty provisions explicitly indicated that they were to serve as the exclusive triggers for LOAC application, they rapidly evolved into such a standard.[39]

Accordingly, LOAC application has since 1949 been contingent on two essential factors: first, the existence of armed conflict and second, the nature of the armed conflict. In the context of inter-state disputes, armed conflict has always been understood as hostilities between the armed forces of two or more States. While the short duration or minimal intensity of such hostilities has at times been asserted as a basis to deny the existence of an inter-state armed conflict, the regular nature of State armed forces and the abnormal nature of inter-state hostilities has produced relative clarity in determining when such armed conflicts exist (when they terminate can be a much more complicated question).[40]

---

36    *See* Commentary, Convention (III) relative to the Treatment of Prisoners of War. Geneva, 12 August 1949 (Jean S. Pictet ed., 1960), at 22–23 [hereinafter ICRC Commentary] (providing additional background on the emphasis on de facto hostilities as a trigger for the protections of the Conventions); *see also* Geoffrey S. Corn and Eric Talbot Jensen, *Untying the Gordian Knot: A Proposal for Determining Applicability of the Laws of War to the War on Terror,* (*available at* http://ssrn.com/abstract=1083849).

37    *See* GWS, *supra* note 17, at Art. 2 stating:

> ... the present Convention shall apply to all cases of declared war or of any armed conflict which may arise between two or more of the High Contracting Parties, even if the state of war is not recognized by one of them.

*Id.*

38    *See* GWS, *supra* note 17 at Art. 3 stating:

> In the case of armed conflict not of an international character occurring in the territory of one of the High Contracting Parties ...

*Id.*

39    *See* Int'l & Operational Law Dep't, The Judge Advocate General's Legal Center & School, The Law of War Deskbook, at Chapter 3 (2000);

40    *See* ICRC Commentary, *supra* note 32, at 32 ("It makes no difference how long the conflict lasts, or how much slaughter takes place. The respect due to human

In contrast, determining the existence of a non-international armed conflict has been much more complex. This is the result of two realities. First, up until September 11, non-international armed conflict was understood to be synonymous with internal armed conflict. Second, unlike interstate hostilities, it is not abnormal for States to use armed force to respond to internal threats that do not rise to the level of intensity of armed conflict. Therefore, defining the line between such non-conflict uses of armed forces and uses that rise to the level of armed conflict against internal dissident groups had always been difficult. Because of this, a number of analytical factors were suggested by the ICRC commentary[41] to Common Article 3. According to the Commentary:

> Nevertheless, these different conditions, although in no way obligatory, constitute convenient criteria, and we therefore think it well to give a list of those contained in the various amendments discussed; they are as follows:
>
> (1) That the Party in revolt against the *de jure* Government possesses an organized military force, an authority responsible for its acts, acting within a determinate territory and having the means of respecting and ensuring respect for the Convention.
>
> (2) That the legal Government is obliged to have recourse to the regular military forces against insurgents organized as military and in possession of a part of the national territory.
>
> (3) (a) That the *de jure* Government has recognized the insurgents as belligerents; or
>
>  (b) that it has claimed for itself the rights of a belligerent; or
>
>  (c) that it has accorded the insurgents recognition as belligerents for the purposes only of the present Convention; or
>
>  (d) that the dispute has been admitted to the agenda of the Security Council or the General Assembly of the United Nations as being a threat to international peace, a breach of the peace, or an act of aggression.
>
> (4) (a) That the insurgents have an organisation purporting to have the characteristics of a State.

---

personality is not measured by the number of victims."); *see generally* Geoffrey S. Corn, *Hamdan, Lebanon, and the Need to Recognize a Hybrid Category of Armed Conflict*, 40 Vand. J. Transnat'l L. 295 (2007).

41    *See* ICRC Commentary, *supra* note 32 at 34–35.

(b) That the insurgent civil authority exercises de facto authority over persons within a determinate territory.

(c) That the armed forces act under the direction of the organized civil authority and are prepared to observe the ordinary laws of war.

(d) That the insurgent civil authority agrees to be bound by the provisions of the Convention.[42]

These criteria became widely regarded as the most authoritative and effective means for making such a determination. As the Commentary indicates, when considered in any combination or even individually, these factors reveal when a situation rises above the level of internal disturbance and crosses the legal threshold into the realm of armed conflict.[43]

Perhaps the most instructive of these factors is the focus on the State response to the threat: when a State resorts to the use of regular (and by "regular" it is fair to presume that the ICRC Commentary refers to combat) armed forces, the situation has most likely crossed the threshold into the realm of armed conflict.[44] While not resolving all uncertainty related to the existence of non-international armed conflicts, the Commentary criteria have proved remarkably effective in practice: Resorting to the use of regular armed forces for sustained operations against internal dissident groups that cannot be suppressed with only law enforcement capabilities makes it difficult for a State to credibly disavow the existence of armed conflict. This conclusion is at the core of the definition of non-international armed conflict adopted by the International Tribunal for the Former Yugoslavia in the first case that tribunal adjudicated when it concluded that "an armed conflict exists whenever there is a resort to armed force between States *or protracted*

---

42   *See* ICRC Commentary, *supra* note 32, at 49–50.

43   *See* ICRC Commentary, *supra* note 32, at 34–35 (the Commentary emphasizes that the limited scope of applicability of common Article 3 was responsive to historic concerns related to the protection of state sovereignty); *see also* Geoffrey S. Corn and Eric Talbot Jensen, *Untying the Gordian Knot: A Proposal for Determining Applicability of the Laws of War to the War on Terror*, (*available at* http://ssrn.com/abstract=1083849) (discussing the objective factors the Commentary laid out to determine whether an internal situation had crossed over into an internal armed conflict. Among the factors discussed are scope, intensity, and duration of military operations, whether the dissident group controlled territory to the exclusion of government forces, and whether the dissident group enjoyed demonstrable popular support).

44   *See* ICRC Commentary, *supra* note 32 at 35.

*armed violence between governmental authorities and organized armed groups or between such groups within a State.*"[45]

The second consideration of this Common Article 2/3 law-triggering paradigm—the nature of the armed conflict—has also caused substantial uncertainty in relation to the evolving nature of warfare. This consideration links LOAC application to what is defined as the international or non-international character of a given armed conflict. Because there is no defined meaning of "international" or "non-international" in Common Articles 2 or 3, uncertainty developed related to application of this prong of the legal trigger.[46] In the inter-state realm, the requirement that hostilities occur between the armed forces of two States reduces this uncertainty. Such conflicts are *ipso facto* "international" in scope, because at least one State's armed forces must act outside its own territory to bring about such a situation. While there have been instances where States have attempted to avoid the Common Article 2 trigger by asserting an absence of a genuine dispute between States (such as in the 2006 Israeli incursion into Lebanon and in the 1989 U.S. invasion of Panama), because there is no plausible basis to assert al Qaeda qualifies as a sovereign state, this Common Article 2 trigger has not been particularly relevant to the characterization of the armed struggle against this transnational enemy. Instead, it has been the meaning of "non-international" within Common Article 3 that has produced substantial uncertainty *vis-à-vis* counter-terror combat operations.[47]

Although the term "non-international" appears broad enough to encompass any armed conflict that does not fall under the definition of "international" within the meaning of Common Article 2—the essential basis

---

45    *See* Prosecutor v. Tadic, Case No. IT-94- 1-AR72, Appeal on Jurisdiction (Oct. 2, 1995), at par. 94, *reprinted in* 35 I.L.M. 32 (1996); *see also* Anthony Cullen, Key Developments Affecting the Scope of Internal Armed Conflict in International Humanitarian Law, 183 Mil. L. Rev. 66 (2005) (providing an excellent analysis of the significance of the *Tadic* ruling).

46    *See generally* Adam Roberts, *Counter-terrorism, Armed Force and the Laws of War,* Survival (quarterly journal of IISS, London), vol. 44, no. 1, (Spring 2002), at 7.

47    *Id.* at 14. *See also* Gabor Rona, *When is a war not a war—The proper role of the law of armed conflict in the "global war on terror,"* "*International Action to Prevent and Combat Terrorism*" Workshop on the Protection of Human Rights While Countering Terrorism, Copenhagen, 15–16 March 2004—Presentation given by Gabor Rona, Legal Advisor at the ICRC's Legal Division, *available at* http://www.icrc.orp/ Web/Eng/siteenvO.nsf/iwpl.ist575/3C2914F52152E565CI256E60005C84CO (last accessed 23 August, 2006).

of the *Hamdan* opinion[48]—the history of Common Article 3 suggests a meaning intended to be synonymous with purely internal, or intra-state armed conflicts.[49] Accordingly, while Common Article 2 was intended to address inter-state hostilities, Common Article 3 was not, as the Supreme Court concluded, created to apply in "contradistinction" to Common Article 2; it was instead developed to respond to the specific problem of intra-state armed conflicts.[50]

Both the military component of the U.S. fight against al Qaeda and the recent conflict between Israel and Hezbollah highlighted the friction between this traditionally understood paradigm for triggering LOAC application and the reality of contemporary counter-terror combat operations.[51] When this inter/intra-state limiting interpretation of the Common Article 2/3 law-triggering paradigm was combined with a rejection of the longstanding practice of applying LOAC principles to any military operation, operational decision makers were deprived of the logical and consistent legal framework that had served them so well over the prior three decades. Instead, the law applicable to these operations— and particularly to the status and treatment of captured and detained al Qaeda operatives—was a true "moving target."

In the years following 9/11 it became increasingly apparent that invocation of the LOAC authority without a counter-balance of LOAC obligation was inconsistent with the historic purpose of the law. This has gradually led to a recognition that the key factor for determining applicability of the most basic LOAC principles must be the mere existence

---

48    Hamdan v. Rumsfeld, 126 S. Ct. 2749, 2795–7 (2006).

49    *See, e.g.* UK Ministry of Defense, THE MANUAL LAW OF ARMED CONFLICT, Oxford University Press (2004), at Para 2.1; INT'L & OPERATIONAL LAW DEPT, THE JUDGE ADVOCATE GENERAL'S LEGAL CENTER & SCHOOL, THE LAW OF WAR DESKBOOK, at Chapter 3 (2000); *see* GWS, *supra* note 17, at Art. 3.

50    Hamdan v. Rumsfeld, 126 S. Ct. 2749, at 2798 (2006). According to Justice Stevens' majority opinion:

> The Court of Appeals thought, and the Government asserts, that Common Article 3 does not apply to Hamdan because the conflict with al Qaeda, being "international in scope," does not qualify as a "conflict not of an international character." That reason is erroneous. The term "conflict not of an international character" is used here as a contradistinction to a conflict between nations.

*Id.*

51    Geoffrey S. Corn, *Hamdan, Lebanon, and the Need to Recognize a Hybrid Category of Armed Conflict,* 40 Vand. J. Transnat'l L. 295 (2007).

of armed conflict. Once that threshold is crossed, the application of these principles becomes essential for providing a logical regulatory framework for forces engaged in combat operations. While the characterization of the conflict remains significant for the purpose of applying specific treaty obligations, denying applicability of core LOAC principles merely because a *de facto* armed conflict does not fit within the inter/intra-state law-triggering paradigm is operationally counter-intuitive.

## RETHINKING THE CORE PURPOSES OF THE 1949 LAW TRIGGERING PARADIGM

Few would dispute that the principal purpose of the LOAC is to ensure that armed conflict is subject to regulatory limits serving both the interests of armed forces and the victims of war.[52] Derived from this proposition is the conclusion that any legitimate application of the LOAC requires a balance between power and restraint. However, as noted above, the advent of armed hostilities between States and transnational non-state entities, when coupled with the limitations of the traditional either/or Common Article 2/3 law-triggering paradigm, produced a conflict between the adherence to this purpose and the policy interests of States. This reality was exposed by the Bush administration's decisions related to LOAC applicability to the conflict with al Qaeda. The legal basis for these policies was influenced by the perceived strategic ramifications of conflict characterization under this law-triggering paradigm. In relation to armed conflict with transnational terrorist groups, it is this context that truly exposes the imperative of endorsing a law-triggering paradigm that is responsive to extraterritorial armed conflicts with non-state enemies.[53]

National security policymakers will almost inevitably seek to accomplish three objectives when assessing the applicability of law to regulate a military operation. First, invocation of the authority derived from the principle of military necessity—authority to take measures needed to bring about the prompt submission of the designated enemy. Second, emphasize to their forces and to the international community uncompromising commitment to the basic humanitarian principles reflected in the Geneva Conventions. The third objective, and perhaps most significant for

---

52    Eric S. Krauss and Michael O. Lacey, *Utilitarians vs. Humanitarian: the battle over the law of war,* PARAMETERS, (Summer 2002).

53    *Id.*

purposes of exposing the deficiency of the "either/or" law-triggering paradigm, is the perceived need to achieve these first two objectives without suggesting that the enemy is vested with any international legal status to which it is not legitimately entitled. The influence of this concern on U.S. policy is emphasized by Adam Roberts:

> For at least 25 years, the United States has expressed a concern, shared to some degree by certain other states, regarding the whole principle of thinking about terrorists and other irregular forces in a laws-of-war framework. To refer to such a framework, which recognizes rights and duties, might seem to imply a degree of moral acceptance of the right of any particular group to resort to acts of violence, at least against military targets. Successive U.S. administrations have objected to certain revisions to the laws of war on the grounds that they might actually favor guerrilla fighters and terrorists, affording them a status that the United States believes they do not deserve.

Exclusive reliance on the Common Article 2/3 triggering paradigm inhibits the ability to satisfy all of these policy objectives. Using the example of military operations directed against an al Qaeda base camp located in the territory of a State unable or unwilling (or perhaps not even given the opportunity) to eliminate the camp illustrates this point. One option would be to stretch the definition of international armed conflict to apply to such operations on the theory that al Qaeda should be treated as a *de facto* State for the purpose of LOAC application. Assuming the credibility of this theory for the sake of argument, it reveals a basic flaw: it allows members of al Qaeda to claim a status reserved for members of regular State-sponsored armed forces, a status in no way justified by either their character or conduct. Thus, while this approach certainly satisfies the objective of invoking the principles of humanity and necessity, it forces policymakers to articulate why the enemy is not entitled to the beneficial status normally associated with international armed conflict, a process that has occurred with respect to individuals captured in Afghanistan.[54]

The second option would be to characterize the military operation as a non-international armed conflict triggering the humane treatment mandate of Common Article 3. This theory certainly seems more plausible

---

54   *See e.g.* U.K. Ministry of Defense, *The Manual for the law of Armed Conflict,* Oxford University Press (2004), at Para. 2.1; *see also* Gabor Rona, *When is a war not a war—The proper role of the law of armed conflict in the "global war on terror,"* supra note 42.

than characterizing such operations as a Common Article 2 conflicts, and if confined to the either/or choice between Common Article 2 and Common Article 3, this second option seems the more acceptable one. However, it not only requires adoption of the questionable interpretation of Common Article 3 endorsed by the *Hamdan* Court;[55] it also ignores the plain language of this article that purports to limit applicability to "the territory of a High Contracting Party."[56] Furthermore, the war on terror revealed another concern among national security policymakers: characterizing an armed conflict that transcends national borders as falling within the scope of Common Article 3 might subtly undermine the legitimacy of extraterritorial military operations. This consequence results from an inference that such conflicts do not trigger the authority to engage in military operations of international scope.[57] As a result, policymakers perceived a Common Article 3 characterization as presenting an unacceptable degradation to their authority to conduct military operations wherever and whenever necessary to defeat the terrorist threat.[58]

What is even more problematic from a pragmatic military perspective is that the Common Article 3 characterization of combat operations against transnational non-state enemies fails to address principles of the law

---

55    Hamdan v. Rumsfeld, 126 S. Ct. 2749.

56    *See* GWS *supra* note 17, at Art. 3 (limits applicability to cases of armed conflict not of an international character occurring in the territory of one of the High Contracting Parties).

57    *See* Mil. Or., Detention, Treatment, and Trial of Certain Non-Citizens in the War against Terrorism, 66 Fed. Reg. 57833 (Nov. 13, 2001); *see also* Counsel on Foreign Relations, *Backgrounder available at* http://www.cfr.org/publication/9126/ (last visited December 5, 2007).

58    *See* Jay S. Bybee, Memorandum for Alberto Gonzales, Counsel to the President, and William J. Haynes II, General Counsel of the DoD (Jan. 22, 2002), *available at* http://news.findlaw.com/hdocs/docs/doj/bybee12202mem.pdf

    Common Article 3, however, covers "armed conflict not of an international character"—a war that does not involve cross-border attacks—that occurs within the territory of one of the High Contracting Parties.

    Common Article 3's text provides substantial reason to think that it refers specifically to a condition of civil war . . . This provision would not reach an armed conflict in which one of the parties operated from multiple bases in several different states.

    *Id.*

    *See generally* Geoffrey S. Corn, *Hamdan, Lebanon, and the Need to Recognize a Hybrid Category of Armed Conflict*, 40 V and. J. Transnat'l L. 295 (2007) *at 29.*

related to the application of combat power.[59] Common article 3's substantive mandate is focused only on the treatment of persons rendered *hors de combat* (unable to fight), and does not regulate the application of combat power. Thus, even when Common Article 3 is applied in "contradistinction" to Common Article 2, the trigger for application of these equally important and relevant regulatory LOAC principles remains undefined.

Abandoning this either/or paradigm associated with Common Articles 2/3 in favor of a more pragmatic armed conflict trigger that responds to these "transnational" combat operations reconciles these typical national policy concerns with the need to provide a logical and relevant operational regulatory framework. As the U.S. Supreme Court implicitly recognized in its *Hamdan* opinion, it is fundamentally invalid to detach the applicability of regulation from the necessity for regulation.[60] Acknowledging that *any* armed conflict triggers fundamental LOAC principles is necessary to reconcile the historical purposes of the LOAC with the rapid evolution of the nature of warfare exemplified by the post-9/11 Global War on Terror. While critics may argue that this conception of a "new" category of armed conflict distorts the meaning of the Common Article 2/3 paradigm, allowing the geographic scope of a combat operation or the non-state nature of a transnational enemy to nullify application of the LOAC regulatory framework is itself inconsistent with the intent of the drafters of the Geneva Convention of 1949:[61] a rejection of a legally formalistic approach to determining LOAC application inspired by the perceived "law avoidance" that occurred during the Second World War.[62]

---

59  *See* Geoffrey S. Corn and Eric Talbot Jensen, *Untying the Gordian Knot: A Proposal for Determining Applicability of the Laws of War to the War on Terror* (*available at* http://ssrn.com/abstract=1083849); *see, e.g.,* U.S. Dep't of Def., DoD Directive 2311.01E, DoD Law of War Program (2006); *see also* Chairman, Joint Chiefs of Staff, CJSCI 5810.01B, Implementation of the DoD Laws of War Program (2002).

60  Hamdan v. Rumsfeld, 126 S. Ct. 2749 (2006).

61  *See supra* note 47.

62  *See* ICRC *supra* note 32 at 22–23. A similar Commentary was published for each of the four Geneva Conventions. However, because Articles 2 and 3 are identical—or common—to each Convention, the Commentary for these articles is similar in each of the four Commentaries.

The ICRC Commentary offers additional background for this emphasis on *de facto* hostilities as a trigger for the protections of the Conventions:

The Hague Convention of 1899, in Article 2, stated that the annexed Regulations concerning the Laws and Customs of War on Land were applicable "in case of

If law avoidance was the underlying motivation for the development of Common Articles 2 and 3, then their significance seems to transcend the formalistic meaning widely attributed to them. Their broader significance, therefore, is that they reflect an effort to ensure that the LOAC regulatory framework could not be disavowed once a *de facto* situation of armed conflict existed. Accordingly, relying on these law-triggering provisions as a basis to *deny* applicability of this regulatory framework to a situation of *de facto* armed conflict represents a perversion of the spirit and intent of this fundamental advancement of the law.[63]

## SEARCHING FOR A DE FACTO INDICATOR OF ARMED CONFLICT

The LOAC is indisputably a *lex specialis*,[64] and as such does not and cannot apply at all times to all situations. Nor can it simply apply to all military operations, for many such operations cannot under any legitimate definition be characterized as armed conflicts. Accordingly, the "war on terror" exposes the need to identify law-triggering conditions beyond those focused on the inter/intra-state conflict paradigm. Identification of such criteria is particularly essential for determining the existence of an extraterritorial non-international armed conflict. Such

---

war." This definition was not repeated either in 1907 at The Hague or in 1929 at Geneva; the very title and purpose of the Conventions made it clear that they were intended for use in war-time, and the meaning of war seemed to require no defining . . . Since 1907 experience has shown that many armed conflicts, displaying all the characteristics of a war, may arise without being preceded by any of the formalities laid down in the Hague Convention. Furthermore, there have been many cases where Parties to a conflict have contested the legitimacy of the enemy Government and therefore refused to recognize the existence of a state of war. In the same way, the temporary disappearance of sovereign States as a result of annexation or capitulation has been put forward as a pretext for not observing one or other of the humanitarian Conventions. It was necessary to find a remedy to this state of affairs and the change which had taken place in the whole conception of such Conventions pointed the same way. The Geneva Conventions are coming to be regarded less and less as contracts concluded on a basis of reciprocity in the national interests of the parties, and more and more as a solemn affirmation of principles respected for their own sake, a series of unconditional engagements on the part of each of the Contracting Parties 'vis-à-vis' the others.

*Id.* at 19–20.

63 *See generally* Geoffrey S. Corn, *Hamdan, Lebanon, and the Need to Recognize a Hybrid Category of Armed Conflict,* 40 Vand. J. Transnat'l L. 295 (2007).

64 Geoffrey S. Corn and Eric Talbot Jensen, *Untying the Gordian Knot: A Proposal for Determining Applicability of the Laws of War to the War on Terror,* (*available at* http://ssrn.com/abstract=1083849), at 22.

conflicts involve characteristics of international armed conflict; but the military operational characteristics of non-international armed conflicts. It is therefore unsurprising that designating the struggle against international terrorism as a "global war" and announcing that the United States was engaged in an "armed conflict" with al Qaeda was both controversial and ultimately confusing for the armed forces required to execute operations associated with this struggle.[65]

While there may be growing consensus (particularly among operational legal advisors) that LOAC principles must apply to combat operations executed to destroy or disable transnational terrorists operatives, identifying the line between non-conflict and armed conflict components of this struggle is and will continue to be extremely difficult. This difficulty is not only the result of the undisputable fact that the drafters of the Geneva Convention law triggers did not contemplate this evolution in the nature of armed conflict; it is also complicated by the reality that many uses of armed force in this struggle cannot be legitimately characterized as armed conflict, but instead fall under a law enforcement legal paradigm.[66] Past and future military operations conducted to destroy, disable, or disrupt the capabilities of such organizations have and will

---

65   *See* Mil. Or., Detention, Treatment, and Trial of Certain Non-Citizens in the War against Terrorism, 66 Fed. Reg. 57833 (Nov. 13, 2001); Hamdan v. Rumsfeld, 126 S. Ct. 2749 (2006) (reflecting an almost unanimous conclusion among the Justices that the struggle between the United States and *al Qaeda* is an armed conflict for purposes of international law); Authorization for the Use of Military Force, Pub. L. No. 107–40, 115 Stat. 224 (2001); Geoffrey S. Corn and Eric Talbot Jensen, *Untying the Gordian Knot: A Proposal for Determining Applicability of the Laws of War to the War on Terror*, (*available at* http://ssrn.com/abstract=1083849), at 52. Authors state:

> President Bush characterized the terror strike against the United States as an "armed attack," and he and the Congress of the United States almost immediately invoked the war powers of the nation to respond to the threat represented by al Qaeda, a non-state entity operating throughout the world . . . Since that time, the executive branch has struggled to articulate, and in many judicial challenges defend, how it could invoke the authorities of war without accepting the obligations of the law regulating war.

*Id.*

66   *Id.* at 47 (the application of either/or law triggers is insufficient because determination of existence of armed conflict is often difficult because of co-mingling of military and law enforcement in some situations).

remain operationally and legally complex.[67] Determining where military operations conducted for this purpose fall along the spectrum between peace and armed conflict is therefore essential for developing a logical and coherent approach to determining when such operations must comply with LOAC principles.

One solution would be to link LOAC applicability—at least applicability of fundamental LOAC principles such as humanity, distinction, proportionality, and the prohibition against inflicting unnecessary suffering—to invocation of the most basic authority of armed conflict: inflicting death as a measure of first resort.[68] When States employ armed forces, they invariably provide their forces with a mandate authorizing the use of combat power. This mandate is then translated into authority for the military to use force for the purpose of mission accomplishment, often taking the form of Rules of Engagement.[69] In this respect, Rules of Engagement, or ROE, are simply use-of-force control mechanisms. At the most basic level, ROE dictate the "shoot/don't shoot" criteria to be followed by operational forces. However, because they are derived from the authority granted by national leaders—either explicit or implicit—for the achievement of the national strategic objective, they reveal where the operation falls along this peace-to-conflict spectrum.

---

67    Geoffrey S. Corn and Eric Talbot Jensen, *Untying the Gordian Knot: A Proposal for Determining Applicability of the Laws of War to the War on Terror* (Sept. 7, 2008) (*available at* http://ssrn.com/abstract=1083849).

68    Chairman, Joint Chiefs of Staff Instruction 3121.01B, Standing Rules of Engagement/ Standing Rules for the Use of Force for U.S. Forces, encl. A, para. 1d (13 June 2005) (U.S. military operations involving armed conflict are to comply with LOAC, and will comply with the principles and spirit of the LOAC during all operations); Susan L. Turley, *Keeping the Peace: Do the Laws of War Apply?*, 73 Tex. L. Rev. 139, (1994); Richard J. Grunawalt, *The JCS Standing Rules of Engagement: A Judge Advocate's Primer*, 42 A.F.L. Rev. 245, 247–48 (1997) (SROE which encompass LOAC are the standing instructions regulating the use of destructive military power that apply to almost everything outside the U.S.).

69    The Joint Chiefs of Staff, Joint Pub 1–02, Department of Defense Dictionary of Military and Associated Terms (14 April 2001 as amended through 14 Sept. 2007) *available at* http://www.dtic.mil/doctrine/jel/new_pubs/jp1_02.pdf. Defining ROE as:

> Directives issued by competent military authority that delineate the circumstances and limitations under which United States forces will initiate and/or continue combat engagement with other forces encountered.

*Id.*

The authority to use combat power granted to the armed forces generally falls into one of two broad categories: either use-of-force is authorized based on the conduct of individuals[70] encountered during the operation, or it is authorized based on a determination of a designated status[71] of an opponent. In the lexicon of ROE, this dichotomy is referred to as either "conduct" based ROE or "status" based ROE. Irrespective of the form of the authorization, what these distinct authorities signify is the true nature of the military operation. When armed forces conduct operations pursuant to a conduct-based use-of-force authority, they are in effect operating within a law enforcement paradigm.[72] This is because their use-of-force is dictated by the demonstration of threat by the object of that use and conditioned on a judgment that no lesser means will ensure the protection of the individual or some other designated person or thing.

In contrast, when armed forces conduct operations pursuant to a status-based use-of-force authority, they are essentially operating within an

---

70   Chairman, Joint Chiefs of Staff Instruction 3121.01B, Standing Rules of Engagement/ Standing Rules for the Use of Force for U.S. Forces, encl. A, para. 1c (13 June 2005); Geoffrey S. Corn and Eric Talbot Jensen, *Untying the Gordian Knot: A Proposal for Determining Applicability of the Laws of War to the War on Terror,* (*available at* http://ssrn.com/abstract=1083849), at 44 (describing conduct based ROE as inherently self-defense/responsive in nature).

71   *Id.* (definition of status based ROE as once identification of a designated enemy force is made deadly force may be used against that enemy based on its status and regardless of its conduct).

72   Chairman, Joint Chiefs of Staff Instruction, 3121.01B, Standing Rules of Engagement/ Standing Rules for the Use of Force for U.S. Forces, encl. A, para. 3f (13 June 2005). (SROE states that conduct based authority for use of force and "the use of force in self-defense should be sufficient to respond decisively to hostile acts or demonstrations of hostile intent. Such use of force may exceed the means and intensity of the hostile act or hostile intent, but the nature, duration, and scope of force should not exceed what is required."); *see also* Geoffrey S. Corn and Eric Talbot Jensen, *Untying the Gordian Knot: A Proposal for Determining Applicability of the Laws of War to the War on Terror,* (*available at* http://ssrn.com/abstract=1083849), at 44. Authors state:

> Because conduct-based ROE are inherently self-defense/responsive in nature, they indicate that the state views the nature of the military mission as insufficient to trigger the targeting authority of the laws of war.

*Id.*

armed conflict paradigm.[73] This is because the use of deadly force is not contingent on identification of a threat to the soldier employing force. Instead, use of force is authorized at the moment the object of that use is determined to fall into a pre-designated category, such as "enemy force," "hostile force," or some other designation of lawful object of attack.[74] Thus, status-based engagement authority is an implicit invocation of the principle of military objective, because it is the nature of the target and not the conduct of the target that triggers use-of-force authority.[75]

---

73    Chairman, Joint Chiefs of Staff Instruction, 3121.02B, Standing Rules of Engagement/ Standing Rules for the Use of Force for U.S. Forces, encl. A, para. 2b (13 June 2005); Geoffrey S. Corn and Eric Talbot Jensen, *Untying the Gordian Knot: A Proposal for Determining Applicability of the Laws of War to the War on Terror*, (*available at* http://ssrn.com/abstract=1083849), at 44. In this excerpt authors describe why status-based ROE ought to trigger laws of war obligations:

> However, because status-based ROE require no justification for the use of force beyond threat recognition and identification, they indicate that the state views the nature of the military mission as sufficient to trigger the targeting authority of the laws of war . . . Because of the approval of status-based ROE implicitly invokes the target engagement authority of the laws of war, it seems logical that such issuance should trigger an analogous requirement to comply with fundamental regulatory obligations derived from the laws of war.

> *Id.*

74    Chairman, Joint Chiefs of Staff Instruction, 3121.02B, Standing Rules of Engagement/ Standing Rules for the Use of Force for U.S. Forces, encl. A, para. 3d (13 June 2005) (defining declared hostile force as "Any civilian, paramilitary or military force or terrorist(s) that has been declared hostile by appropriate US authority." U.S. forces, according to SROE may always engage a declared hostile force, irrespective of their conduct—unless that conduct clearly indicates that they are *hors de combat*).

75    *See* Geoffrey S. Corn and Eric Talbot Jensen, *Untying the Gordian Knot: A Proposal for Determining Applicability of the Laws of War to the War on Terror*, (*available at* http://ssrn.com/abstract=1083849), at 40 where authors assert that

> If the military mission is to destroy, defeat, or neutralize a designated enemy force or organization . . . personnel associated with that force will be declared hostile pursuant to the ROE. The consequence of this designation is that once individuals are identifies as a member of such a group or organization . . . U.S. forces have the authority . . . to immediately attack these "targets."

> *Id.* It is, of course true that in operational environments where the line between civilian and enemy is blurred the determination that an individual falls into a designated status category may be contingent on that individuals conduct. But this does not nullify the conclusion that the use of force remains fundamentally status based, for what is significant for an assessment of use of force authority is

THE WAR ON TERROR AND THE LAWS OF WAR

This dichotomy between conduct-based and status-based use-of-force authority mirrors the dichotomy between the law enforcement and armed conflict legal paradigms. This conclusion is derived from a simple truism: the most fundamental distinction between law enforcement and armed conflict is manifested in the scope of use of deadly force authority—a distinction between use of deadly force as a last resort and use of deadly force as a first resort.[76] As a result, use-of-force authority provides an effective *de facto* indicator of the line between non-conflict and conflict operations—a line that indicates when the regulatory principles of the LOAC must come into force. If operations fall into the category of law enforcement, application of LOAC principles would be inconsistent with the fundamental restraint associated with the use-of-force during such operations.[77] Law enforcement activities, regulated by domestic law and international human rights standards, reserve the use of deadly force as a measure of last resort.[78] However, if use of force is authorized based on status determinations, application of a law enforcement use-of-force paradigm would not only be inconsistent with the fundamental nature of the operation; it would disable the effectiveness of the armed forces by depriving them of the type of "first resort" use-of-force authority necessary for mission accomplishment. This basic distinction between relative authorities reveals in the starkest manner the fundamental fallacy of characterizing all transnational counter-terror military operations as "militarized"

---

not the particular threat identification criteria that triggers that authority, but the scope of the authority triggered by the threat identification. In other words, so long as the armed forces are authorized to employ deadly force as a measure of first resort upon the identification of a certain status, that employment is fundamentally status based.

76 McCann and Others v. the United Kingdom, application no. 18984/91 (24 May 1995) para. 213 (European Court of Human Rights case that held that British officials that had conducted an anti-terror raid against members of the IRA did not comply with Geneva Convention Common Article II which states that force used by a state must be proportionate to the aim of protecting persons against unlawful violence and such operations must be so as to minimize to the greatest extent possible, the recourse to the use of lethal force. An excerpt of the opinion indicates that:

"...the Court is not persuaded that the killing of the three terrorists constituted the use of force which was no more than absolutely necessary in defense of persons from unlawful violence within the meaning of Article 2 ..."

*Id.*

77 *See* Chairman, *supra* note 67.

78 *Id.*

law enforcement, and why focus on the nature of the use-of-force authority can effectively expose the line between law enforcement and armed conflict.

The example of an air strike conducted against a terrorist training facility operating with impunity in the territory of another State is instructive.[79] It is inconceivable that the authority to employ deadly force relied on by the air assets executing the mission will be contingent on a provocation from the terrorist target. It is equally inconceivable that the air assets will be obliged to offer the potential targets the opportunity to submit to apprehension as a condition precedent to the employment of combat power. Instead, the authority to employ that power will almost certainly be based on an inherent invocation of the principle of military objective, allowing the use of deadly combat power based solely on the identification of the target as one falling into the category of a defined terrorist enemy.[80]

Employment of combat power under this type of authority is not law enforcement. Accordingly, based on the nature of the use-of-force authorization, the *de facto* nature of the operation justifies an armed conflict characterization, if for no other reason than the State's implicit invocation of the principle of military objective as a justification for the use of deadly force.[81] Characterizing such operations as law enforcement creates an immediate incongruity: the suggestion that the use of deadly force is limited to a measure of last resort and that less destructive means must be attempted prior to such use.[82]

No such incongruity would result from acknowledging that operations targeting terrorist operatives with combat power are armed conflicts. Instead, such acknowledgment achieves a critical effect: the authority

---

79   *See* Orna Ben-Naftali and Keren R. Michaeli, *We Must Not Make a Scarecrow of the Law: A Legal Analysis of the Israeli Policy of Targeted Killings*, 35 Cornell Int'l L.J. 233, (2003); *see also* Karen De Young, *U.S. Strike in Somalia Targets Al Qaeda Figure*, http://www.washingtonpost.com/wp-dyn/content/article/2007/01/08/AR2007010801635.html (article discussing U.S. strike within Somalia aimed at targeting Al Qaeda members in 2007).

80   Geoffrey S. Corn and Eric Talbot Jensen, *Untying the Gordian Knot: A Proposal for Determining Applicability of the Laws of War to the War on Terror*, (*available at* http://ssrn.com/abstract=1083849), at 35.

81   *Id.*

82   McCann and Others v. the United Kingdom, application no. 18984/91 (24 May 1995).

implicitly invoked by the State is counter-balanced by the limiting humanitarian principles of this law. In short, if such operations are categorized as armed conflicts, the law essentially creates a "package deal" for participants. While the principle of military necessity/military objective may justify the employment of deadly force as a measure of first resort, other principles limiting the methods and means of warfare and establishing baseline standards of treatment for captured and detained personnel also become applicable. Unless combat operations conducted against terrorist operatives are understood to trigger this "package" of principles, States will continue to be free to adopt a selective invocation of the fundamental authority derived from the LOAC to take measures necessary to disable terrorist capabilities while disavowing legally mandated obligations derived from the same source of law.

It would be overly optimistic (or perhaps pessimistic, depending on perspective) to assert that the concept of transnational armed conflict is gaining substantial traction within the international legal community. There is, however, a growing recognition that hostilities between States and non-state transnational groups must be subject to LOAC-based regulation, manifested in the international reaction to both U.S. and Israeli combat operations against terrorist organizations.[83] Thus, while there may be consternation in acknowledging the limits of the Common Article 2/3 law-triggering paradigm, there seems to be an equally determined effort to demand the application of rules those articles trigger. Whether this will ultimately lead to widespread recognition, this hybrid category of armed conflict is yet to be seen.

What is indisputable, however, is that States are routinely invoking the authority of the LOAC to justify the application of combat power against transnational terrorist entities. These invocations of authority should, therefore, serve as the trigger for application of complementary humanitarian LOAC principles. In short, when States employ combat power pursuant to an inherent invocation of the principle of military objective—as will often be revealed by the authorization of status-based targeting authority—it is logical to require compliance with complimentary LOAC humanitarian obligations. And, because such status-based

---

83    *See* Human Rights Watch, Lebanon/Israel: U.N. Rights Body Squanders Chance to Help Civilians, Aug. 11, 2006, http://hrw.org/english/docs/2006/08/11/lebano13969_txt.htm; *see also* Human Rights Watch, U.N.: Open Independent Inquiry into Civilian Deaths, Aug. 8, 2006, http://hrw.org/english/docs/2006/08/08/lebano13939.htm (containing statements by Kofi Annan).

targeting authorizations have been (and will likely continue to be) issued for military operations that fall in the twilight zone between Common Articles 2 and 3, this indication that the State is invoking the LOAC in support of mission accomplishment provides the missing ingredient in determining when these principles apply outside this established law-triggering paradigm.[84] Clinging to the restrictions of this paradigm in such situations produces a dangerous anomaly: Military forces will execute operations with the force and effect of expansive authority without being constrained, as a matter of law, by any balancing principles. Such an anomaly may be explicable in purely treaty-interpretation terms, but it is inconsistent with the historical underpinnings of the LOAC.[85]

Opponents to this concept of transnational armed conflict often argue that the war on terror is not really a "war," and as a result it cannot trigger LOAC authorities or obligations.[86] What is striking about such criticism is how it seems to ignore the pragmatic realities of military operations. Such realities are the day-to-day business of the armed forces tasked to

---

84    Geoffrey S. Corn and Eric Talbot Jensen, *Untying the Gordian Knot: A Proposal for Determining Applicability of the Laws of War to the War on Terror*, (*available at* http://ssrn.com/abstract=1083849), *at* 51 where authors state:

> For them, the line between armed conflict and non-armed conflict operations is easily defined: when they are authorized to engage opponents based solely on status identification, opponents who ostensibly seek to kill them, they know they are engaged in armed conflict.

> When ROE authorizes engagement based solely on status determinations, it represents an inherent invocation of the laws of war as a source of operational authority, for it is the rules of necessity and military objective that will provide the parameters for implementing such ROE.

85    *Id.* at 50–52 (discussion of how adoption of status based ROE as trigger for application of LOAC would ensure that armed forces operate within framework of essential regulation derived from the history of warfare); *see* GWS at Art. II; GWS at Art. III.

86    See Gabor Rona, *When is a war not a war?—The proper role of the law of armed conflict in the "global war on terror,"* "International Action to Prevent and Combat Terrorism" *supra* note 42; Kenneth Watkin, *Controlling the Use of Force: A Role for Human Rights Norms in Contemporary Armed Conflict*, 98 AM. J. INTL. L. 1, 2–9 (Jan. 2004) (discussing the complex challenge of conflict categorization related military operations conducted against highly organized non-state groups with transnational reach); *see also* Kirby Abbott, Terrorists: Combatants, Criminals, or . . . ? in The Measures of International Law: Effectiveness, Fairness, and Validity, Proceedings of the 31st Annual Conference of the Canadian Council on International Law, Ottawa (Oct. 24–26, 2002); CRS Report, *supra* note 22 (analyzing whether the attacks of September 11 triggered the law of war).

execute operations under the GWOT rubric. These forces have been and will continue to be called upon to execute military operations to destroy or disable terrorist personnel and/or assets. Unlike politicians, policy makers, scholars, and pundits, they do not have the luxury of debating the legal niceties of whether the law of war should or should not apply to their operations. For them, the line between armed conflict and non-conflict operations is easily defined: When they are authorized to engage opponents based solely on status identification, opponents who ostensibly seek to kill them, they know they are engaged in armed conflict.[87]

It is therefore both logical and essential to treat such operations as bringing into force all fundamental LOAC principles. Doing so will ensure that the armed forces operate within the framework of essential regulation derived from the history of warfare,[88] prevent a non-state enemy from claiming a status or legitimacy unjustified by the conflict, and prevent national policy makers from avoiding the most basic humanitarian obligations through the assertion of technical legal arguments devoid of pragmatic military considerations.[89]

---

87   This section is a lightly edited extract from Geoffrey S. Corn and Eric Talbot Jensen's previous article, *Untying the Gordian Knot: A Proposal for Determining Applicability of the Laws of War to the War on Terror*, (*available at* http://ssrn.com/abstract=1083849).

88   Leslie C. Green, The Contemporary Law of Armed Conflict, at 20–33 (2d Ed.) (2000); *see also* Leslie C. Green, *What is—Why is There—the Law of War*, The Law of Armed Conflict: Into The Next Millennium Vol. 71, 176 U.S. Naval War College International Studies, Naval War College, Newport, Rhode Island (1998). Professor Green reminds readers not only that the regulation of warfare is as ancient as warfare itself, but that the logic of such regulation transcends hyper-technical legal paradigms defining what is "war" and when such rules should apply.

89   Geoffrey S. Corn and Eric Talbot Jensen, *Untying the Gordian Knot: A Proposal for Determining Applicability of the Laws of War to the War on Terror*, (*available at* http://ssrn.com/abstract=1083849) *at* 56 where authors state:

  More importantly, consistent with the underlying objective of the Geneva Conventions, the probability that an ROE based trigger for law of war application will be manipulated to avoid application of the law is *de minimis*. This is because of one simple reality: the state is unlikely to deprive its forces of the authority to effectively accomplish a military mission in order to avoid obligations imposed by the laws of war.

  *Id.*

## CONCLUSION

While the proposition that transnational armed conflicts must trigger LOAC principles may be gaining increasing acceptance, deciding how to define such conflicts, when these principles are legally applicable, and the substantive scope and content of these principles will continue to vex all the constituents involved in the conflict-regulation process. Asserting the logic of applying LOAC principles to all combat operations does not and simply cannot resolve perhaps the most complicated questions related to the regulation of conflict to emerge in decades: how does a State determine what triggers this law outside the Common Article 2/3 paradigm? As illustrated above, relying on the existing law-triggering criteria is insufficient to provide an effective answer to this question. This insufficiency has led to confusion as to when this law applies to contemporary operations, criticism of decisions related to its application, and uncertainty for the armed forces called upon to execute missions against non-state entities.

The answer to this question therefore must be derived from a new perspective, and it is the perspective of the warrior where it is found. Warriors understand the difference between conflict and non-conflict operations. This understanding is not based on the nature of the opponent, nor the geographic location of the operation, nor the scope, duration, or intensity of the operation. Instead, it is based on the pragmatic and simple reality that authorization to engage an opponent based solely on a status determination means the line has been crossed. Thus, for the warrior, the most fundamental indication of armed conflict is the nature of the authority that defines how combat power may be applied to accomplish a given mission.[90]

Until this uncertainty is resolved, armed forces will almost certainly endeavor to comply with the LOAC principles during military operations, even if only as a matter of national policy. The LOAC is, after all, an operational legal framework intended to serve the interests not only of the victims of war, but also of the warriors called upon to engage

---

90    *Id.* at 32; Chairman, Joint Chiefs of Staff Instruction 3121.01B, Standing Rules of Engagement/Standing Rules for the Use of Force for US Forces, encl. A, para. 1c (13 June 2005).

in war.[91] The mere fact that these warriors have and will continue to embrace the applicability of this framework during operations that fall into a realm of legal uncertainty is perhaps the most compelling indication of the validity of a transnational armed conflict trigger, and the invalidity of attempting to characterize such operations under some alternate legal paradigm.

*Entre armes, sine leges*[92] is a flawed concept. History demonstrates that the effective and disciplined execution of combat operations necessitates a regulatory framework. Fundamental LOAC principles—principles that ensure not only the humane treatment of captured and detained opponents but also the regulation of the employment of combat

---

91   *See* Derek Jinks and David Sloss, *Is the President Bound by the Geneva Conventions?*, 90 Cornell L. Rev. 97, 108–09 (November, 2004) where authors state:

> Embodied principally in the 1899 and 1907 Hague Conventions, Hague law prescribes the acceptable means and methods of warfare, particularly with regard to tactics and general conduct of hostilities. Though Geneva law and Hague law overlap, the terminology distinguishes two distinct regimes: one governing the treatment of persons subject to enemy's authority (Geneva law), and the other governing the treatment of persons subject to the enemy's lethality (Hague law). International humanitarian law embraces the whole *jus in bello*, in both its Geneva and Hague dimensions.

*Id.*

Geoffrey S. Corn and Eric Talbot Jensen, *Untying the Gordian Knot: A Proposal for Determining Applicability of the Laws of War to the War on Terror*, (*available at* http://ssrn.com/abstract=1083849) at 6. In this excerpt authors state the inherent purposes of the laws of war:

> Over time, this body of conflict regulation has come to be known as the "laws of war, the law of armed conflict, or more recently international humanitarian law" . . . they serve three broad purposes: 1) protecting both combatants and noncombatants from unnecessary suffering, 2) safeguarding both all persons who fall into the hands of the enemy, and 3) helping with the reestablishment of peace.

*Id.*

Int'l. & Operational Law Dep't, The Judge Advocate General's Legal Center and School, U.S. Army, JA 422, Operational Law Handbook, 12 (John Rawcliffe ed. 2007).

92   This section is lightly edited extract from Geoffrey S. Corn and Eric Talbot Jensen's previous article, *Untying the Gordian Knot: A Proposal for Determining Applicability of the Laws of War to the War on Terror*, (*available at* http://ssrn.com/abstract=1083849) at 62;*see* Gregory P. Noone, *The History and Evolution of the Law of War Prior to WWII*, 47 Naval. L. Rev. 176, 182–85 (2000) where author asserts that laws regulating conflict have developed in almost every culture.

power—provide this framework. Depriving warriors of the value of such an important set of principles—a value validated by hundreds of years of history[93]—on the basis of technical legal analysis of two treaty provisions is no longer acceptable. Instead, all warriors must understand that when they "ruck up" and "lock and load" to conduct operations during which an opponent will be destroyed on sight, the laws of war go with them.

---

93   *See* Howard S. Levie, *History of the Law of War on Land*, International Review of the Red Cross No. 838, 339 (2000); *see also* A.P.V. Rogers, Law on the Battlefield, (1996); Leslie C. Green, The Contemporary Law of Armed Conflict, at 20–33 (2d Ed.) (2000).

# CHAPTER 2

# TARGETING OF PERSONS AND PROPERTY

By Lieutenant Colonel Eric T. Jensen[†]

It is a simple reality of warfare that in order to defeat an enemy it is necessary to attack and destroy the enemy's combat capability. Employment of combat power for this purpose is referred to in the lexicon of military operations as targeting. The targeting process involves identifying a potential target or desired effect and determining it as a military objective; selecting the most appropriate capability, whether kinetic or non-kinetic, to achieve the desired operational effect; executing military operations to employ the combat capability; and assessing the effects achieved. Once the effects are assessed, that information is fed back into the targeting process, and the cycle continuously repeats itself.[1]

Executing such operations within the bounds of the law of armed conflict is undoubtedly challenging in any operational context. However, in the context of transnational armed conflict (TAC) against terrorists, this challenge is exacerbated by the uncertainty regarding the boundaries of military objective and the unconventional nature of the non-state enemy. Questions concerning the identity of terrorists, their mixture within the civilian populace, the desire to interdict those who support them in their terrorist acts, and the length of time those conducting and supporting terrorist acts can be targeted are all questions that highlight the increased difficulty in applying the core principles of targeting to a terrorist conflict. It is therefore critical to identify and embrace a meaningful and effective regulatory framework for targeting operations in this context, one that does not disregard the fundamental principles of wartime targeting upon

---

[†]  Chief, International Law Branch, Office of The Judge Advocate General, U.S. Army. LTC Jensen holds an LL.M. from Yale Law School, and LL.M. from The Judge Advocate General's Legal Center and School and a Juris Doctor degree from University of Notre Dame Law School. He has served for twenty years in the U.S. Army and been deployed as a legal advisor to operations in Bosnia, Macedonia, and Iraq. He was also an assistant professor at The Judge Advocate General's Legal Center and School where he taught international law and law of war topics.

[1]  U.S. Dep't of the Army, Field Manual 6-20-10, Tactics, Techniques and Procedures for the Targeting Process, Chapter 2 (8 May 1996).

which militaries have consistently trained, but also one that accounts for the unique difficulties of targeting in this complex TAC environment.

While a characteristic of TAC is often its proximity to the civilian population, warfare has always affected the local population and seldom ever occurred on a contained, sterile battlefield where two combatant groups who were easily recognizable to each other fought under the same rules, with the victor conquering the vanquished and leaving hostilities on the battlefield while moving through the conquered territory. More often, the fighting forces have moved freely in and out of the population not only during, but also before and after the major battles. Despite this historical reality, the percentage of civilian casualties injured during armed conflict has risen steadily in the twentieth century, from 19 percent in World War I to 48 percent in World War II and to 90 percent in the armed conflicts of the 1990s.[2]

Though there are undoubtedly numerous reasons for these statistics, it is interesting to note that concurrent with this increase in risk to those not directly involved in combat has been a dramatic increase in technological advancement of weaponry and in the codification of rules on how to employ those weapons. Ironically, the purposes of both these advances has included mitigation of the risk of harming innocent civilians and their property, a primary purpose of the law that regulates targeting and an inherent purpose of developing weapons that can more accurately strike legitimate objects of attack. It is a matter of debate as to whether these technological and legal innovations have had their desired effect.

This disparity between intent and execution is nowhere more apparent than in the "Global War on Terror," including the recent conflicts in Afghanistan and Iraq where terrorists have not only fueled insurgencies but taken an active part in both military and support operations. Armed forces in both conflict areas have been confounded in their attempts to properly apply the targeting principles in areas where fighters, financiers, suppliers, and trainers intentionally integrate themselves into the civilian populace to accrue undeserved protections.[3] These militaries are

---

2   Ronald R. Lett, Olive Chifefe Kobusingye, & Paul Ekwaru, *Burden of Injury During the Complex Political Emergency in Northern Uganda*, 49 CANADIAN JOURNAL OF SURGERY 1, 51 (2006) *available at* http://www.cma.ca/multimedia/staticContent/HTML/N0/l2/cjs/vol-49/issue-1/pdf/pg51.pdf.

3   *See* Kelly McCann, *CNN Live Sunday: U.S. Helicopter Shot Down in Iraq, Both Pilots Killed; 7 Chinese Citizens Taken Hostage in* Iraq (CNN television broadcast,

committed to applying the core principles of the law of war by refraining from attacking the civilian population. However, they also recognize that they still have to be able to conduct military operations in an effective manner.

This chapter will analyze the targeting of persons and property in the war on terror. This analysis will begin by exploring the legal principles related to targeting that apply in combat operations generally, including the origins of these principles and how they form the foundation of the hostility regulation prong of the law of war. The chapter will then address how these principles apply in operations directed against transnational terrorist enemies, with particular attention to the challenging aspects of their application, such as dealing with co-mingled civilian and enemy forces and limitation on collateral damage in densely populated areas. The chapter will conclude with the assertion that though the law of war is highly developed, nations are now imposing policy limitations on their militaries that are far more restrictive than the law of armed conflict would require, making the targeting process in TAC even more complex.

## A. ORIGINS OF THE LAW OF TARGETING

Laws of war are not a modern conception. Many ancient cultures have had rules concerning the conduct of hostilities, including the Chinese, Babylonians, Hittites, Persians, Greeks, and others.[4] These rules concerned

---

Apr. 11, 2004) (041104CN.V36) LEXIS, News File where the author quotes a military spokesperson as saying:

> We are working at a disadvantage … The lack of uniforms, so that you can't define the enemy very well. And the intertwining of the enemy with combatants is very, very difficult. So you've got combatants and non-combatants mixed together intentionally.

*Id.*

4   For information on the historical development of the laws of war, *see* William Bradford, *Barbarians at the Gates: A Post-September 11th Proposal to Rationalize the Laws of War*, 73 Miss. L. J. 639 (2004); Chris af Jochnick and Roger Normand, *The Legitimation of Violence: A Critical History of the Laws of War*, 35 Harv. Int'l L.J. 49 (Winter, 1994); Gregory P. Noone, *The History and Evolution of the Law of War Prior to WWII*, 47 Naval. L. Rev 176 (2000); Thomas C. Wingfield, *Chivalry in the Use of Force*, 32 U. Tol. L. Rev. 111 (2001); Scott R. Morris, *The Laws of War: Rules by Warriors for Warriors*, 1997 Army Law. 4 (Dec., 1997); Nathan A. Canestaro, *"Small Wars" and the Law: Options for Prosecuting the Insurgents in Iraq*, 43 Colum. J. Transnat'l L. 73 (2004); Eric Krauss & Michael Lacey, *Warriors vs. Humanitarians: The Battle Over the Law of War*, Parameters, Summer 2002, at 74–75; Eric Talbot Jensen, *Combatant Status: It is Time for Intermediate Levels of*

a broad range of actions, from what weapons could be used in combat, to the proper treatment of captives. While the rules often differed from civilization to civilization and from era to era, almost every armed force was guided by some rules that limited its actions.

During the age of chivalry, the customs and usages of war developed rather intricate rules for actions when attacking an enemy, such as the rules for plunder, siege, ransom, and parole, as well as combat rules, such as the distinction between ruses and perfidy. These rules not only helped regulate methods of attack, but also relations generally between fighting factions. As the feudal system gave way to the rise of the nation state, and its dominance as the major player in international relations, use of knights also gave way to the use of professional armies who represented the State. This transition broadened the scope of who participated in hostilities and turned greater focus on the laws governing war.

In response to the renewed focus on the laws of armed conflict, nations began in the nineteenth century to codify these rules that had developed over time. Examples of this include the 1863 Lieber Code, which established rules for the conduct of hostilities by Union forces in the American Civil War, and the Hague Conventions of 1899 and 1907, which codified the customs of war that were accepted by the major European nations.[5] These conventions and others like them came to be known as the "Hague tradition." The Hague tradition, typified by the 1907 Hague regulations, became the foundation upon which all modern laws of armed conflict are built and embody concepts still valid today.

Though not extensive, the Annex to Hague Convention (IV) Respecting the Laws and Customs of War on Land[6] contains several articles that concern the targeting of persons and property during armed conflict. Article 22 states that "The right of belligerents to adopt means of injuring the enemy is not unlimited." While not announcing a specific prohibition, this article presents a general premise that even in warfare, there are limits. The next article announces some specific limits, including the proscription on the use of poisonous weapons, treacherous killing or

---

*Recognition for Partial Compliance*, 46 Va J. Int'l L. 214 (2005); Rosa Ehrenreich Brooks, *War Everywhere: Rights, National Security Law, and the Law of Armed Conflict in the Age of Terror*, 153 U. Pa. L. Rev. 675, 706 (2004).

5    *See generally* Dietrich Schindler & Jiri Toman, The Laws of Armed Conflicts (3rd ed. 1988).

6    *Available at* http://www.icrc.org/ihl.nsf/FULL/195?OpenDocument.

wounding, killing or wounding those who have surrendered or are *hors de combat*, and employing weapons that will cause unnecessary suffering. Article 25 prohibits the attack or bombardment of undefended places, and Article 26 requires warnings by the attacker in certain circumstances. Article 27 protects certain buildings from attack, such as hospitals and other civilian structures, as long as they are not being used for military purposes.

While these provisions will seem antiquated and incomplete to the modern soldier, they are the foundation upon which current law is constructed. The Hague tradition contained not only general rules such as those mentioned above, but also embraced specific prohibitions, such as the 1868 Declaration of St. Petersburg that prohibited explosive projectiles under 400 grams, and the 1925 Protocol for the Prohibition of the Use in War of Asphyxiating, Poisonous, or Other Gases, and of Bacteriological Methods of Warfare.

As previously mentioned, WWII exhibited an exponential rise in wartime costs in both human lives and property. In the years immediately following WWII, once again the world community turned its focus to regulating warfare. Codification began with the 1949 Geneva Conventions, which dealt with the wounded and sick; wounded, sick, and shipwrecked; prisoners of war (hereinafter GPW), and civilians during times of armed conflict (hereinafter GCC).[7] While the first three Geneva Conventions built upon preexisting established principles that survived WWII and were aimed at members of the military, the GCC extended certain protections to civilians based on the fact that they are not covered by

---

7 *See* Convention (I) for the Amelioration of the Condition of the Wounded and Sick in Armed Forces in the Field, Article 2 *opened for signature* Aug. 12, 1949, 6 U.S.T. 3114, 75 U.N.T.S. 31, *reprinted in* DIETRICH SCHINDLER & JIRI TOMAN, THE LAWS OF ARMED CONFLICTS 373, 376 (3d ed. 1988) (hereinafter GWS) *available at* http://www.icrc.org/ihl.nsf/Full/365Open-Document; Convention (II) for the Amelioration of the Condition of Wounded, Sick, and Shipwrecked Members of Armed Forces at Sea, *opened for signature* Aug. 12, 1949, 6 U.S.T. 3217, 75 U.N.T.S. 85, *reprinted in* SCHINDLER & TOMAN, *supra*, at 404 (hereinafter GSW) *available at* http://www.icrc.org/ihl.nsf/Full/370OpenDocument; Convention (III) Relative to the Treatment of Prisoners of War, *opened for signature* Aug. 12, 1949, 6 U.S.T. 3316, 75 U.N.T.S. 135, *reprinted in* SCHINDLER & TOMAN, *supra*, at 429-30 (hereinafter GPW) *available at* http://www.icrc.org/ihl.nsf/Full/375OpenDocument; and Convention (IV) Relative to the Protection of Civilian Persons in Time of War, *opened for signature* Aug. 12, 1949, 6 U.S.T. 3516, 75 U.N.T.S 287, *reprinted in* SCHINDLER & TOMAN, *supra*, at 501 (hereinafter GCC) *available at* http://www.icrc.org/ihl.nsf/Full/380OpenDocument.

provisions of the other three Conventions. None of those provisions dealt specifically with targeting of persons and property, but they codified the idea that civilians were victims of armed conflict, not participants, and deserved certain protections from hostilities.

In the two decades that followed the 1949 Geneva Conventions, world politics developed into a bi-polar world, with the United States and its North Atlantic Treaty Organization members directly opposing the Soviet Union and its supporting Warsaw Pact members. The most significant aspect of this bi-polar world was the lack of armed conflict between the major powers. While many conflicts erupted across the globe, the two superpowers did not come into direct military conflict and avoided unleashing their massive weapons arsenals and armies against each other. Rather, they fought through surrogates or on the side of an embattled "ally" where direct confrontation with the other superpower was unlikely. During one such war, the Vietnam War, there were numerous allegations that many of the provisions of the law of war were disregarded.[8]

Partially in response to these violations and in an attempt to update the 1949 Geneva Conventions, the International Committee of the Red Cross (ICRC) led the world in adopting the 1977 Protocols to the Geneva Conventions.[9] These Protocols revisited the rules of warfare and produced the most complete codification of those rules to date. Their applicability will be discussed below, but it is sufficient here to mention

---

8    *See* Cara Levy Rodriguez, *Slaying the Monster: Why the United States Should Not Support the Rome Treaty*, 14 AM. U. INT'L L. REV. 805, at note 130 (1999) (referencing the alleged American violations of the Law of War); Major Jeffrey F. Addicott and Major William A. Hudson, JR., *The Twenty-Fifth Anniversary of My Lai: A Time to Inculcate the Lessons*, 139 MIL. L. REV. 153, 174–75 (Winter, 1993) (referencing the alleged North Vietnamese violations of the Law of War). *Cf.* Adam Roberts, *The Laws of War: Problems of Implementation in Contemporary Conflicts*, 6 DUKE J. COMP. & INT'L L. 11, 43 (1995) (where the author states that law of war violations were not prosecuted during this time period because of the superpower deadlock between the United States and the Soviet Union); Earl H. Lubensky, *Internal Security & Human Rights: Militarism and Diplomacy, available at http://www.unc.edu/depts/diplomat/archives_roll/2002_01-03/lubensky_internal/ lubensky_internal.html.*

9    Protocol Additional to the Geneva Conventions of Aug. 12, 1949, and Relating to the Protection of Victims of International Armed Conflicts (Protocol I) [hereinafter GPI]; and Protocol Additional to the Geneva Conventions of 12 August 1949, and Relating to the Protections of Victims of Non-International Armed Conflicts (Protocol II)[hereinafter GPII], *opened for signature* Dec. 12, 1977, 16 I. L. M. 1391.

that the vast majority of the world accepts the provisions of these two Protocols as binding on all nations when in armed conflict.

GPI and GPII were focused largely on rules for the conduct of warfare and were meant as supplements to the existing Geneva Conventions and Hague tradition. As supplements, they added substantive rules in many areas of the law of armed conflict, including key provisions on the targeting of persons and property. Though not ratified by the United States, GPI and GPII have quickly become accepted as customary law by most of the nations of the world.[10]

As well as more general rules, regulation on specific weapons systems and tactics has also continued in the post-WWII era. The 1980 Convention on Prohibitions or Restrictions on the Use of Certain Conventional Weapons which may be Deemed to be Excessively Injurious or to have Indiscriminate Effects (CCW) with its Protocols,[11] the 1993 Convention on the Prohibition of the Development, Production, Stockpiling, and Use of Chemical Weapons and on their Destruction (CWC),[12] and the 1997 Convention on the Prohibition of the Use, Stockpiling, Production, and Transfer of Anti-Personnel Mines and on their Destruction[13] are examples of this. In each case, State parties have agreed to limit their warfighting capabilities or methods, often despite the objection of their militaries.[14]

The regulation of targeting of persons and property is an ongoing history as illustrated by the recent initiative to prohibit cluster munitions. The means and methods of warfare will always be a topic of discussion, not only amongst militaries and governments, but also amongst

---

10 *See* Michael J. Matheson, *The United States Position on the Relation of Customary Law to the 1977 Protocols Additional to the 1949 Geneva Conventions,* 2 Am. U. J. Int'l L. & Pol'y 419 (1987) (discussing which articles of GPI the U.S. believes are customary international law and to which the U.S. objects).

11 *Available at* http://www.icrc.org/IHL.nsf/5a780f680129b33841256739003e6367/ 396eb56361f2e5e3c12563cd0051eca4?OpenDocument&Highlight=0,conventional.

12 *Available at* http://www.opcw.org/.

13 *Available at* http://www.icrc.org/IHL.nsf/52d68d14de6160e0c12563da005fdb1 b/d111fff4b9c85b0f41256585003caec3?OpenDocument.

14 *See* Major Christopher W. Jacobs, *Taking the Next Step: An Analysis of the Effects the Ottawa Convention May Have On the Interoperability of United States Forces With the Armed Forces of Australia, Great Britain, and Canada,* 180 Military Law Review 49 (Summer 2004).

non-governmental organizations and other like-minded groups who are concerned about the effects of war, both on participants and non-participants alike. It is appropriate next, therefore, to look at where this history has left the current law on targeting of persons and property.

## B. THE LAW OF TARGETING PERSONS AND PROPERTY

As addressed previously in this book, there are generally two types of armed conflict, as defined by Articles 2 and 3 of the Geneva Conventions. Article 2 defines international armed conflict as "armed conflict which may arise between two or more of the High Contracting Parties."[15] Such conflicts explicitly invoke the full body of the law of war, including the Geneva Conventions and Hague tradition, as well as other conventional and customary international law. For those who have ratified GPI, it also applies to international armed conflict and contains many provisions that apply to the law of targeting.

In contrast, Article 3 conflicts are conflicts "not of an international character,"[16] and the provisions concerning this type of armed conflict are much less extensive. This is particularly true in the area of targeting, where Article 3 is completely silent. However, for those who have ratified GPII, several provisions apply fundamental principles of the law of targeting to non-international armed conflicts. In fact, there is general consensus now that the principles of targeting apply to armed conflict generally, whether Article 2 or 3.[17] No distinction need be made between international and non-international armed conflict. Rather, the principles of targeting apply generally to all forms of armed conflict. This is exemplified by the fundamental targeting principle of distinction.

Distinction is a principle of warfare that has existed as long as organized conflict itself.[18] The codified statement of distinction comes from GPI and requires militaries to "distinguish between the civilian population and combatants and between civilian objects and military objectives and

---

15    GPW, *supra* note 7, article 2.

16    GPW, *supra* note 7, article 3.

17    International Institute of Humanitarian Law, The Manual on the Law of Non-International Armed Conflict, Sanremo, March 2006 (hereinafter NIAC Manual).

18    NIAC Manual, *supra* note 17, at 10 (quoting API Commentary); A.P.V. ROGERS, LAW ON THE BATTLEFIELD (1996) ("The great principles of customary law, from which all else stems, are those of military necessity, humanity, distinction and proportionality.").

accordingly [to] direct their operations only against military objectives."[19] To support this principle, the law of armed conflict evolved to establish three general categories of individuals on the battlefield: combatants, non-combatants, and civilians. Combatants are those persons who meet the criteria of GPW art. 4a(1), (2), (3), or (6).[20] Non-combatants include medical personnel and chaplains who are authorized to be on the battlefield but lose their protections if they engage in combat acts.[21] All other persons are classified as civilians[22] and benefit from presumptive immunity from being made the object of attack. Both the International Criminal Tribunal for the former Yugoslavia (ICTY) in the *Tadić* decision[23] and

---

19    GPI, *supra* note 9, article 48.

20    *See* Convention (III) Relative to the Treatment of Prisoners of War, Aug. 12, 1949, 6 U.S.T. 3316, 75 U.N.T.S. 135, *reprinted in* DIETRICH SCHINDLER & JIRI TOMAN, THE LAWS OF ARMED CONFLICTS 430–31 (2d ed. 1981) which requires:

>     A. Prisoners of War, in the sense of the present Convention, are persons belonging to one of the following categories, who have fallen into the power of the enemy:
>
>     (1) Members of the armed forces of a Party to the conflict as well as members of militias or volunteer corps forming part of such armed forces.
>
>     (2) Members of other militias and members of other volunteer corps, including those of organized resistance movements, belonging to a Party to the conflict and operating in or outside their own territory, even if this territory is occupied, provided that such militias or volunteer corps, including such organized resistance movements, fulfill the following conditions:
>
>>     (a) that of being commanded by a person responsible for his subordinates;
>>
>>     (b) that of having a fixed distinctive sign recognizable at a distance;
>>
>>     (c) that of carrying arms openly;
>>
>>     (d) that of conducting their operations in accordance with the laws and customs of war.
>
>     (3) Members of regular armed forces who profess allegiance to a government or an authority not recognized by the Detaining Power.
>
>     …
>
>     (6) Inhabitants of a non-occupied territory, who on the approach of the enemy spontaneously take up arms to resist the invading forces, without having had time to form themselves into regular armed units, provided they carry arms openly and respect the laws and customs of war.

21    Protocol Additional to the Geneva Conventions of 12 August 1949, and relating to the Protection of Victims of International Armed Conflicts (Protocol I), 8 June 1977 [hereinafter GPI], arts. 13, 43, para. 2 June 8, 1977.

22    *Id.* at art. 50.

23    Prosecutor v. Tadić, *supra* note 34, at ¶¶ 102–104 where the appellate chamber opined that the principle of distinction was so fundamental to the conduct of hostilities that it applied to equally to all armed conflicts.

the NIAC Manual embrace this interpretation. The NIAC Manual states that it is "indisputable that the principle of distinction is customary international law for both international and non-international armed conflict."[24]

Distinction is really about target selection. When a targeter analyzes who he may target, he is really applying the concept of distinction. Because armed forces are showing an increased proclivity to conduct their operations in close proximity to civilian population centers and to co-mingle their forces with civilians, the principle of distinction is increasingly central to the effective regulation of all armed conflicts. The difficulty arises when defining what actions by civilians make them targetable, particularly in an environment where one side of the armed conflict is presumably composed completely of civilians who have decided to take up arms without meeting all the criteria of a nation's armed forces.

The law makes it clear that civilians are not targetable. The clearest statement of this standard is found in GPI. Article 51 states:

> Art 51.—Protection of the civilian population
>
> 1. The civilian population and individual civilians shall enjoy general protection against dangers arising from military operations. To give effect to this protection, the following rules, which are additional to other applicable rules of international law, shall be observed in all circumstances.
>
> 2. The civilian population as such, as well as individual civilians, shall not be the object of attack. Acts or threats of violence the primary purpose of which is to spread terror among the civilian population are prohibited.
>
> 3. Civilians shall enjoy the protection afforded by this section, unless and for such time as they take a direct part in hostilities.[25]

Paragraphs 1 and 2 state the civilian populations' immunity from attack. The international community was anxious to restate and codify the desire to preserve the civilian population from the effects of conflict. However, this immunity is not absolute as paragraph 3 makes clear.

The immunity granted to civilians is subject to divestment, but only "unless and for such time as they take a direct part in hostilities." There is a great deal of discussion and disagreement on what that provision actually means. This is a discussion of no small import. Though these

---

24    NIAC Manual, *supra* note 17, at ¶ 1.2.2.3.

25    GPI, *supra* note 9, article 51.

words are clearly recognized as the standard in the law of armed conflict, there is great disagreement on how those words actually apply in practice. In recent conflicts, there has been a tendency for at least one side in the conflict to intermingle itself with the local population, making it extremely difficult for nations that wish to comply with the distinction rule. Therefore, Article 51 is key to the correct application of targeting.

There are two elements to a civilian's involvement in hostilities. The first, direct participation, has become an issue of great debate, particularly in transnational armed conflicts with terrorists. In an attempt to provide "interpretive guidance" on the issue, the ICRC has convened a group of experts from a number of different nations and a wide variety of backgrounds and attempted to clarify or provide a framework for analysis of this difficult concept. The report is due to be released in June of 2009, but the ICRC's legal adviser responsible for the project provided an insight at the American Society of International Law's annual meeting into what the final report will likely say.[26] According to the report, acts amounting to direct participation in hostilities must meet three cumulative criteria. The first criterion is the threshold of harm: the act in question must be likely to adversely affect the military operations or military capacity of a party to the conflict, or, to inflict death, injury or destruction on persons or objects protected against direct attack. To meet this criterion, the action must create harm of a sufficient degree to the enemy or to civilians.

If the first criterion is met, the second criterion is to establish a direct link between the action and the harm. This second criterion is direct causation and requires that there must be a direct causal link (i.e., "one step" causation) between the act in question and the harm likely to result from that act, or from a concrete and coordinated military operation of which that act constitutes an integral part. This does not include an indirect link (which would amount to indirect participation), such as working in a munitions factory or an oil refinery which supplies the enemy's military with war-sustaining capability. Rather, the action must be an integral part of a concrete military action.

Finally, the third criterion requires a belligerent nexus, or that the act must be designed to directly cause the required threshold of harm in support of a party to the conflict and to the detriment of another. If all three

---

26  Presentation by Nils Melzer, International Committee of the Red Cross, at the American Society of International Law Annual Meeting, 26 March 2009.

criteria are met, the first element of a civilian's direct participation is established. That is, there is sufficient participation to allow targeting while the civilian in question engaged in the specific act. This raises the question of the temporal scope of the ensuing loss of protection. As the commander contemplates targeting that individual, he may not be able to target him at the exact moment the individual takes direct part in hostilities. At what point and for how long does that individual remain targetable? On one end of the spectrum is the civilian who directly participates one time and then ceases his participation. Is he targetable until the end of hostilities? On the other end of the spectrum is the civilian by day and guerilla by night who carries out a continuous pattern of hostile acts against his foes. Is he only targetable while conducting the actual nighttime raid? This element of time is the second element of a civilian's participation in hostilities and is based on the phrase "unless and for such time."

Many nations' scholars have taken a restrictive view on the time element and read very narrowly the requirements for a time nexus, arguing that the time window for targeting is very narrow. The contrary position to the narrow reading of the "for such time" dilemma is that once an individual has directly participated in hostilities, he must either abstain from further participation or affirmatively opt out of direct participation to regain the protections of his civilian status. The ICRC study is also attempting to assist in defining this provision more concretely and setting a more generally accepted standard. The published guidance will likely assert that civilians lose protection against direct attack for the duration of each specific act amounting to direct participation in hostilities. This loss of protection only occurs only for the duration of the act, including concrete preparatory measures, deployments to the location of their execution, and return from the location of their execution. Responding to the often raised "revolving door" problem where civilians are farmers by day but become insurgents every night, the ICRC recognizes that these individuals should have an expanded window of targetability. However, to fall into that expanded window, they must be members of an organized group operating as the armed wing of a non-state party to an armed conflict. According to the report, the concept of membership in an organized armed group includes only persons who assume a continuous function involving their direct participation in hostilities ("continuous function"). Only then could they be assimilated to State combatants and, therefore, also targeted outside the concrete preparation, attack, and return.[27]

---

27    *Id.*

As was pointed out at the same conference, it is unclear how States will respond to the ICRC's approach. However, there are certainly some issues that will bear consideration. For example, what does it take to establish a "continuous" combat function within an organized armed group, and how does an individual disassociate himself from an armed group if he later becomes disaffected? Is it appropriate that individuals who form a part of the fighting unit without assuming a continuous combat function that involves direct participation in hostilities (e.g., cooks) are immunized from direct attack when their counterparts in nations' uniformed armed forces can be targeted under the laws of war? These are valid questions that will be discussed by both States and academics (once the ICRC report is released) and that will hopefully, over time, clarify these important targeting principles.

In addition to the targeting of persons, there are also specific provisions concerning the law of targeting civilian objects. The current statement on this portion of the law of targeting is found in GPI, Article 52. The article states:

Art 52. General Protection of civilian objects

1. Civilian objects shall not be the object of attack or of reprisals. Civilian objects are all objects which are not military objectives as defined in paragraph 2.

2. Attacks shall be limited strictly to military objectives. In so far as objects are concerned, military objectives are limited to those objects which by their nature, location, purpose or use make an effective contribution to military action and whose total or partial destruction, capture, or neutralization, in the circumstances ruling at the time, offers a definite military advantage.

3. In case of doubt whether an object which is normally dedicated to civilian purposes, such as a place of worship, a house or other dwelling, or a school, is being used to make an effective contribution to military action, it shall be presumed not to be so used.[28]

The first paragraph of this article grants the same immunity to civilian objects as is granted in the prior article to the civilian populace—immunity from attack. As in the case of actual civilians, this immunity can be forfeited.

---

28 *See* GPI, *supra* note 9, article 52.

Paragraph 2 of Article 52 requires the commander to analyze an object's nature, location, purpose, or use to determine if it is a valid military objective. Some objects are military by their nature, such as tanks, artillery, and military aircraft. Commanders can target these objects without further analysis. Objects that are by nature civilian may become military objects, based on their location, purpose, or use. For example, a building that normally houses a civilian business would normally be a civilian object. However, if a portion of the building were used to house a military command post, its nature would be transformed into a military one. This would be true even if the rest of the building were still being used by civilians for non-military purposes.[29] Objects that are concurrently both military and civilian are known as dual-use objects. The commander

---

29  COMMENTARY ON THE ADDITIONAL PROTOCOLS OF 8 JUNE 1977 TO THE GENEVA CONVENTIONS OF 1949, para. 2020–23 (S. Pictet et al. eds., 1958) [hereinafter GPI Commentary] defines the terms nature, location, purpose, and use:

> 2020 A closer look at the various criteria used reveals that the first refers to objects which, by their 'nature,' make an effective contribution to military action. This category comprises all objects directly used by the armed forces: weapons, equipment, transports, fortifications, depots, buildings occupied by armed forces, staff headquarters, communications centers, etc.

> 2021 The second criterion is concerned with the 'location' of objects. Clearly, there are objects which by their nature have no military function but which, by virtue of their location, make an effective contribution to military action. This may be, for example, a bridge or other construction, or it could also be, as mentioned above, (13) a site which is of special importance for military operations in view of its location, either because it is a site that must be seized or because it is important to prevent the enemy from seizing it, or otherwise because it is a matter of forcing the enemy to retreat from it. It should be noted that the Working Group of Committee III introduced the location criterion without giving reasons.

> 2022 The criterion of 'purpose' is concerned with the intended future use of an object, while that of 'use' is concerned with its present function. Most civilian objects can become useful objects to the armed forces. Thus, for example, a school or a hotel is a civilian object, but if they are used to accommodate troops or headquarters staff, they become military objectives. It is clear from paragraph 3 that in case of doubt, such places must be presumed to serve civilian purposes.

> 2023 Other establishments or buildings which are dedicated to the production of civilian goods may also be used for the benefit of the army. In this case the object has a dual function and is of value for the civilian population, but also for the military. In such situations the time and place of the attack should be taken into consideration, together with, on the one hand, the military advantage anticipated, and on the other hand, the loss of human life which must be expected among the civilian population and the damage which would be caused to civilian objects.

can still attack dual-use objects, such as the building in our example, but must move to the next step of the analysis.

Paragraph 2 contains two further qualifiers on the commander's ability to target property. Once the commander has determined that the piece of property is a military object by its nature, location, purpose, or use, he must also determine that the property makes an effective contribution to the military action and that the "total or partial destruction, capture or neutralization, in the circumstances ruling at the time, offers a definite military advantage." The first of these is a relatively low standard. One might argue that a piece of military equipment such as a tank that is in disrepair and nonfunctional may not be making an effective contribution to the military effort. However, the commander may determine that it could be used for spare parts or in a ruse or for some other military purpose and legitimately determine to target it.

The latter end of the paragraph requires a similar analysis but with a slightly higher standard. Once the commander has determined that the object's nature, location, purpose, or use provide the enemy with a military benefit, he must determine that the destruction of the object will provide his forces a "definite military advantage." While these words are not clearly defined in the text, the commentary states:

> it is not legitimate to launch an attack which only offers potential or indeterminate advantages. Those ordering or executing the attack must have sufficient information available to take this requirement into account; in case of doubt, the safety of the civilian population, which is the aim of the Protocol, must be taken into consideration.[30]

Unless the target meets both the nature, location, purpose, or use test *and* the "definite military advantage" test, the commander is precluded from attacking an object.

Once it has been determined that the individual or object is a legitimate target, the person doing the targeting must then consider the means used to target and the method of munition employment—both of which are an integral part of targeting, and both of which present legal proscriptions within the law of targeting. The means of targeting generally refers to the weapon used to engage the person, whether that be an infantryman's rifle, an explosive round fired from an artillery tube, or a bomb dropped from

---

30   *See* GPI Commentary, *supra* note 30, para. 2024, *available at* http://www.icrc.org/ihl.nsf/1a13044f3bbb5b8ec12563fb0066f226/5f27276ce1bbb79dc12563cd00434969!OpenDocument.

an aircraft. Every weapon used by the United States must pass a legal review to ensure that it complies with international law[31] and is not specifically prohibited.[32] As long as the weapon is not prohibited and has been appropriately reviewed, it is a valid means of targeting. However, it may be employed in a method that is a violation of the law of armed conflict.

The method of targeting is most often a matter of tactics, deciding how and when to employ a weapon system. However, it also has legal implications, particularly in light of the principle of proportionality.[33] The rule of proportionality is "an attempt to balance the conflicting military and humanitarian interests (or to balance military necessity and humanity) and is most evident in connection with the reduction of incidental damage caused by military operations."[34] As mentioned in the Commentary to Protocol II, proportionality, like distinction, is among the "general principles relating to the protection of the civilian population which apply irrespective of whether the conflict is an international or an internal one."[35]

The authoritative statement on proportionality is found in GPI, Articles 51.5(b) and 57.2(iii), which compel a member of the military to "refrain from deciding to launch any attack which may be expected to cause incidental loss of civilian life, injury to civilians, damage to civilian objects, or a combination thereof, which would be excessive in relation to the concrete and direct military advantage anticipated."[36]

The NIAC Manual provides an excellent explanation of the terms and meaning of proportionality[37] that need not be repeated here. The rule of

---

31   *See* U.S. Dep't of the Army, Army Regulation 27-53, Review of Legality of Weapons Under International Law (1 January 1979).

32   For example, the Convention on the Prohibition of the Development, Production, Stockpiling and Use of Chemical Weapons and on Their Destruction, *available at* http://www.icrc.org/ihl.nsf/Full/553OpenDocument, made the use of chemical weapons illegal as a method of warfare.

33   *See generally* Eric Talbot Jensen, *Unexpected Consequences from Knock-On Effects: A Different Standard for Computer Network Operations?*, 18 American University International Law Review 1145, 1170–73 (2003).

34   *See* Rogers, *supra* note 18.

35   *See* Jean Pictet, et. al., Commentary on the Additional Protocols of 8 June 1977 to the Geneva Conventions of 12 August 1949 [hereinafter Protocol I & II Commentary] 1449 (1987).

36   GPI, *supra* note 9, article 57.2(iii).

37   NIAC Manual, *supra* note 16, at ¶ 2.1.1.4.

proportionality applies only to civilians and civilian property.[38] There is no requirement that a combatant limit the quantum of his force when engaging another combatant or civilians who take a direct part in hostilities. The rule of proportionality only affects the method of targeting if the commander anticipates that it may be expected to cause incidental injury to civilians or damage civilian property. There are several key words in this definition, including "may be expected," "concrete and direct," and "anticipated."

For the commander to be required to refrain from an attack, there must be some expectation of collateral damage. Therefore, if after reviewing the target, the commander determines that, given the information he has, there are no civilians in the area or civilian objects, he need not expect collateral damage. If that expectation, based on faulty information, proves to be wrong after the attack, there is no violation. This determination prior to the attack is made based on the best information available to him at the time the decision must be made.[39] It is the targeter's reasonable expectation that is the standard. If the targeter is relying on information from a source that has been faulty in the recent past, he may need to take additional steps to confirm the information before launching the attack. However, if the information comes from a trusted source, the commander can place full reliance on that information.

Once the targeter has ascertained the expected collateral damage, he must balance the damage against the anticipated concrete and direct military advantage. Concrete and direct military advantage is discussed in the commentary to GPI. The Commentary states, "A military advantage can only consist in ground gained and in annihilating or weakening the enemy armed forces. In addition, it should be noted that the words

---

38   See Michael N. Schmitt, Ethics and Military Force: The *Jus in Bello*, Address before the Carnegie Council of Ethics and International Affairs workshop on European and North American perspectives on ethics and the use of force, at 9 (January 2002) [hereinafter Schmitt, *Jus in Bello*] *available at* http://www.carnegiecouncil.org/test/about/transcript_schmitt.html.

39   See Matthew Lippman, *Conundrums of Armed Conflict: Criminal Defenses to Violations of the Humanitarian Law of War*, 15 Dick. J. Int'l L. 1, 63 (1996) (discussing the Rendulic case where German General Rendulic was acquitted of charges of unnecessarily destroying civilian property based on the ground that "the conditions, as they appeared to the defendant at the time, were sufficient upon which he could honestly conclude that urgent military necessity warrant the decision made.").

'concrete and direct' impose stricter conditions on the attacker than those implied by the criteria defining military objectives in Article 52."[40]

While concrete and direct is a fairly high standard, it is based on the advantage anticipated by the targeter. In other words, if the attack is carried out and there is little military advantage gained, that is not relevant in the consideration of whether the commander appropriately applied the standard. The standard is completely forward looking, not retrospective. Of course, as with the expectation of collateral damage, the anticipation must be reasonable, but it need not be perfect.

Even if these conditions are not met, that does not necessarily preclude the overall attack. Instead, the commander may reconsider his means or methods of attack in order to produce different results. The Air Force has developed an intricate modeling process for estimating collateral damage that is not available outside of military channels but provides the commander with an accurate picture of the damage a munition will do in a particular scenario.[41]

In summary, when engaging a target, a targeter must first determine that the target is a combatant or a civilian who is taking direct part in hostilities by committing or having committed an act that is designed to directly harm the enemy. That civilian can be targeted "for such time" as he is participating directly. When targeting, the targeter must apply a reviewed and approved weapon system in a method that is not expected to cause collateral damage that would be excessive in relation to the concrete and direct military advantage anticipated from the attack.

## C. TARGETING IN TRANSNATIONAL ARMED CONFLICT AGAINST TERRORISTS

As demonstrated above, there is virtually no dispute within the international community or within the armed forces that civilians are and must remain immune from attack. Nor is there much dispute that, at times, the legitimate needs of an armed force justify divesting civilians and their property of this immunity when, as the result of their conduct, they participate directly in hostilities. As discussed above, the proverbial devil is in the details. Nowhere is this truer than in TAC against terrorists.

---

40    *See* GPI Commentary, *supra* note 30, para. 2218.

41    United States Joint Forces Command, Doctrinal Implications of Low Collateral Damage Capabilities, 16 (27 January 2003).

The complexity of complying with the distinction obligation is exponentially increased in the context of any TAC. This is because such conflicts are not, by definition, armed conflicts between the armed forces of warring states. Instead, at least one party to the conflict will be composed of non-state fighters. Much like the typical non-international or internal armed conflict, these fighters will normally appear to be civilians and utilize objects that would otherwise be civilian in nature and protected from attack. However, in addition to the traditional difficulties of internal armed conflict, TAC produces further complicating factors—decentralized organizational command and control and the dispersion of fighters.

Unlike traditional "internal" armed conflicts, where the control of the opposition forces is centralized and the fighters are geographically bounded, TAC is characterized by the lack of geographic proximity for both forces and organization. Instead, the head of the organization stays far away from the actual battle and exercises almost no control of the day-to-day actions of his fighters. Rather, he sends intermittent messages through various media, mostly carried over the Internet with general instructions, and then relies on his fighters to implement those instructions as they are able. Further, his fighters are not in communication with each other and may not even recognize each other as members of the same organization. They congregate in very small cells that are purposefully dispersed throughout the world and remain insular, acting with relative freedom on the general guidance that comes from the organization's leadership. As a result, using the traditional armed conflict methodology to discern what members of these organizations may be lawfully targeted is particularly challenging.

Therefore, it is vital to determine what rules apply to regulate the targeting of non-state actors and assets to mitigate as much as possible the potentially devastating devaluation of the civilian protections through the effects of armed conflict. At the same time, it seems utterly illogical to suggest that outside the context of international armed conflict, there is no such thing as an "enemy" for purposes of targeting, but only civilians who temporarily lose their immunity by virtue of taking a direct part in hostilities which result in some "actual harm." Such a conception is fundamentally inconsistent with the history of non-international armed conflicts during which government forces routinely treated organized opposition groups as much like an "enemy" as they would the armed forces of opposing States during international armed conflicts. That conception also ignores the realities of armed transnational terrorist groups. Governments deserve the same authority to respond to organized terrorist "cells" whose intent is equally dangerous and destructive.

Application of targeting principles to TAC therefore warrants a broader scope of targeting authority than merely responding to civilians who take a direct part in hostilities. It requires some methodology to distinguish individuals who remain immune from attack by virtue of their abstention from any participation in hostilities from those individuals who, by virtue of their connection with and conduct in support of an armed hostile group, are justifiably characterized as lawful objects of attack. This methodology must be consistent with the underlying purposes of the Law of Armed Conflict (LOAC).

Returning to the fundamental LOAC principle, that everyone on the battlefield may be divided into three categories: combatants, noncombatants, and civilians, targeting of terrorists in TAC must remain true to the principle of distinction which underlies this division. Transnational armed terrorists are seldom, if ever, going to qualify as combatants under LOAC principles because they do not meet the requirements of GPW, Article 4.[42] They are also clearly not noncombatants. Therefore, they appear to be civilians. However, as stated above, designating individuals devoted to committing hostile acts that will kill or injure large numbers of innocent civilians is inconsistent with the principles of the law of war. The United States has resolved this dilemma by designating such persons as unlawful enemy combatants, a term which has its pedigree in the law of war. While this term is also much maligned as a method of treatment or legal status, as a tool of targeting it remains consistent with LOAC principles and provides a reasonable methodology for targeting in TAC.

In the 2006 Military Commissions Act, an Act dealing with treatment and prosecution of detainees, not targeting, "unlawful enemy combatant" is defined as:

> (i) a person who has engaged in hostilities or who has purposefully and materially supported hostilities against the United States or its co-belligerents who is not a lawful enemy combatant (including a person who is part of the Taliban, al Qaeda, or associated forces); or

> (ii) a person who, before, on, or after the date of the enactment of the Military Commissions Act of 2006, has been determined to be an unlawful enemy combatant by a Combatant Status Review Tribunal or another

---

42    Memorandum from Office of the Assistant Att'y Gen. to Alberto R. Gonzales, Counsel to the President (Aug. 1, 2002).

**THE WAR ON TERROR AND THE LAWS OF WAR**

competent tribunal established under the authority of the President or the Secretary of Defense.[43]

The key phrase in the statute is "purposefully and materially supported hostilities." This is a very general definition and can be read very broadly to include persons who merely supply financial support to an organization involved in hostilities against the United States, though in practice the definition has not been used in that manner. For targeting purposes, this broad definition provides the commander with great discretion while providing a discernible standard upon which to base his judgment. If the commander discovers a person who is purposefully or materially supporting hostilities, he can take action to target that individual, including the use of deadly force.

This standard would overcome the problem presented by the individual who constructs improvised explosive devices to be used on the streets of Baghdad but is not the person who actually places or triggers the device. On a strict reading of "actual harm," the individual who merely builds the device is not causing actual harm. However, it is clear that that individual is participating in terrorist activities and the fight against Iraqi and coalition forces. Similarly, the individual who is recruiting and paying individuals to act as suicide bombers is certainly participating in the hostilities but would not be targetable under a strict requirement of causing actual harm.

Another aspect of adopting such an approach is that it is presumably a permanent status. The statute provides no time limit for automatic expiration of the designation of unlawful enemy combatant status. While it appears unreasonable to allow that individual to be targeted years after the particular hostilities he participated in are over, it appears equally unreasonable to determine he is either untargetable, or can only be targeted for the short time period that he is conducting his business.

The alternative to defining terrorists as targetable unlawful enemy combatants is to adopt the approach briefly introduced above of an expanded application of the "for such time" element of direct participation in hostilities to allow for a membership theory. In other words, while transnational armed terrorists remain civilians, once they join the armed wing of a terrorist organization, they have surrendered their immunity from

---

43    10 U.S.C. sec. 948a(1)(i) and (ii).

attack and become targetable until such time as they affirmatively opt out of that organization and permanently eschew all hostile acts.

This methodology also supports the underlying principles of the LOAC, particularly the principle of distinction, because it removes from these fighters their civilian protections, thus emphasizing the immunity from targeting that civilians inherently possess.

This analysis has its analogy in a State's armed forces. Each military throughout the world has persons who do not normally serve a combat role, such as cooks, paymasters, clerks, and legal personnel. However, each of these persons who are members of the military are equally targetable with infantrymen, artilleryman, and aircraft pilots. Because they have joined the military, the equivalent to the armed wing of a transnational terrorist organization, they have surrendered their civilian status as part of the organization they have embraced. Under a membership theory of direct participation in hostilities, it would be a similar argument for terrorists. Once a civilian joined the armed wing of Hamas, as opposed to the political wing, he becomes targetable based on his membership, regardless of whether he is functioning as a cook, a paymaster, a clerk, or a legal specialist. Until he affirmatively renounces that membership and restricts his participation in Hamas, he remains targetable.

In practical application, such a result would require a targeter (1) to distinguish between transnational armed terrorists who may be targeted even when not directly engaged in hostilities and civilians who may not be the object of attack, and (2) to apply the principle of distinction in the targeting process. While this may be practically difficult amongst groups who do not wear uniforms or any other distinguishing mark, it is no more difficult than a more restrictive reading of "unless and for such time." Commanders must still embrace the responsibility of distinguishing between targetable individuals and those who retain their immunity from targeting and apply their force only against the former.

This application of the distinction principle would also support the LOAC principle of proportionality. Because of the nature of the fighters and the fact that they are civilians who are either part of armed groups or persons who are taking part in hostilities, the proportionality analysis must reflect the reality of the situation. By participating in hostilities, these civilians have surrendered the protections they would otherwise be granted. Therefore, when a commander conducts his proportionality analysis, he need not account for the civilians who are fighters but must then apply the principle as he would under the Protocol to any other civilians and civilian property that will be affected by his attack. In applying this proportionality analysis, the commander must still determine that danger of death or injury to non-targetable civilians is not excessive to the concrete and direct military advantage anticipated from the attack. However, in doing so, he must balance that against the military advantage gained from the death of the targetable terrorists.

There is no doubt that TAC creates difficulties in the targeting of persons and property. The complexity of the situations that commanders face is dramatically increased in TAC. A restrictive view of targeting of terrorists will act as an incentive for terrorists to continue to move and work amongst the civilian population, thus increasing the danger to civilians. A less restrictive view that either embraces the U.S. approach of declaring terrorists as unlawful combatants, or the approach currently being studied by the ICRC, where membership in the armed wing of a terrorist organization forfeits an individual's civilian immunity, will not only increase a State's ability to respond to terrorists but will also reinforce the fundamental principles of the LOAC that are designed to protect civilians from the effects of hostilities.

## D. MODERN POLICY IN THE LAW OF TARGETING

While this is a vitally important discussion for the continued viability of the LOAC, current military practice makes much of this discussion unnecessary, at least with regard to the proportionality analysis. Current military targeting procedures have placed such restrictions on a commander's ability to engage targets where collateral damage is anticipated, that the targeting commander never gets to the point of applying the LOAC standard.

With the ubiquitous nature of media coverage in modern warfare, few military operations happen without immediately being broadcast throughout the world over television, radio, and the Internet. The arrival of the U.S. Marines on the beaches of Somalia to awaiting news crews was but the precursor to the in-depth media coverage and scrutiny in today's armed conflicts. In recognition of the role of media, the U.S. Department of Defense solicited media outlets to provide reporters that could be embedded within military units throughout its recent operations in Iraq. While the value and benefits of such a plan may be open to discussion, the recognition of the effect of media on armed conflict is virtually uncontested.

One of the areas where the media's effect has been the most pronounced is in the area of targeting. The real-time broadcast of military operations and their effects have brought each collateral damage assessment made by a commander into sharp focus for hundreds of millions of people who read or listen to the media reports of the attack. After each engagement, the media lists in great detail the number of civilians killed or injured and the civilian property damaged by the attack, with special emphasis if any of the casualties were children. The general outrage at each civilian death, whether considered necessary by the attacking commander or not, has created immense pressure on governments, particularly those in Europe and North America, to alter their military procedures and operations to account for the negative effects of any collateral damage. They have done this in two ways: the establishment of procedures and approval levels for an attack where collateral damage is anticipated that completely overlay the LOAC targeting standard; and the increased focus on information warfare and non-kinetic targeting to both prevent the need for kinetic targeting and to counter the effects of kinetic targeting when it occurs.

As noted above, the law-of-armed-conflict standard clearly is based on the "anticipated" advantage of the attack by the commander conducting the attack. The commander is not required to be able to predict the future. Nor is he required to search out every possible misapplication of force that could occur from his targeting strategy, only those that may be expected. The standard is the reasonableness of the commander's decision, and the reasonableness of the commander's decision is determined in light of the anticipated results, not the actual results. Despite this clear standard, many governments have placed additional restrictions on a military commander targeting that are not required by the LOAC. Two examples are illustrative.

In a recent case brought before the Israeli Supreme Court,[44] petitioners argued that the Israeli military practice of "targeted killings" violated both human rights and the law of war. The Court limited its consideration of the principle of proportionality in this case to its application in the law of armed conflict and then restated the principle thus:

> The proportionality test determines that attack upon innocent civilians is not permitted if the collateral damage caused to them is not proportionate to the military advantage (in protecting combatants and civilians). In other words, attack is proportionate if the benefit stemming from the

---

44     The Public Committee Against Torture in Israel, et al. v. The Government of Israel, et al. HCJ 769/02, 14 December 2006 (hereinafter "Public Committee").

attainment of the proper military objective is proportionate to the damage caused to innocent civilians harmed by it.[45]

The Court then went on to state "the law dealing with preventative acts on the part of the army which cause the deaths of terrorists and of innocent bystanders requires *ex post* examination of the conduct of the army. That examination must—thus determines customary international law—be of an objective character."[46] It is unclear where in customary international law that the Court found this requirement. It is certainly not contained within the LOAC.

The Court continued by stating that when doing a post operation review, "[t]he question is whether the decision of the military commander falls within the zone of reasonable activity on the part of the military commander. If the answer is yes, the Court will not exchange the military commander's security discretion with the security discretion of the Court."[47] The Court further stated "[t]he decision of the question whether the benefit stemming from the preventative strike is proportionate to the collateral damage caused to innocent civilians harmed by it is a legal question, the expertise about which is in the hands of the judicial branch."[48] By turning the collateral damage analysis into a judicial question, the Court has removed what has traditionally been a commander's decision from the military and placed it in the judicial branch. This is, again, not part of the LOAC, but a domestic attempt to provide greater overview of military operations that may cause collateral damage.

In the end, the Israeli Supreme Court refused to grant the petitioners' request to strike down the Government's policy of target killings, but it did remove the ultimate discretion of the commander because he could now assume that, on a case-by-case basis, the Court would review his decision and determine the legality of the attack. There is no doubt that this will cause increased hesitation on the part of the commander when making a targeting decision. While there is a normative aspect to this development, the important point for this chapter is that modern policy and procedure are injecting different and more constraining requirements on the LOAC principle of targeting that make targeting of terrorists in TAC much more difficult than the LOAC standard would require.

---

45    Public Committee, *supra* note 45, para. 45.

46    Public Committee, *supra* note 45, para. 54.

47    Public Committee, *supra* note 45, para. 57.

48    Public Committee, *supra* note 45, para. 58.

Another example of this phenomenon is the escalation of approval authority for launching an attack where collateral damage is anticipated. As
explained above, the decision for this attack lies with the commander who
is ordering the attack. While the Israeli court has added a post-hoc review,
the United States has elevated the initial decision approval authority to
levels well above the commander at the scene of the attack. Rather than
the attacking commander making that determination, the request must be
sent to higher authorities and acted upon at levels far from the battlefield.

Much of the information about the targeting process is available only
within the military and is kept secret from the outside world. However,
there have been enough reports to clearly indicate that decisions concerning attacks that will result in collateral damage have been withheld
from the battlefield commander and elevated to superior commanders
or civilian leaders who analyze the decision and then approve or disap-
prove the attack. This step is not required by the LOAC and actually
makes the LOAC principles virtually meaningless. As responsive as the
military systems are, there is no doubt that seeking approval authority
from commanders or civilians away from the battlefield must increase
the time necessary to launch the attack. In a world where terrorists are
fleeting targets, any delay may mean an opportunity is missed.

Additionally, if the anticipated death of a certain number of civilians as
collateral damage in an attack will disqualify that attack, this serves the
perverse purpose of incentivizing terrorists to continue to operate among
innocent civilians. The more civilians the terrorists can surround themselves with, the less responsive the targeting decision will be, and the less
likely it will be that the attack is even launched. Thus, modern law and
policy in TAC against terrorists is not only detached from the LOAC
principles of targeting but ironically may be encouraging the most undesirable outcome, for terrorists to operate amongst civilians to the maximum extent possible.

In addition to the increased approval levels and post-decision review of
targeting, modern militaries have also turned their targeting against terrorists in TAC to non-kinetic methods in an effort to increase effectiveness and to decrease public outcry over the death of innocent civilians.
Over the past decade, the military discipline of information operations
has moved farther to the forefront of planning both at the tactical and
strategic levels. Military manuals have been written and doctrine promulgated to raise the level of focus on these non-kinetic tools at the
commander's disposal. Much of this has been in response to increased

capability through advancing technology, but it has also been viewed as an effective non-kinetic method of target engagement that removes the risk of collateral damage and its resulting popular outcry. Two of the most prominent aspects of information operations include psychological operations and computer network operations.

Psychological operations are defined as "planned operations to convey selected information and indicators to foreign audiences to influence their emotions, motives, objective reasoning, and ultimately the behavior of foreign governments, organizations, groups, and individuals."[49] It is not a new capability in the military arsenal, but increased focus has been put on its effectiveness in TAC. The idea behind psychological operations is to use information as your weapon. In practice, the information is most often true, but the method of using the information becomes an effective tool to target specific audiences.

Unfortunately it is not only western militaries that are making effective use of psychological operations. One of the best examples of the effective use of psychological operations is that being used against coalition forces in both Afghanistan and Iraq. Knowing that the civilian populace and governments of the coalition partners have little patience for civilian casualties, they purposely conduct their attacks in ways that will put the local civilian populace at risk to any military response. As the military responds, it is inevitable that some civilian casualties result. The terrorists have become experts at then publicizing these civilian casualties and emphasizing the fact that the deaths and injuries were caused by military action, but downplaying their own role in creating the target amongst the civilian populace. While this is a clear violation of Article 58, GPI,[50]

---

49  THE JOINT CHIEFS OF STAFF, JOINT PUB 3–53, DOCTRINE FOR JOINT PSYCHOLOGICAL OPERATIONS I-1 (5 Sept. 2003)

50  Article 58 states:

Article 58 — Precautions against the effects of attacks

The Parties to the conflict shall, to the maximum extent feasible:

(a) without prejudice to Article 49 of the Fourth Convention, endeavour to remove the civilian population, individual civilians and civilian objects under their control from the vicinity of military objectives;

(b) avoid locating military objectives within or near densely populated areas;

(c) take the other necessary precautions to protect the civilian population, individual civilians and civilian objects under their control against the dangers resulting from military operations.

See GPI, *supra* note 8, article 58.

the terrorists are able to present the facts through various cooperative media outlets in a very effective manner that focuses the attention on the military response, as opposed to the terrorist actions.

Of course, those fighting TAC are also engaged in psychological operations on a grand scale, targeting both the local populaces and the terrorists themselves. This war of words and ideas is an essential, and mostly bloodless, part of the conflict. Sometimes, the only way to victory is to somehow exchange one set of ideas in the minds of an enemy with another set of ideas.

Computer network operations, or CNO, are another non-kinetic means of targeting. CNO "stems from the increasing use of networked computers and supporting IT infrastructure systems by military and civilian organizations. CNO, along with [electronic warfare] is used to attack, deceive, degrade, disrupt, deny, exploit, and defend electronic information and infrastructure."[51] CNO consists of computer network attack (CNA), computer network defense (CND), and computer network exploitation (CNE).[52] While CND is mostly focused on protecting computer networks from adversarial attacks,[53] CNA and CNE include proactive methods of gathering intelligence and then acting on that intelligence electronically to disrupt terrorist plans or potential activities.

---

51    THE JOINT CHIEFS OF STAFF, JOINT PUB 3–13, INFORMATION OPERATIONS II-4,5 (13 Feb. 2006).

52    Joint Pub 3–13 defines CNA, CND, and CNE.

> CNA consists of actions taken through the use of computer networks to disrupt, deny, degrade, or destroy information resident in computers and computer networks, or the computers and networks themselves. CND involves actions taken through the use of computer networks to protect, monitor, analyze, detect, and respond to unauthorized activity within DOD information systems and computer networks. CND actions not only protect DOD systems from an external adversary but also from exploitation from within, and are now a necessary function in all military operations. CNE is enabling operations and intelligence collection capabilities conducted through the use of computer networks to gather data from target or adversary automated information systems or networks.

> THE JOINT CHIEFS OF STAFF, JOINT PUB 3-13, INFORMATION OPERATIONS II-5 (13 Feb. 2006).

53    *See generally* Sean M. Condron, *Getting it Right: Protecting American Critical Infrastructure in Cyberspace,* 20 HARV. J.L. & TECH. 403 (2007); Eric Talbot Jensen, *Computer Attacks on Critical National Infrastructure: A Use of Force Invoking the Right of Self-Defense,* 38 STAN. J. INT'L L. 207 (2002).

These methods of targeting have the potential to be extremely effective in TAC against terrorists. Because of the nature of the dispersion of terrorist organizations, much of their communication travels over the Internet. Attacking that method of communication, or even exploiting it for one's own purposes could potentially yield significant benefits in combating transnational terrorists. If it were possible to gain access over the Internet to information that was being sent from one terrorist operative to another, it would be a great intelligence-gathering technique. Perhaps even more beneficial would be gaining access to a terrorist leader's email or messaging system and sending out false or inaccurate communications that would potentially foil future plots or lead to the capture or death of terrorist operatives.

Of course, particular actions that have been or may be taken by governments in the fight against terrorists are cloaked in secrecy. However, there are examples of reported uses of CNO. The United States may have accessed Serbian leader Milosevic's bank accounts to apply pressure on him to end the fighting in Kosovo.[54] Russia has used cyber attacks against both Estonia and Georgia. And both official and unofficial attacks are reported to have come out of China, where the government has created an entire branch of the military dedicated to information warfare and computer operations.

There is no doubt that as this TAC against terrorists continues, both psychological operations and CNO can be very effective non-kinetic means of targeting terrorists, not only for information, but also to disrupt activities and potentially lead to the capture or death of terrorists. Further, because of the strain on governments caused by traditional targeting methods and the resulting collateral damage as amplified by ubiquitous media coverage, modern policy will drive governments to more comprehensive reliance on these non-kinetic tools. The current constraints on targeting procedures, such as heightened approval levels, demonstrate the government's desire to avoid the media scrutiny collateral damage brings. Non-kinetic alternatives may reduce this public outcry and become an effective tool in this fight. However, it is important to note that some CNO may have kinetic effects and would be

---

54    Gregory L. Vistica, *Cyberwar and Sabotage*, NEWSWEEK 38 (May 31, 1999) *quoted in* Charles J. Dunlap, Jr., *The End of Innocence: Rethinking Noncombatancy in the Post-Kosovo Era*, STRATEGIC REVIEW 9, 13 (Summer 2000).

required to comply with the traditional law of war principles in those instances.[55]

## E. CONCLUSION

Though the transnational armed conflict against terrorists is neither a traditional international armed conflict, nor a non-international armed conflict, the LOAC still applies to all military operations supporting this fight. Questions such as the identity of terrorists and the ability to target them while intermixed within the civilian populace can be answered by the application of traditional LOAC principles. Further, the desire to interdict those who support them in their terrorist acts, and the length of time those conducting and supporting terrorist acts can be targeted, are all questions that can be answered based on the core principles of targeting.

Some adaptation will be necessary to allow a commander to target terrorists, whether considered unlawful combatants or civilians participating directly in hostilities, over an extended period of time. Further, a broadened application of a "membership" theory will be necessary to prevent terrorists from using their civilian status to protect their actions. Otherwise, the fundamental principles of LOAC, such as distinction and proportionality, will eventually be eroded because of the realities of fighting transnational armed conflicts.

---

55   *See generally* Eric Talbot Jensen, *Unexpected Consequences from Knock-On Effects: A Different Standard for Computer Network Operations?*, 18 AMERICAN UNIVERSITY INTERNATIONAL LAW REVIEW 1145, 1170–73 (2003).

# CHAPTER 3

# DETENTION OF COMBATANTS AND THE GLOBAL WAR ON TERROR

By James A. Schoettler Jr.[†]

## OVERVIEW

In the conduct of armed conflict, a State may not only kill or wound combatants fighting on behalf of its enemies, but it also may take them prisoner and hold them until the end of the conflict.[1] Indeed, where an enemy combatant clearly is no longer capable of fighting due to wounds, or where an enemy combatant has clearly signaled his or her desire to cease fighting, a State's only option to remove an enemy combatant from the battlefield will be to take that person prisoner.

The principal sources of law regarding the detention of enemy combatants are (i) the Regulations concerning the Laws and Customs of War on Land annexed to Fourth Hague Convention of 1907 (hereinafter Hague IV Regulations);[2] (ii) the 1949 Geneva Convention relative to

---

[†]    Adjunct Professor, Georgetown University Law Center. Professor Schoettler holds a Juris Doctor degree (magna cum laude) from Georgetown University Law Center, a Master's of Science in Foreign Service degree from Georgetown University and a Bachelor of Arts degree from The Johns Hopkins University. He has served for over twenty-five years as a reserve officer in the U.S. Army's Judge Advocate General's Corps, holds the rank of Colonel, and was formerly the Assistant Chief of the International and Operational Law Division in the Office of The Judge Advocate General. The views or opinions expressed in this article are not attributable to Georgetown University, the U.S. Department of Defense or the U.S. Army, but are strictly the views and opinions of the author. All statements are based on information drawn from the public record.

[1]    Hamdi v. Rumsfeld, 542 U.S. 507, 518, 588–589. *See also* article 18 of GPW, *infra* note 3, which requires that prisoners of war be "released and repatriated without delay after the cessation of hostilities."

[2]    Regulations Respecting the Laws and Customs of War on Land, annexed to Convention Respecting the Laws and Customs of War on Land, Oct. 18, 1907, 36 Stat. 2277, 1 Bevans 631 [hereinafter Hague IV Regulations].

the Treatment of Prisoners of War (hereinafter GPW);[3] and (iii) certain provisions of the Protocol Additional to the Geneva Conventions of 12 August 1949 relating to the Protection of Victims of International Armed Conflicts (hereinafter "Additional Protocol I" or "API").[4] Together, these treaties define a highly protective regime that ensures that captured enemy soldiers are humanely treated by their captors, properly accounted for, and set free once hostilities are over. Importantly, enemy soldiers who are treated as prisoners of war under these treaties cannot be prosecuted by the capturing State for belligerent acts against lawful targets (such as killing combatants who are fighting on behalf of the capturing State) provided such acts were done in accordance with the law of war. This protection against prosecution, typically called "combatant immunity," is an important protection under international law.

In the global war on terror (GWOT)[5] and other modern conflicts, however, belligerent acts are often carried out by persons who do not fit neatly into the categories of combatants covered by the Hague IV Regulations, the GPW and the applicable provisions of Additional Protocol I, often called "privileged belligerents." These individuals typically wear civilian clothes, operate in a non-conventional manner and do not enjoy any connection with any State. Their actions can be as lethal and disruptive as those taken by enemy military personnel and therefore a State attacked by these individuals has just as strong an interest in neutralizing them, including by detaining them, as it would in neutralizing an enemy's conventional military units. Yet, law of war treaties provide only limited guidance as to their status and treatment.

An important distinction between individuals who fall within the categories of combatants who, upon capture would be treated as prisoners of war under the Hague IV Regulations, the GPW and the applicable provisions of Additional Protocol I (hereinafter referred to as "lawful combatants" or "privileged belligerents") and those who engage in combatant

---

3    Geneva Convention (III) Relative to the Treatment of Prisoners of War, Aug. 12, 1949, 6 U.S.T. 3316, 75 U.N.T.S. 135 [hereinafter GPW].

4    Protocol (I) Additional to the Geneva Conventions of 12 August 1949, and Relating to the Protection of Victims of International Armed Conflicts, June 8, 1977, 1125 U.N.T.S. [hereinafter API].

5    The term "Global War on Terror" was widely used by the Bush Administration but reportedly has been abandoned by the Obama Administration. For ease of reference, I use the term in this chapter, without endorsing it as the correct way to view the conflict with al Qaeda and associated groups.

activities but are not entitled to be treated as prisoners of war under the applicable treaties (hereinafter "unlawful combatants" or "unprivileged belligerents") is that unprivileged belligerents do not enjoy combatant immunity, and can be prosecuted by the capturing State under its domestic law for any belligerent acts they have committed. Thus, the unprivileged belligerent is not only a captured enemy combatant, but also presumptively a criminal subject to prosecution. Rightly or not, the criminality associated with his or her status tends to color the nature of the detention and the attitude of the capturing State toward the prisoner.

In GWOT, the Bush Administration used its right under the law of war to detain and punish unlawful combatants, as a method of warfare in its fight against terrorist groups like al Qaeda and the Taliban. Individuals suspected of being terrorists are seized both on and off active battlefields and held by the United States as combatants who can be prosecuted by military commissions for their terrorist activities, which today are characterized by U.S. legislation as belligerent acts in violation of the law of war. As discussed further in this chapter, to the extent an individual can be shown to be an unprivileged belligerent, the Bush Administration's position has enjoyed considerable support in the law of war and under U.S. law. However, many of these detained individuals assert that they are not combatants, but rather civilians who should be freed or provided benefits under the Convention (IV) relative to the Protection of Civilian Persons in Time of War (hereafter "GCIV").[6] Others assert that they are entitled to be treated as lawful combatants who should be held as prisoners of war but not prosecuted. At the heart of these arguments is a challenge to the means by which the United States has concluded that these individuals can be detained as unprivileged belligerents.

This chapter looks closely at the treaty law applicable to the determination of a person's status as a combatant, the approach taken by the Bush Administration to these status determinations in GWOT, the principal court decisions evaluating the U.S. government's approach, and the Bush Administration's response. In so doing, it provides insight into one of the most important questions affecting the treatment of combatants, namely their status once captured. It concludes with observations on how the experience in GWOT in dealing with this issue may complicate the U.S. military's ability to make those status determinations in the

---

6    Geneva Convention Relative to the Protection of Civilian Persons in Time of War, Aug. 12, 1949, 6 U.S.T. 3516, 75 U.N.T.S. 287 [hereinafter GCIV].

future, and suggests that greater application of treaty law to all detainees in GWOT could be useful in addressing concerns of the Judicial branch regarding long-term military detentions under the law of war.

## DETENTION AND THE TERRORIST-COMBATANT

Under the law of war, detention of an enemy combatant is not a form of punishment. Instead, the purpose of detention is to take the combatant off the battlefield and to neutralize any threat he or she may pose to the capturing State and its forces.[7] Once the combatant is off the battlefield, his or her status as a privileged or unprivileged belligerent then determines what may be done about the belligerent acts that led to detention. While detained combatants may be punished for acts committed before detention if those acts constitute crimes, the detention itself is not supposed to serve as punishment for those acts.[8] Indeed, the conflict that led to the combatant's detention is not a conflict against the combatant personally, but rather against the country or group for which he or she is fighting. Thus, in the absence of proof that acts committed by the combatant are crimes, the combatant should be set free once the conflict is over; but, until that time, the combatant remains a prisoner of his or her enemy.

The combatant detention paradigm described in the preceding paragraph has been severely tested in the GWOT. In the GWOT as conducted by the U.S. government, the terrorist has been treated as an unprivileged belligerent, who, as a combatant, can be detained for the duration of the conflict in the same manner as an enemy soldier. Application of this paradigm is complicated by the fact that most of the detainees in the GWOT are nationals of States who are not at war with the United States, and indeed, may even be allies in the war on terror. Further, the "battlefield" for these purposes is not limited to contested territory of a single country, but potentially includes any nation where a terrorist cell could be located or where terrorist acts could be committed. Also, because the scope and length of the conflict is uncertain, the detentions have been lengthy and could last years, if not decades.

---

7    *In re* Territo, 156 F.2d 142, 145 ("The object of capture is to prevent the captured individual from serving the enemy. He is disarmed and from then on must be removed as completely as practicable from the front, treated humanely, and in time, exchanged, repatriated or otherwise released.") (citations omitted).

8    Hamdi v. Rumsfeld, 542 U.S. at 518.

The terrorist-combatant is not a privileged belligerent and therefore, it has not been clear what protections, if any, apply to him or her under international law. The three Geneva Conventions (the GPW and two other conventions dealing with the protection of certain categories of wounded, sick, and shipwrecked individuals belonging to, or accompanying, armed forces fighting for a State) do not apply, by their terms. GCIV, the one treaty dealing with civilians, is generally viewed as only protecting civilians in occupied territory or in the territory of an enemy; it is not applicable to civilians worldwide.[9] Further, all these treaties apply only in an international armed conflict, *i.e.*, a conflict between States.[10] Except for the short period after the U.S. intervention in

---

9    This is the position under the express terms of the treaty. The U.S. Army's Field Manual on Land Warfare takes a broader position that, as a matter of policy, GCIV protects "all persons who have engaged in hostile or belligerent conduct but who are not entitled to treatment as a prisoners of war." Dep't of Army, Field Manual 27–10, Law of Land Warfare, para. 247 (July 1956) [hereinafter FM 27–10].

10   API art. 1 states that the Protocol applies only to situations covered by article 2 of GPW, GCIV and the two other 1949 Geneva Conventions, *i.e.*, an armed conflict between States who are party to the Geneva Conventions (each a "State Party") and a partial or total occupation of the territory of such a State Party by another State Party. However, API art. 1(4) also treats as international armed conflicts, conflicts in "which peoples are fighting against colonial domination and alien occupation and against racist régimes in the exercise of their right of self-determination" under the U.N. charter. The United States objected to API in part because it believed this provision would grant combatant status under API to terrorist groups. Abraham D. Sofaer, *Agora: The U.S. Decision Not to Ratify Protocol I to the Geneva Conventions on the Protection of War Victims (Cont'd), The Rationale for the United States Decision*, 82 Am. J. Int'l L. 784, 786–787 (1988). Whether the GWOT is an armed conflict falling within API art. 1(4) is open to question, but even if it was, it would not appear that al Qaeda or other terrorist groups have the internal disciplinary system required to be entitled to be treated as armed forces of a Party under API art. 43.

API art. 2 raises the possibility that, even if API does not apply, a conflict with a non-State entity such as al Qaeda would be governed by customary international law.

> In cases not covered by this Protocol or by other international agreements, civilians and combatants remain under the protection and authority of the principles of international law derived from established custom, from the principles of humanity and from dictates of public conscience.

While this is undoubtedly true, it is not easy to divine what customary law requires regarding detention in a conflict such as the GWOT, beyond the general obligation of humane treatment and minimal due process expressed in Common Article 3 of the 1949 Geneva Conventions and API art. 75.

Afghanistan, before the emergence of a new Afghan government to replace the Taliban, the GWOT has not involved a conflict among States, but rather a conflict between States and a worldwide terrorist movement.

Yet, in the absence of at least some protection under international law, a State's use of the combatant detention paradigm to detain its enemies, no matter how nefarious they may be, can have uncomfortable or even ominous implications for those concerned about unchecked executive power. Detention is potentially indefinite, without any possibility of judicial review. Treatment of detainees who do not fall under the protection of the GPW is not regulated by international law, but instead governed by the capturing State's internally drafted and implemented policies, subject only to limitations or prohibitions on mistreatment imposed by domestic law.[11] While detention is allegedly not a form of punishment, it may appear to have the same effect, particularly if used to encourage or coerce disclosure of useful intelligence from the detainee. Regardless of its track record, the detaining State's commitment to humane treatment may be questioned where it is based on a policy choice, rather than a sense of legal obligation. And incidents of abuse will only further strengthen arguments that the paradigm is unfair in the absence of legally binding protections.

In short, even if legally correct, the use of the combatant detention paradigm is politically vulnerable, absent an overlay of some level of binding legal protection for the detainee who is determined by the capturing State to be an unprivileged belligerent.[12] As discussed further, *infra*, this political reality has had significant consequences for the application of

---

11  Some domestic laws may be based on international obligations, such as the Convention Against Torture, although the application of such treaties to conduct of a nation outside its own borders has been debated.

12  In these circumstances, detention of the terrorist-combatant has provided a rich field for advocates who argue that the terrorist-combatant should enjoy greater protections, either under the regime established for privileged belligerents, or those afforded to non-combatants under human rights standards. While neither argument has yet achieved success in U.S. courts, they have succeeded in establishing that a minimum set of standards, generally founded on the rules applicable to non-international armed conflicts under the Geneva Conventions of 1949, should apply. These standards impose a base line requirement for humane treatment and due process that generally conforms to the bare minimums required under human rights treaties.

the combatant paradigm in the GWOT and potentially could affect its application in more traditional conflicts as well.

## STATUS AND DETENTION

In armed conflict, an individual's status under international law determines his or her treatment when captured in connection with an armed conflict, including which treaty protections apply, and whether he or she is subject to prosecution for combatant activities. That status will be determined by (i) the type of armed conflict, (ii) the nature of the belligerents involved; and (iii) the depth of the individual's involvement, if any, in the armed conflict.

At the beginning of the twentieth century, the law of war consisted principally of rules for the conduct of conflicts between States in which the active participants were limited to citizens of each State in military formations, *i.e.*, soldiers. Non-soldiers, *i.e.*, civilians, were bystanders and generally not involved in the conflict, except in limited cases where civilians performed peripheral functions (e.g., suppliers, war correspondents) which did not involve engaging in belligerent acts against the enemy. Whether conflicts at that time actually conformed to that model, conflicts today do not, with complexities emerging in a number of areas.

The twentieth century revolutionized armed conflict in terms of scope and lethality. Further, civilians were far from bystanders. Not only did they produce the weapons and equipment that wars were fought with and the supplies that supported the combatants, as the century progressed they moved closer and closer to the battlefield. Today, civilians transport military equipment and ammunition, service weapons, collect and interpret intelligence, and advise military commanders on certain military operations. In the case of a nation's senior leadership, civilians may also direct the activities of combatants. These are accepted roles for civilians and are to some degree sanctioned in treaty law in the case of "persons who accompany the armed forces without actually being members thereof".[13] However, in many twentieth century conflicts, civilians also took up arms and conducted attacks against their enemies, perhaps using civilian status as cover for their military actions.

---

13    GPW art. 4A(4). *See also* Hague IV Regulations art. 13. No treaty specifically addresses the status of a civilian senior leader who also serves as the head of a nation's armed forces, but such persons certainly have been targeted in the same manner as combatants in recent conflicts.

The law of war only changed slowly to meet these developments. The four Geneva Conventions adopted in 1949 were designed principally to provide more detailed rules for international armed conflicts based on World War II experiences. Yet, the next several decades were characterized by conflicts that did not comply with the WW II model. Conflicts resulting in, or resulting from, the break-up of Western European empires were most often guerrilla wars or "low intensity conflicts," in which one or both sides consisted of indigenous forces that often did not conform to the model of a modern western army and that made up for a lack of fire power and resources with, *inter alia*, the use of force against their enemies that included indiscriminate attacks on civilians and civilian property.

In 1977, nations agreed on Additional Protocol I,[14] which applies to international armed conflict, and a companion Additional Protocol II,[15] applicable to non-international armed conflicts, to supplement the four Geneva Conventions. These protocols expanded the scope of the conflicts that could be subject to the law of war treaties. However, even under this expanded scope, the conflicts covered by these protocols generally fit one of two categories: (i) conflicts between nations and other nations; or (ii) conflicts between a nation and a movement or organized force within its borders (or the borders of its colonies) or within territory occupied by it.

GWOT is not a conflict among States or a conflict within a State. The terrorist enemy in GWOT is completely independent of any particular State and has substantial military capabilities equal to or better than those of some States. It is capable of projecting force into third countries as effectively as any State (e.g., the terrorist attack in Mumbai in 2008, which was organized and executed as well as any State-sponsored commando raid). Indeed, the terrorist enemy may challenge or even supplant State authority in a country in which it is based to such an extent that it becomes the true power in that country (e.g., Afghanistan under the Taliban). Thus a conflict with a terrorist enemy of this type may not be an international armed conflict as traditionally conceived, but it is a conflict on an international scale that is potentially just as destructive as a traditional armed conflict.

---

14    *See supra*, note 4.

15    Protocol (II) Additional to the Geneva Conventions of 12 August 1949, and Relating to the Protection of Victims of Non-International Armed Conflicts, Dec. 12, 1977, 1125 U.N.T.S. 609 [hereinafter APII].

The regulation of combatants under law of war treaties is focused on the traditional category of fighters who would fight the wars covered by the treaties, *i.e.*, soldiers in armies raised by States, militias, resistance fighters, and civilians who rise up spontaneously to repel an invasion. Except in the case of a force rebelling against a State (covered by Additional Protocol II and one common article of the four Geneva Conventions) or a limited category of conflicts involving "peoples ... fighting against colonial domination and alien occupation and against racist regimes" pursuant to the right of self-determination recognized in the UN Charter,[16] all these categories envision fighters acting on behalf of a State. Further, only treaties dealing with international armed conflicts specifically provide for the treatment of combatants as prisoners of war, and there is no specific coverage in law of war treaties for combatants who fight on behalf of a force that is neither sponsored by a State nor rebelling against a State.

The traditional categories of combatants protected by the law of war can be found in the GPW. The GPW affords prisoner of war treatment to the following specific six categories of persons, all of whom upon capture are considered "prisoners of war":

(1) Members of the armed forces of a Party to the conflict, as well as members of militias or volunteer corps forming part of such armed forces.

(2) Members of other militias and members of other volunteer corps, including those of organized resistance movements, belonging to a Party to the conflict and operating in or outside their own territory, even if this territory is occupied, provided that such militias or volunteer corps, including such organized resistance movements, fulfill the following conditions:

(a) that of being commanded by a person responsible for his subordinates;

(b) that of having a fixed distinctive sign recognizable at a distance;

(c) that of carrying arms openly; and

(d) that of conducting their operations in accordance with the laws and customs of war.

(3) Members of regular armed forces who profess allegiance to a government or an authority not recognized by the Detaining Power.

---

16    API art. 1(4). The United States has cited the provision on "peoples ... fighting against colonial domination and alien occupation and against racist regimes" as one of the reasons it will not ratify API. *See supra* note 10. Note that the States where most of the conflict in the GWOT has been waged—Afghanistan, Iraq and the United States—have yet to ratify API.

(4) Persons who accompany the armed forces without actually being members thereof, such as civilian members of military aircraft crews, war correspondents, supply contractors, members of labor units, or of services responsible for the welfare of the armed forces, provided that they have received authorization from the armed forces which they accompany, who shall provide them for that purpose with an identity card.

(5) Members of crews, including masters, pilots, and apprentices of the merchant marine and the crews of civil aircraft of the Parties to the conflict, who do not benefit by more favorable treatment under any other provisions of international law.

(6) Inhabitants of a non-occupied territory, who on the approach of the enemy spontaneously take up arms to resist the invading forces, without having had time to form themselves into regular armed units, provided they carry arms openly and respect the laws and customs of war.[17]

Individuals falling within these categories are entitled under the GPW to a number of protections upon capture, including the right to be interned, rather than confined; to receive adequate food, shelter, medical treatment, and other benefits from the capturing State; to be protected against all forms of abuse and coercion; and importantly to be released upon the conclusion of hostilities. The GPW also requires the capturing State to report the fact of their capture, and the state of their health, and to provide information on how they may be contacted by their families. Prisoners of war under the GPW are entitled to receive visits by the International Committee of the Red Cross or a neutral Protecting Power to ensure that the capturing State is fulfilling its treaty obligations under the GPW.

There are important limitations on the scope of these protections under the GPW:

First, they only apply to individuals falling within the six categories listed above. Thus, combatants who do not fit any of these categories are not protected by the GPW. Even under the broader standards found

---

17    The six categories are set out in GPW art. 4A. GPW art. 4B permits a State Party occupying another State Party to take, as prisoners of war under the GPW, persons belonging, or having belonged, to the armed forces of the occupied State Party, if the occupying State Party considers it necessary by reason of their allegiance to the occupied State Party, to intern them, even though it has originally liberated them while hostilities were going on outside the territory it occupies, in particular where such persons have made an unsuccessful attempt to rejoin the armed forces to which they belong and which are engaged in combat, or where they fail to comply with a summons made to them with a view to internment.

in Additional Protocol I, international terrorists would not qualify as prisoners of war, because they do not carry arms openly, which is the minimum requirement for treatment as a prisoner of war under Article 44(3) of Additional Protocol I. In any case, the United States and a number of other nations (including Afghanistan and Iraq) that have detained alleged terrorists in the GWOT have not yet ratified Additional Protocol I.

Second, with the exception of one important article, the protections under the GPW only apply to prisoners taken by a State in an international armed conflict (including the occupation of an enemy State). Thus, the protections are not applicable even to the six categories of individuals listed above if they are captured during a non-international armed conflict.

Third, as a corollary to the second point, the protections under the GPW do not apply with respect to an entity that is not a State party to the GPW, or at least a State that accepts and applies the provisions of the GPW. While nearly all States are party to the GPW today, entities such as al Qaeda are not, and are not capable of becoming party to the GPW because they are not States. Thus, members of terrorist organizations in GWOT are not specifically protected by the GPW.[18]

The fact that an individual does not qualify under one of the GPW categories does not mean that he or she cannot be detained. Under international law, any person who is a combatant in an armed conflict against another State may be detained for the duration of hostilities. On the other hand, a State generally may not detain persons who are not combatants (*i.e.*, "innocent civilians"), even if they are citizens of an enemy State.[19]

---

18    Under API art. 96, an authority representing "peoples... fighting against colonial domination and alien occupation and against racist regimes in the exercise of their right of self-determination" may, by unilateral declaration undertake to apply Additional Protocol I and thereby make the protocol and the four Geneva Conventions applicable. However, the terrorist organizations in the GWOT do not fit this description, have not made such a declaration and have not demonstrated by the nature of their activities and attacks that they would comply with any international law of war treaty or rule.

19    GCIV does permit an enemy civilian to be detained if he or she is a clear security threat. *See* GCIV art. 78 (permitting an occupying power to intern civilians where the occupying State "considers it necessary, for imperative reasons of security....."). However, unlike military detention of combatants, such detention is subject to periodic review to determine if the reasons for detention still apply. *Id.*

Thus, for States fighting al Qaeda and others in the GWOT, determining that terrorists are combatants who can be detained under the law of war, and not "innocent civilians" entitled to protection under international humanitarian law, is the foundation of the military detention paradigm being used in the GWOT.

The law-of-war treaties do not provide a clear definition of who should be treated as a combatant for purposes of detention. Clearly, anyone who falls into one of the six categories in the GPW may be interned under the conditions specified in the GPW, even if not committing a combatant act at the time detained, provided the detention is in connection with an international armed conflict. However, there is no guidance in the treaties with respect to persons who fall outside the six categories, and in particular members of terror networks who may have committed or are planning terrorist acts, but at the point or time of capture are not involved in such acts.

Additional Protocol I suggests that a line can be drawn between an individual who should be considered a combatant and an individual who should not, based on the "direct" or "active" participation of the individual in hostilities.[20] Specifically, paragraph 2 of Article 43 of Additional Protocol I provides:

> Members of the armed forces of a Party to a conflict (other than medical personnel and chaplains covered by Article 33 of the Third Convention [*i.e.*, GPW]) are combatants, that is to say, they have the right to participate directly in hostilities.

Paragraph 3 of Article 51 of Additional Protocol I uses similar terminology in prohibiting the targeting of civilians, "unless and for such time as they take a direct part in hostilities", thereby suggesting that civilians, who cannot be targeted, are those who do not participate directly in hostilities, and combatants, who can be targeted, are those who do so participate.[21]

---

20   API art. 50 defines a civilian as anyone who does not fall within the categories laid out in GPW art. 4A or API art. 43 (defining armed forces of a Party), and requires that in cases of doubt a person will be considered a civilian.

21   Similar language is used in APII art. 13(3). The language suggests that a civilian can become a combatant by directly participating and then regain protection against the attack and the civilian's belligerent acts are done. The ambiguity this creates with respect to civilians who engage in combatant activities is a significant problem with determining how to categorize such civilians for purposes of detention, treatment, and prosecution.

These provisions address targeting, and not status, and therefore do not purport to define who is a "combatant" for purposes of military detention under the law of war. Further, the line drawn by Additional Protocol I can be interpreted narrowly to suggest that a civilian is only a combatant when directly participating in hostilities. The "revolving door" effect of this language is problematic with respect to detention, because the detainee, when captured, may or may not be engaged in the belligerent acts that are the reason for detaining him or her.

For purposes of determining whether members of al Qaeda and other terrorist groups should be treated as combatants, the United States has adopted a broad definition that includes persons who are either "part of or supporting forces hostile to the United States or its coalition partners and engaged in an armed conflict against the United States."[22] This definition has been adopted by U.S. courts in evaluating combatant status determinations.[23] Additionally, 10 U.S.C. § 948a defines "unlawful enemy combatant" for purposes of determining who is subject to trial by military commission, as:

(i) a person who has engaged in hostilities or who has purposefully and materially supported hostilities against the United States or its co-belligerents who is not a lawful enemy combatant (including a person who is part of the Taliban, al Qaeda, or associated forces); or

(ii) a person who, before, on, or after the date of the enactment of the Military Commissions Act of 2006, has been determined to be an unlawful enemy combatant by a Combatant Status Review Tribunal or another competent tribunal established under the authority of the President or the Secretary of Defense.[24]

---

22 Hamdi v. Rumsfeld, 543 U.S. at 517. The definition can also be found in the procedures governing Combatant Status Review Tribunals, discussed *infra* at notes 110–117 and accompanying text. *See* Memorandum from Dep. Sec'y Defense to Sec'y of Navy, July 7, 2004, Subject: Order Establishing Combatant Status Review Tribunal [hereinafter 2004 CSRT Order] *available at* http://www.defenselink.mil/news/Jul2004/d20040707review.pdf (last visited Mar. 9, 2009).

23 Boumediene v. Bush, 583 F. Supp. 2d 133 (D.D.C. 2008) (identifying combatant definition that court will use in habeas corpus proceedings.)

24 10 U.S.C. § 948a (2006) (as enacted by Military Commissions Act of 2006, Pub. L. No. 109–366, § 3, 120 Stat. 2600 (2006) [hereinafter MCA]). To be subject to trial by military commission, a person meeting the definition of unlawful enemy combatant also must be an alien (*i.e.*, not a U.S. citizen.) *Id.*

Both definitions indicate that persons who materially support a terrorist group need not actually commit belligerent acts in order to be treated as enemy combatants.

The most comprehensive statement of the U.S. government's claim to detention authority in the GWOT can be found in a March 2009 memorandum submitted by the U.S. Justice Department to the U.S. District Court for the District of Columbia in connection with ongoing *habeas corpus* proceedings involving detainees at Guantanamo Bay, Cuba.[25] In the memorandum, the Justice Department proposed the following "definitional framework" for its authority to detain persons held at Guantanamo Bay:

> The President has the authority to detain persons that the President determines planned, authorized, committed, or aided the terrorist attacks that occurred on September 11, 2001, and persons who harbored those responsible for those attacks. The President also has the authority to detain persons who were part of, or substantially supported, Taliban or al Qaida[sic] forces or associated forces that are engaged in hostilities against the United States or its coalition partners, including any person who has committed a belligerent act, or has directly supported hostilities, in aid of such enemy armed forces.[26]

The memorandum explains that the authority to detain is derived from the Authorization to Use Military Force ("AUMF") passed by Congress in response to the attacks on September 11, 2001.[27] The AUMF authorized the use of "all necessary and appropriate force against those nations, organizations, or persons ... [the president] determines planned, authorized, committed, or aided the terrorist attacks that occurred on September 11, 2001, or harbored such organizations or persons, in order to prevent any future acts of international terrorism against the United States by such nations, organizations or persons."[28] Arguing that this authorization of force necessarily included the authority to detain under the law of war, the memorandum reasons that this

---

25 Respondent's Memorandum Regarding the Government's Detention Authority Relative to Detainees Held at Guantanamo Bay, In re: Guantanamo Bay Detainee Litigation, Misc. No. 08–442 (TFH) (March 13, 2009) [hereinafter Detention Authority Memorandum].

26 *Id.* at 2.

27 Authorization for Use of Military Force, S.J. Res. 23, 107th Congress, 1st Sess. P.L. 107–40, 115 Stat. 224 (2001) [hereinafter AUMF].

28 *Id.* § 2(a).

authority permits the detention of anyone who was "part of" the groups targeted by the AUMF just as the law of war permits detention of any member of an enemy armed force.[29] Determining whether an individual was "part of" such a force depends on a "formal or functional analysis" of the individual's role in the groups targeted by the AUMF, in which, "given the nature of the irregular forces, and the practice of their participants or members to try to conceal their affiliations, judgments about the detainability of a particular individual will necessarily turn on the totality of the circumstances."[30]

Other than the use of the phrase "substantially supporting" in lieu of "supporting", the definitional framework differs little from the definition of "enemy combatant" employed during the Bush Administration, although the memorandum does provide much greater insight into how judgments about the application of the "definitional framework" should be applied.[31] The individualized "totality of the circumstances" approach taken by the Justice Department in its March 2009 memorandum, however, underscores the importance to detainees of the quality and thoroughness of the procedures that will be employed to evaluate those circumstances, including the opportunity for the detainee to be heard by the tribunal making the determination about the lawfulness of detention. Accordingly, it is not surprising that the courts taking up the question of detention in the GWOT have focused attention on these questions, as discussed in greater detail below.

---

29     Detention Authority Memorandum, *supra* note 25, at 5–6.

30     *Id*. at 7. As of this writing, three judges of the U.S. District Court for the District of Columbia have issued decisions evaluating the Government's definitional framework as legal basis for detention. Geherebi v. Obama, — F.Supp.2d —, 2009 WL 1068955 (D.D.C.) (Judge Walton); Hamlily v. Obama, — F.Supp.2d —, 2009 WL 1393113 (D.D.C.) (Judge Bates); and Mattan v. Obama, — F.Supp.2d —, 2009 WL 1425212 (D.D.C.) (Judge Lamberth). In each case, the District Court upheld the authority of the President to detain those who are members of (*i.e.*, "part of") the terrorist groups covered by the definition, but rejected "support" of these groups as an independent basis for detention.

31     Notably, the "definitional framework" applies only to detainees at Guantanamo Bay, and the Obama Administration has yet to extend it to detainees in other places, such as in Afghanistan. *Id*. at 2 ("[The Definitional Framework] is not meant to define the contours of authority for military operations generally, or detention in other contexts.").

## COMBATANT STATUS AND PROSECUTION

The statement in Article 43 of Additional Protocol I that "combatants" have a right to participate directly in hostilities is somewhat misleading. Not all combatants have this right. Only those who belong to the armed forces of a State or otherwise fall into the categories of combatants recognized in the GPW (categories (1), (2), (3) and (6) in the list above) have such a right, because they have "combatant immunity," meaning that they cannot be prosecuted for the personal injury or destruction they cause while acting as a combatant, provided they otherwise follow the law of war in conducting hostilities. Those combatants who do not fall into these favored categories of fighters not only do not qualify for protection under the GPW, but they may also be prosecuted for their belligerent acts.

Entitlement to combatant immunity is not expressly spelled out in the GPW or other law of war treaties, but has long been recognized as a key principle of the law of war. For example, Article 57 of General Order No. 100, "Instructions for the Government of Armies of the United States in the Field."[32] which governed Union forces during the American Civil War, provided, in pertinent part:

> So soon as a man is armed by a sovereign government and takes the soldier's oath of fidelity, he is a belligerent; his killing, wounding, or other warlike acts are not individual crimes or offenses.

A similar point is made in Colonel Winthrop's classic treatise on military law:

> The State is represented in active war by its contending army, and the laws of war justify the killing or disabling of members of the one army by those of the other in battle or hostile operations.[33]

The "combatant immunity" principle is recognized in the first sentence of Article 87 of the GPW, which provides:

> Prisoners of war may not be sentenced by the military authorities and courts of the Detaining Power to any penalties except those provided for in respect of members of the armed forces of the said Power who have committed the same acts.

---

32    Also known as the Lieber Code after its author, Professor Francis Lieber.

33    WILLIAM WINTHROP, MILITARY LAW AND PRECEDENTS 778 (2nd ed. 1920).

The principle is also reflected in Article 1 of the Hague IV Regulations, which provides:

> The laws, rights, and duties of war apply not only to armies, but also to militia and volunteer corps fulfilling the following conditions:
>
> 1. To be commanded by a person responsible for his subordinates;
>
> 2. To have a fixed distinctive emblem recognizable at a distance;
>
> 3. To carry arms openly; and
>
> 4. To conduct their operations in accordance with the laws and customs of war.
>
> In countries where militia or volunteer corps constitute the army, or form part of it, they are included under the denomination "army."

The reference to the "rights" as well as the "duties" of individuals falling into these categories includes the combatant immunity against prosecution for belligerent acts enjoyed by members of the armed forces, militias, and other State-sponsored forces taking part in an international armed conflict.

Perhaps because the doctrine is so widely respected, there are few cases in which the issue of combatant immunity has been litigated. A recent case, *U.S. v. Lindh*, involved an allegation by a U.S. citizen who was captured fighting with the Taliban against U.S. forces in Afghanistan in 2001, that, as a Taliban soldier, he was entitled to invoke the doctrine of combatant immunity as a defense to prosecution for his combat activities against U.S. and allied forces.[34] The court rejected the claim, noting:

> Importantly, this lawful combatant immunity is not automatically available to anyone who takes up arms in a conflict. Rather, it is generally

---

34  212 F. Supp. 2d 541, 552 (E.D.Va. 2002). In analyzing the defendant's claim, the court noted:

> Lawful combatant immunity, a doctrine rooted in the customary international law of war, forbids prosecution of soldiers for their lawful belligerent acts committed during the course of armed conflicts against legitimate military targets. Belligerent acts committed in armed conflict by enemy members of the armed forces may be punished as crimes under a belligerent's municipal law only to the extent that they violate international humanitarian law or are unrelated to the armed conflict. This doctrine has a long history, which is reflected in part in various early international conventions, statutes and documents.

*Id.* at 553. Other cases that have referred to or discussed combatant immunity include *Ex Parte* Quirin, 317 U.S. 1, 30–31 (1942) and Johnson v. Eisentrager, 339 U.S. 763, 793 (1950) (Black, J., dissenting).

accepted that this immunity can be invoked only by members of regular or irregular armed forces who fight on behalf of a state and comply with the requirements for lawful combatants.[35]

Absent combatant immunity, an individual committing belligerent acts is subject to prosecution for those acts by the detaining State. Thus, absent combatant immunity, a combatant who kills, wounds or captures other combatants could be prosecuted for murder, battery or assault, and kidnapping. Similarly, a combatant without combatant immunity who destroys enemy property of any kind, including military weapons and equipment, would be subject to prosecution.[36]

The crimes with which combatants would be charged would be crimes under the law of the detaining State and not the international law of war. Violations of the international law of war, or war crimes, generally involve the conduct of hostilities in a manner contrary to law of war treaties or customary law. A person who participates in hostilities by attacking an enemy's military forces without combatant immunity risks prosecution for such belligerent acts, but those acts are not violations of international law if otherwise conducted in accordance with the law of war.[37]

---

35    U.S. v. Lindh, 212 F. Supp. 2d at 554 (footnotes omitted).

36    A number of the detainees held by the United States at Guantanamo are being prosecuted before military commissions on charges that they committed murder or engaged in unauthorized destruction of property, because they engaged in combat against U.S. or allied military forces, without the benefit of combatant immunity. Counsel for these defendants have opposed these charges on a number of grounds, including that the crimes are not recognized under international law and raised the point that the Military Commissions Act, which authorizes the substantive offenses with which the detainees are charged, requires that the murder and destruction be a violation of the "law of war." Since murder of a combatant by another combatant is considered a violation of the domestic law of the various States with an interest in the crime (e.g., the State of the victim, or, if different, the State of the perpetrator or the State where the crime occurred), but not a crime under international law. In a recent military commission decision, the Military Judge held that the fact that the defendant "might fail to qualify as a lawful combatant does not automatically lead to the conclusion that his conduct violated the law of law." D-007 Ruling on Defense Motion to Dismiss—Lack of Subject Matter Jurisdiction, United States v. Jawad (U.S. Military Commission *available at* http://www.defenselink.mil/news/RULING%20D-007%20(subject%20matter%20jurisdiction)%20(2).pdf (last visited on Mar. 9, 2009).

37    Thus, none of the war crimes listed in Article 8 of the Rome Statute of the International Criminal Court include attacks on enemy combatants who are not *hors de combat*.

## DETENTION AND PROSECUTION OF PERSONS OTHER THAN COMBATANTS

The foregoing discussion has focused on the detention and prosecution of combatants. Yet, it is also possible that on the battlefield or in occupied territory, a commander may detain civilians who were not combatants, but otherwise pose a security threat. Article 5 of GCIV specifically provides that, where a State occupies the territory of its enemy, civilians in occupied territory detained "as a spy or saboteur, or as a person under definite suspicion of activity hostile to the security of the Occupying Power" shall "in those cases where absolute military security so requires, be regarded as having forfeited rights of communication" under GC IV, but "shall nevertheless be treated with humanity and, in case of trial, shall not be deprived of the rights of fair and regular trial" under GC.[38] They also are to be granted "the full rights and privileges of a protected person" under GC "at the earliest date consistent with the security of the State or Occupying Power, as the case may be."[39] Consistent with the latter requirement, GCIV requires that a civilian detainee be permitted to appeal his detention, with such appeals to be decided "with the least possible delay."[40] Further, if the decision to detain is upheld, "it shall be subject to periodical review, if possible every six months, by a competent body set up by the [Occupying] Power."[41] It is worth noting, however, that, with exceptions, GCIV's protections are generally limited to civilians either in occupied territory or in the home territory of a belligerent State. By its terms, it does not protect civilians in enemy territory that has not been occupied (e.g., on the battlefield or in neutral countries.) The applicability of GCIV to the GWOT is uncertain, and it is not clear what protection it affords to civilians who are enemy combatants.[42]

---

38    GCIV art. 5.

39    *Id.* art. 5.

40    *Id.* art. 78.

41    *Id.* A similar right can be found in GCIV art. 43 regarding alien enemies detained in a State's home territory.

42    During the GWOT, the Department of Justice's Office of Legal Counsel ("OLC") defined the scope of GCIV very narrowly, to exclude, *inter alia*, persons who voluntarily came into occupied territory from third countries to engage in combatant activities, such as "operatives of the al Qaeda terrorist organization who are not Iraqi nationals or permanent residents of Iraq" during the period in which the United States was an occupying power, since such persons did not "find themselves" in occupied territory but rather had elected to come there. Memorandum,

Many would argue that the provisions applicable to occupied territory should be broadly construed to apply in all situations in which civilians are detained during military operations.[43]

As the foregoing suggests, the difference in treatment of those considered to be combatants and those considered to be civilians is quite significant. If the capturing State concludes that an individual is an enemy combatant, he or she can be held until the end of hostilities. The legal protections afforded the detained combatant during captivity will be determined by whether the combatant is considered to be a lawful combatant entitled to prisoner of war status and protection under the GPW or an unprivileged belligerent, who is not entitled to such status and protection. However, there is no express requirement under the GPW to grant the detained combatant an opportunity to appeal his or her status once that status had been determined under the GPW, or to obtain any subsequent review of whether continued detention is required.

On the other hand, if the detaining State determines that the detained individual is a civilian, there is no authority under the Geneva Conventions for indefinite detention; rather, detention may only continue for so long as the situation requires, consistent with the security of the detaining State.[44] Further, the detainee must be granted a right of periodic appeal to determine if detention is still required.[45]

## DETERMINATION OF STATUS

As the preceding discussion suggests, an individual detained by a State in connection with an armed conflict has a significant stake in the determination of his status. If the individual can demonstrate that he or she is not a combatant, the detaining State may release the detainee or, if he or

---

Office of the Legal Counsel to Counsel to the President, subject: Protected Person Status in Occupied Iraq under the Fourth Geneva Convention, 14–23 (Mar. 18, 2004) *available at* http://www.usdoj.gov/olc/2004/gc4mar18.pdf (last visited Mar. 9, 2009).

43    It is DoD policy to broadly apply the law of war. *See* U.S. Dep't of Defense, Dir. 2311.01E, DoD Law of War Program, para. 4.1 (May 9, 2006) (Stating DoD "policy" that "Members of the DoD Components comply with the law of war during all armed conflicts, however such conflicts are characterized, and in all other military operations.") However, a policy leaves open the possibility of a future change and therefore is not legally binding.

44    GCIV arts. 5, 42 & 78.

45    *Id.* art. 78.

she is retained for reasons of security, the detention must be periodically reviewed. On the other hand, if the individual is determined to be a combatant, he or she will want an opportunity to establish his or her status as a prisoner of war who enjoys combatant immunity and is entitled to the protections afforded by the GPW. In either case, the scope, nature and quality of the process by which the status determination will be made is critically important to the treatment and disposition of the individual.

There is surprisingly little guidance in the GPW on the question of status determinations. Article 5 of the GPW directs that "[s]hould any doubt arise as to whether persons, having committed a belligerent act and having fallen into the hands of the enemy, belong to any of the categories in Article 4 [the applicable article regarding the persons covered by the GPW], such persons shall enjoy the protection of the present Convention until such time as their status has been determined by a competent tribunal."[46] As stated, the rule provides for the protection of the GPW as the default in cases of doubt, but it does not stipulate which person or entity is entitled to make the decision whether or not there is any doubt. The absence of guidance on this point leaves enormous latitude for different practices among the various States who are party to the GPW, who presumably could leave the decision as to doubt to the lower echelons of command of the capturing unit, or require such authority to be exercised by higher levels.

Also missing from Article 5 is any detail about the nature of the tribunal that will make the status determination in cases of doubt.[47] This lack is arguably helpful to implementation of Article 5, as it affords each State party to the GPW the flexibility to adopt procedures commensurate with the circumstances in which Article 5 is to be applied. For example, it would be difficult to follow a very formal procedure on the battlefield, where there may be large numbers of detainees, and where the armed

---

46   GPW art. 5.

47   The ICRC's Commentary on the GPW, which is influential (albeit not binding) on how States interpret their obligations under the GPW and related law of war treaties, notes that, in earlier drafts of this Article, it was initially proposed by the ICRC to have the status determination made by a "responsible authority." Concerns about leaving this important decision to an individual led the drafters to replace the phrase with "military tribunal" and later with "competent tribunal," which was ultimately adopted. JEAN S. PICTET, COMMENTARY ON THE GENEVA CONVENTION RELATIVE TO THE TREATMENT OF PRISONERS OF WAR 77 (1960) [hereinafter GPW COMMENTARY].

forces of the capturing State are operating under austere conditions. On the other hand, formal procedures could be followed where the number of detainees is limited and they are being held at locations suitable for such process.[48] Therefore, the flexibility provided by the generality of the language used in the article has practical value. However, absolutely nothing in the GPW guides the capturing State in fashioning its procedure.[49]

Article 45 of Additional Protocol I provides some additional detail regarding the status determination. First, it allows the detained person, or the State party on whom he depends (*i.e.*, the State on whose behalf he or she is fighting) to claim prisoner of war status, thereby allowing him or her to raise the issue and require a tribunal to be held before the status could be denied. Second, Article 45 grants any individual being tried for an offense arising from hostilities to litigate the issue of his or her entitlement to prisoner of war status (which would then allow the defendant to claim combatant immunity) before a "judicial tribunal". Finally, it provides that even if prisoner of war status is denied, the individual is still entitled to the protections of Article 75 of Additional Protocol I, which applies to all persons detained in connection with an armed conflict subject to Additional Protocol I (generally international armed conflicts).[50] While Article 75 would not provide a detainee with combatant immunity, it does ensure that the detained individual stills retains certain protections under international law even if he or she is determined to be a combatant who is not entitled to be treated as a prisoner of war.

---

48 The objective and length of detention might also influence the degree of formality in any procedures adopted by a State to implement the "tribunal" requirement. Detentions that are anticipated to last only a very short time before release would seem to merit a less formal procedure as compared to detentions that could last indefinitely or that might also be accompanied by prosecution for the detainee's belligerent acts.

49 The Commentary's view of the meaning of the reference to a tribunal perhaps tilts toward the more formal:

> The matter should be taken to a court, as persons taking part in the fight without the right to do so are liable to be prosecuted for murder or attempted murder, and might even be sentenced to capital punishment.

GPW COMMENTARY, *supra* note 47, at 77. This view seems farsighted in light of recent U.S. court decisions discussed more fully *infra* affording detainees held by the United States to seek review of their detention in U.S. courts under writs of habeas corpus.

50 APII arts. 4–6 provide similar protections in non-international armed conflicts.

Like Article 5 of the GPW, Article 45 of Additional Protocol I does not provide any detail regarding the nature of the tribunal or the procedure it is to follow in making status determinations. Article 45 includes the same presumption that a detainee whose status is in doubt is entitled to prisoner of war treatment until a tribunal determines otherwise. However, there is a notable difference between the presumptions in the two articles. In Article 5 of the GPW, it is only individuals who have "committed a belligerent act" and then are later detained who are afforded the presumption. The reason, which is not addressed in the ICRC Commentary to the GPW, appears to be that a person committing a belligerent act has at least established, by that act, that he or she is a combatant. The only question then is whether he or she belongs in one of the categories of combatants protected by the GPW.

By contrast, Article 45 of Additional Protocol I affords this presumption to any person who "takes part in hostilities". The phrase is broader and could include persons committing acts that are not clearly "belligerent" in that they do not involve the use of arms or otherwise are not easily recognized as combatant activities, but are nonetheless directly related to the hostilities and indicate that the individual is or intends to be a combatant. In such a situation, the person might be treated as a prisoner of war if he or she is a member of one of the categories of armed forces protected by Additional Protocol I. By expanding the presumption to apply to these individuals as well, Additional Protocol I expands the numbers of individuals who are presumed to be prisoners of war absent a determination by a tribunal under Article 5 of the GPW that they are not. As the ICRC Commentary on Additional Protocol I notes:

> [T]he capture can occur in conditions when the captor has no way of finding out whether or not the person concerned is a prisoner of war, or perhaps in circumstances which give him some indication, but no proof on this point. This provision has therefore introduced a system of legal presumptions in favour of the prisoner. If the captor wants to contest such a presumption, it is up to him to present evidence that the person concerned is not a prisoner of war. . . .[51]

Thus, unlike under Article 5 of the GPW, the burden clearly falls on the captor under Additional Protocol I to establish that a detainee is not entitled to prisoner of war status.

---

51    COMMENTARY ON THE ADDITIONAL PROTOCOLS OF 8 JUNE 1977 TO THE GENEVA CONVENTIONS OF 12 AUGUST 1949 ¶ 1733, at 547 (Yves Sandoz *et al* eds., 1987).

The United States has not ratified Additional Protocol I and has identified various aspects of its provisions that are unacceptable because they would afford prisoner of war status to persons and groups that the United States does not believe should be given such treatment. However, the United States has not objected to the principles reflected in Article 45, including the principle that where there is doubt as to the status of a detainee, he or she should be accorded prisoner of war treatment until that doubt is resolved.[52]

The United States has implemented Article 5 of the GPW in a manner that provides more due process protections than is required by the GPW or Additional Protocol I. The U.S. military services, with the U.S. Army acting as Executive Agent for the Department of Defense on detainee matters, has promulgated a multi-service regulation, designated as Army Regulation (AR) 190–8, but also falling within the regulation series of each of the other services (U.S. Air Force, Marine Corps and Navy) that includes procedures for the tribunals required by Article 5 of the GPW. The current version of AR 190–8 was promulgated in 1997, based in part on lessons learned in the Gulf War and in prior conflicts. It provides for tribunals consisting of three commissioned officers, one of whom must be in the grade of Major (or its Navy equivalent) or higher, assisted by a recorder, which the regulation says "preferably" should be a judge advocate (*i.e.*, a military lawyer).[53] The tribunal's procedure includes a number of due process protections, including notifying the detainee of his or her rights at the beginning of the tribunal's hearings and granting the detained person the right to attend all open hearings (hearings may be closed where

---

52 Michael J. Matheson, *Session One: The United States Position on the Relation of Customary Law to the 1977 Protocols Additional to the 1949 Geneva Conventions*, 2 Am. U. J. Int'l L. & Pol'y 419, 425–426 (1987) (remarks of Deputy Legal Advisor, U.S. Department of State). It is U.S. policy, as expressed in Army Regulation (AR) 190–8, that "all persons taken into custody by U.S. forces will be provide the protections of the GPW until some other legal status is determined by competent authority." U.S. Dep't Army, Reg. 190–8 Enemy Prisoners of War, Retained Personnel, Civilian Internees and Other Detainees, para. 1–5.a.(2) (1997) [hereinafter AR 190–8].

53 Although not required by AR 190–8, *supra* note 52, military lawyers could serve as the three members of the tribunal, and in fact this is what has occurred in most recent U.S. operations where Article 5 tribunals have been required. *See* U.S. Army Center for Law and Military Operations, Forged in the Fire: Legal Lessons Learned During Military Operations 1994–2006 at 35 (2006) [hereinafter Forged in the Fire 2006] *available at* http://www.loc.gov/rr/frd/Military_Law/pdf/forged-in-the-fire.pdf (last visited on Mar. 9, 2009).

open hearings would "compromise security"), to question witnesses, and to have the assistance of an interpreter. The detainee may testify or otherwise address the tribunal, but may not be compelled to do so.

The tribunal decides, by majority vote and applying a "preponderance of the evidence" standard, whether the detainee is an "innocent civilian who should be immediately returned to his home or released or a prisoner of war under the GPW, who will be accorded prisoner of war status.[54] The tribunal may also decide that the person is a civilian who should be detained for reasons of operational security or probable cause incident to criminal investigation". This latter category of "civilian" includes combatants who are not entitled to prisoners of war status but who must nonetheless continue to be held.[55] They are not entitled to protection under the GPW, although they would benefit from the protections

---

54    The tribunal may also determine that the person is a member of certain categories of "retained personnel," *i.e.*, medical or religious personnel who are part of an enemy armed force or the staff of voluntary aid societies who work with the enemy armed force. AR 190–8, *supra* note 52, para. 1–6e.(10). These categories of non-combatants may be released, but are entitled to be treated as prisoners of war if retained with other prisoners of war, rather than released. *Id*. para. 3–15.

55    Chapters 5–7 of AR 190–8, *supra* note 52, describe the "internment" of persons considered to be a "civilian internee" or "CI," which the Regulation defines as "[a] civilian who is interned during armed conflict or occupation for security reasons or for protection or because he has committed an offense against the detaining power." *Id*. Glossary, Section II. CIs are entitled to treatment similar to that accorded to prisoners of war under GPW, but under the provisions of GCIV. The applicability of the CI category is unclear. AR 190–8 para. 6–2.a(2) provides that only civilian persons entitled to "protected status" and that meet the requirements set forth in GCIV will be classified as CI. GCIV only explicitly protects enemy civilians in occupied territory and in the home territory of a belligerent, and indeed the applicable provisions of AR 190–8 suggest that its provisions on CI are directed toward civilians in those specific circumstances. *See, e.g.*, AR 190–8, para. 5–1.c. Thus, it is not explicitly clear that the provisions of AR190–8 applicable to CI apply to persons detained in other areas (e.g., on a battlefield) who are determined not to be either a prisoners of war entitled to protection under GPW or an innocent civilian entitled to be released. Nevertheless, consistent with the position taken as a matter of policy in FM 27–10, *supra* note 9, U.S. policy is to apply to all detainees, "without regard to a detainee's legal status," a minimum humane treatment standard that includes the provisions of Common Article 3 plus some enhancements. U.S. Dep't of Defense, Dir. 2310.01E, The Department of Defense Detainee Program, para. 4.2 & Enclosure 4 (Sept. 5, 2006). Further, under DOD Dir. 2310.01E, any detainee is to be treated as prisoners of war under GPW "until some other legal status is determined by competent authority." *Id*. Enclosure 4.

afforded to internees under GCIV if they are considered "protected persons".[56]

A written report of the proceedings is prepared and forwarded to a higher headquarters for legal review within three days after the tribunal's decision is completed. The record of every proceeding resulting in a determination denying prisoner of war status is reviewed for legal sufficiency by the legal office of the general officer who convened the tribunal.[57]

Although extensive, the procedures adopted by the United States in AR 190–8 do not accord a detainee the full panoply of rights that could have been granted in light of the significant interest the detainee may have in either (a) proving that he or she is an innocent civilian entitled to be released or, if that is not possible, at least (b) securing prisoner of war status under the GPW (and hence the protection of combatant immunity.) Indeed, in Vietnam, U.S. military authorities issued directives that required the tribunals to consist of three officers, generally military lawyers, assisted by a non-voting counsel who handled administrative tasks, including advising the detainee of his rights, arranging for witnesses, presenting evidence, and preparing the report of the tribunal's proceedings. The detainee was permitted to be present at all open sessions of the tribunal, to present evidence, and to have the assistance of an interpreter.

Unlike the procedures in AR 190–8 (which do not include a right to counsel), the detainee in the Vietnam War procedure could select his

---

56   AR 190–8 does not expressly state under which circumstances a person would be considered to be a "protected person." This term is defined in GCIV art. 4 to be "those who, at a given moment and in any manner whatsoever, in case of a conflict or occupation, find themselves in the hands of a Party to the conflict or Occupying Power of which they are not nationals" (with certain exclusions for nationals of a neutral State or a co-belligerent.) As indicated in note 42, *supra*, during the GWOT, the Department of Justice's Office of Legal Counsel defined the phrase "find themselves in the hands of a Party" very narrowly, to exclude, *inter alia*, persons who voluntarily came into occupied territory from third countries to engage in combatant activities.

57   An important element of the procedure under AR 190–8 is that tribunals can only be convened by a commander exercising "general courts-martial convening authority," which is generally reserved to higher ranking general officers or admirals. AR 190–8, *supra* note 52, para. 1–6.d. Such authority is generally exercised only by senior military commanders and others designated by the president, the Secretary of Defense or the Secretary of a Military Department. *See* Article 22, Uniform Code of Military Justice [hereinafter UCMJ].

own counsel, including a fellow detainee to help him, but if he failed to appoint someone, a military lawyer familiar with the Geneva Conventions was appointed for him. Counsel for the detainee had a number of rights, including conferring with the detainee, examining evidence and presenting (and cross-examining) witnesses and testimony on the detainee's behalf. The Tribunal would decide by vote, in a closed session, whether the detainee was a prisoner of war, and a record would be prepared for further review, particularly in cases where the tribunal determined that the detainee was not entitled to prisoner of war status.

The extensive procedures used in Vietnam reflected a broader U.S. policy of liberally granting prisoner of war status to combatants, other than those engaged in terrorism, spying or sabotage.[58] The policy was driven in part by the reality that the government of South Vietnam did not have the resources and facilities to try and punish as civil defendants those who engaged in belligerent acts, but did not qualify as prisoners of war.[59] The policy was also driven by the belief that humane treatment accorded to captured North Vietnamese and Vietcong forces would be reciprocated by the North Vietnamese and Vietcong who captured Americans.[60] As noted by a senior military lawyer, who was the chief military legal advisor to the U.S. military forces in Vietnam from 1964–66:

> U.S. policy was to do all in its power to alleviate the plight of American prisoners. It was expected that efforts by the United States to ensure humane treatment for Vietcong and North Vietnamese Army captives would bring reciprocal benefits for American captives.[61]

---

58   GEORGE S. PRUGH, LAW AT WAR: VIETNAM 1964–1973, at 66 (1975) ("The MACV policy was that all combatants captured during military operations were to be accorded prisoner of war status, irrespective of the type of unit to which they belonged. Terrorists, spies and saboteurs were excluded from consideration as prisoners of war.")

59   *Id.* at 66 ("By broadly construing Article 4 [GPW], so as to accord full prisoner of war status to Viet Cong Main Force and Local Force troops, as well as regular North Vietnamese Army troops, any Viet Cong taken in combat would be detained for a prisoner of war camp rather than a civilian jail.")

60   *Id.* at 62 ("In the south, where the government of South Vietnam had tried and publicly executed some Viet Cong agents, there had been retributory executions of Americans by Viet Cong. In the north, . . . Hanoi repeatedly threatened to try United States pilots in accordance with Vietnamese laws, but never carried out this threat.")

61   *Id.* The procedures used in Vietnam were set out in Annex A of U.S. Military Assistance Command (MACV), Directive No. 20-5 (Mar. 15, 1968), an excerpt

As the foregoing suggests, the procedures were tailored to Vietnam and not applicable to all U.S. military operations. In subsequent conflicts, it was left to commanders at the theater level or lower to determine what procedures would be used to make status determinations. As a result, in those conflicts, U.S. military officials used more informal procedures that were better suited to the circumstances of the conflict.[62] The procedures for Article 5 tribunals set out in AR 190–8 now provides a bottom line standard to be applied.[63]

As an obligation under international law, Article 5 has proven to be sufficiently flexible for the United States to tailor its implementation to meet the circumstances on the ground.[64] Importantly, however, Article 5's

---

from which is reprinted in *Contemporary Practice of the United States Relating to International Law*, 62 AM. J. INT'L LAW 770–774. The Article 5 tribunals held in Vietnam are also briefly described in FRED L. BORCH, JUDGE ADVOCATES IN COMBAT: ARMY LAWYERS IN MILITARY OPERATIONS FROM VIETNAM TO HAITI 20–21 (2001) [hereinafter JUDGE ADVOCATES IN COMBAT].

62  For example, in U.S. operation "Just Cause" in Panama in December 1989, then U.S. Army Major Richard B. Jackson (one of the co-authors of this book) developed an informal procedure to deal in a short time with the classification of a large number of Panamanian prisoners taken by U.S. forces:

> Reaffirming that Article 5 of the GPW Convention required that a three-person tribunal determine the status of detainees, Jackson, along with a representative of the camp commander and a military intelligence officer, began the process of sorting out the individuals in question. In determining their status, Major Jackson and the two other officers acted as a *de facto* Article 5 tribunal, examining any paperwork accompanying the detainees and questioning the individuals concerned when necessary.

JUDGE ADVOCATES IN COMBAT, *supra* note 61, at 104. While this procedure did not employ all the formalities of the procedures used in Vietnam, it nonetheless met the requirements of Article 5, GPW. Further, the procedure allowed Major Jackson and his colleagues to reduce from 4100 to 100 the number of individuals who required continued detention and greatly facilitate repatriation and release of the others. *Id.* at 105.

63  In practice, commanders have varied the procedures to fit the specific situation while still complying with the regulation's requirements.

64  In addition, in the case of captures made on a battlefield, U.S. military practice is that the Article 5 tribunal is typically only a part of a lengthy screening process that begins with a determination by a commander at the time of capture on the battlefield, based on evidence on the ground and continues as the detainee is processed by military authorities as he or she is moved to more centralized internment facilities away from the battlefield. *See* Brief for the Respondents at 3, Hamdi v. Rumsfeld, 542 U.S. 528 (2004), 2004 WL 724020 (U.S.) [hereinafter "Government Response Brief in Hamdi"] ("Those taken into U.S. control [in the conflict in

requirement that, in cases of doubt, a person must be treated as a prisoner of war until a tribunal determines otherwise, means that there is little risk that an individual will be afforded less rights than he or she is entitled to under international law.[65] On the other hand, where the capturing State concludes there is no doubt, Article 5 is not applicable and provides no protection against an erroneous conclusion.

## DETENTION AS A METHOD OF WARFARE IN GWOT

The scale and lethality of the attacks on the United States on September 11, 2001, led the U.S. government to view its struggle with the terrorist elements that launched the attacks and the nations that harbored them in terms of armed conflict. In his statement of September 11 on the attacks, the president said: "The United States will hunt down and punish those responsible for the cowardly acts", adding "[o]ur military around the world is on high alert status...." On September 14, the president declared a national emergency to respond to "the continuing and immediate threat of further attacks on the United States" and authorized the call to duty of reserve military personnel.

On September 18, 2001, citing the "threat to the national security and foreign policy of the United States posed by these grave acts of violence", both houses of Congress approved the "Authorization for Use of Military Force", which authorized the president to:

> ...use all necessary and appropriate force against those nations, organizations, or persons he determines planned, authorized, committed, or aided the terrorist attacks that occurred on September 11, 2001, or harbored such organizations or persons, in order to prevent any future acts of international terrorism against the United States by such nations, organizations or persons.[66]

---

Afghanistan] are subjected to a multi-step screening process to determine if their continued detention is necessary.")

65   In the past decade or so, U.S. military lawyers have "used an informal screening process to make the initial determination whether to release a detainee or to conduct an Article 5 tribunal if classification was not possible after initial screening," FORGED IN THE FIRE 2006, *supra* note 53, at 35. This approach, from which come the "doubt" that is the predicate for convening an Article 5 tribunal, is not precluded by GPW, which does not specify from whence doubt should come.

66   AUMF § 2(a), *supra* note 27. The AUMF declared that it constituted specific statutory authorization within the meaning of section 5(b) of the War Powers Resolution, which relates to the need for Congressional authority for any extended

The president signed the AUMF the same day it was passed by Congress.

On October 7, 2001, the president announced military operations against al Qaeda training camps and Taliban military installations in Afghanistan, noting that "[t]oday we focus on Afghanistan, but the battle is broader. . . . In this conflict, there is no neutral ground."[67]

That detention and prosecution of terrorists as unlawful combatants would be a key element of the GWOT was made clear with the issuance of the President's Military Order of November 13, 2001.[68] Finding that, among other things, "[i]nternational terrorists, including members of al Qaida[sic], have carried out attacks . . . on a scale that has created a state of armed conflict that requires the use of the United States Armed Forces", the order authorized the Secretary of Defense to detain any individual who is not a U.S. citizen with respect to whom the president has made the following determinations:

"(1) there is reason to believe that such individual, at the relevant times,

(i) is or was a member of the organization known as al Qaida[sic];

(ii) has engaged in, aided or abetted, or conspired to commit, acts of international terrorism, or acts in preparation therefor, that have caused, threaten to cause, or have as their aim to cause, injury to or adverse effects on the United States, its citizens, national security, foreign policy, or economy; or

(iii) has knowingly harbored one or more individuals described in subparagraphs (i) or (ii) . . .; and

(2) it is in the interest of the United States that such individual be subject to this order."[69]

---

involvement of U.S. forces in hostilities. Thus, as the title suggested, the Congress in passing the AUMF was authorizing the use of military force to fight terrorists.

67   Presidential Address, Oct. 7, 2001.

68   Military Order of November 13, 2001—Detention, Treatment and Trial of Certain Non-Citizens in the War Against Terrorism, 66 Fed. Reg. 57,833 (2001) [hereinafter Military Order].

69   *Id.* sec. 2. While detention is authorized under the Military Order, few detainees were actually designated as subject to the Military Order for purpose of detention. CONG. RESEARCH SERV., ENEMY COMBATANT DETAINEES: HABEAS CORPUS CHALLENGES IN FEDERAL COURTS DETENTIONS (Order Code No. RL33180) at 9 n. 59 (last updated Jan. 29, 2009) *available at* http://www.fas.org/sgp/crs/natsec/RL33180.pdf (last visited Mar. 9, 2009). Rather such detention generally occurs

The order authorized not only detention, but also prosecution of the detained individuals by military commission.[70]

The order directed that the detained individuals be:

"(a) detained at an appropriate location designated by the Secretary of Defense outside or within the United States;

(b) treated humanely, without any adverse distinction based on race, color, religion, gender, birth, wealth, or any similar criteria;

(c) afforded adequate food, drinking water, shelter, clothing, and medical treatment;

(d) allowed the free exercise of religion consistent with the requirements of such detention; and

(e) detained in accordance with such other conditions as the Secretary of Defense may prescribe."[71]

The order also directed that regulations to be prescribed by the Secretary of Defense would provide for "a full and fair trial, with the military commission sitting as the triers of both fact and law."[72] It also provided that military tribunals would have exclusive jurisdiction with respect to offenses by the detainees, and that detainees would not have the privilege to seek any remedy or maintain any action, or to have others seek a remedy or maintain an action on the individual's behalf, in any U.S. or foreign court or any international tribunal.[73]

Of course, the U.S. military did not need the military order to authorize detention of battlefield combatants. It already enjoyed that right under the law of war. However, the order significantly expanded the authority to detain by including a potentially broader category of individuals who may not have committed belligerent acts, but who supported or aided

---

under the authority granted in the AUMF, which courts have interpreted to include the right to detain.

70    Military Order, *supra* note 68, sec. 4.

71    *Id.* sec. 3.

72    *Id.* sec. 4. The provisions of the military order related to military commissions was superseded by Executive Order 13425, which implemented provisions of the Military Commissions Act of 2006, *supra* note 24. Executive Order 13425 of February 14, 2007, "Trial of Alien Unlawful Enemy Combatants by Military Commission," 72 Fed. Reg. 7737 (2007).

73    Military Order, *supra* note 68, sec. 7.

those committing or preparing to commit such acts, or who harbored such individuals.[74] Also, the detention authority granted under the order was not limited to any particular theatre of operations, and potentially included any person in the world who was not a U.S. citizen and with respect to whom the president had made the required determinations.

Given the authority granted to the Defense Department to try detainees by military commission, it was clear that detention was not simply to take these individuals off the battlefield, but also to prosecute them for war crimes. An important question in implementing this strategy was whether the detainees would be entitled to prisoner of war status under the GPW. Were they to have prisoner of war status, the United States would not be able to try terrorists for any crimes that involved attacking military installations or personnel, as the combatant immunity enjoyed by prisoners of war would shield them from prosecution for such acts. On the other hand, if they were not prisoners of war and did not enjoy combatant immunity, the detainees could be prosecuted for belligerent acts, even against military personnel and military targets.

The issue of the application of the GPW in the GWOT first arose with respect to the conflict in Afghanistan, where it was anticipated that U.S. military operations would yield detainees who would be held under the president's military order. In January 2002, the Justice Department's Office of Legal Counsel (OLC) concluded that neither the Taliban nor al Qaeda fighters could qualify for prisoner of war status under the GPW.[75] Thus, the GPW could not apply to a conflict with al Qaeda as a matter of law, because, according to Article 2 of the GPW, the GPW only applies in conflicts between "two or more of the High Contracting Parties" to the GPW. Al Qaeda is not a State, nor does it belong to a State. Further, al Qaeda fighters did not meet the requirements of any of the six categories of prisoners covered by the GPW.[76] They were not

---

74   For some helpful perspectives on the tests that might be applied in designating terrorists as enemies under the law of war, see Jack Goldsmith, Long-Term Terrorist Detention and Our National Security Court (2009) (a Working Paper of the Series on Counterterrorism and American Statutory Law) *available at* http://www.brookings.edu/~/media/Files/rc/papers/2009/0209_detention_goldsmith/0209_detention_goldsmith.pdf (last visited on Mar. 9, 2009).

75   Neither Afghanistan nor the United States is a party to Additional Protocol I and therefore OLC did not need to consider whether the provisions of Additional Protocol I would have expanded the applicability of prisoner of war status.

76   *See supra* note 17 and accompanying text for the six categories.

THE WAR ON TERROR AND THE LAWS OF WAR

members of a regular armed force of a State, nor do they qualify as a volunteer force, militia, or organized resistance force under the GPW, because they did not meet the treaty's requirements that such forces distinguish themselves from civilians by wearing uniforms or insignia, carrying their arms openly and obeying the laws of war.

Taliban fighters, on the other hand, did fight on behalf of a state party to the GPW (Afghanistan) but, like al Qaeda fighters, did not come within any of the six categories of prisoners covered by the GPW. The Taliban lacked an organized command structure, with responsibility for subordinates, and was dominated by al Qaeda. Taliban did carry their arms openly and in some cases had a tribal flag, but they otherwise did not distinguish themselves from civilians. Perhaps most importantly, they did not comply with the law of war, did little to distinguish between civilians and combatants in hostilities and in fact intentionally killed civilians and committed other atrocities. For these and other reasons, the OLC concluded that there were sufficient factual grounds for the president to determine that the GPW did not apply to any member of al Qaeda or the Taliban.[77]

On February 7, 2002, the White House announced that the president had made a determination that the "Geneva Convention will apply to the Taliban detainees, but not to the al Qaeda international terrorists", adding that:

> Taliban detainees are not entitled to POW [prisoner of war] status. To qualify as POWs under Article 4, al Qaeda and Taliban detainees would have to have satisfied four conditions: They would have to be part of a military hierarchy; they would have to have worn uniforms or other distinctive signs visible at a distance; they would have to have carried arms openly; and they would have to have conducted their military operations in accordance with the laws and customs of war.

> The Taliban have not effectively distinguished themselves from the civilian population of Afghanistan. Moreover, they have not conducted their operations in accordance with the laws and customs of war. Instead, they

---

77    *See* Department of Justice, Office of Legal Counsel, Memorandum for the Office of the President, *"Status Of Taliban Forces Under Article 4 Of The Third Geneva Convention Of 1949," (February 7, 2002), available at* http://www.usdoj.gov/olc/2002/pub-artc4potusdetermination.pdf (last visited on Mar. 9, 2009).

have knowingly adopted and provided support to the unlawful terrorist objectives of the al Qaeda.[78]

This announcement served two purposes. First, it affirmed that even though the Taliban did not qualify for prisoner of war status, the Geneva Conventions did apply to the conflict. This had the important effect of underscoring that the United States expected any members of regular forces taken during the conflict, including U.S. soldiers, to be treated as prisoners of war. Second, by categorically determining that al Qaeda and Taliban fighters did not qualify for prisoner of war status, the president eliminated any need to hold tribunals to make individual determinations of their status under Article 5 of the GPW. Had such a determination not been made, then a Taliban prisoner wishing to claim the benefits of prisoner of war status might have claimed there was sufficient doubt to merit convening an Article 5 tribunal and, until such a tribunal was convened, he or she would have to be treated as a prisoner of war.[79]

At the time of the announcement, the Administration emphasized that there would not be significant differences in the treatment accorded al Qaeda and Taliban prisoners as a matter of U.S. policy, and the treatment that they would receive would be substantially similar to what they would have received if held as prisoners of war under the GPW. Indeed, a fact sheet issued on the date the president's announcement noted:

The detainees will receive much of the treatment normally afforded to POWs by the [GPW]. However, the detainees will not receive some of the specific privileges afforded to POWs, including:

- access to a canteen to purchase food, soap, and tobacco
- a monthly advance of pay
- the ability to have and consult personal financial accounts
- the ability to receive scientific equipment, musical instruments, or sports outfits[80]

---

78    White House Press Secretary announcement of President Bush's determination re legal status of Taliban and al Qaeda detainees (February 7, 2002), Digest of United States Practice in International Law 2002, *available at* http://www.state.gov/s/l/38727.htm (last visited on Mar. 9, 2009).

79    This was never even an option for al Qaeda fighters, because the president had already determined that the GPW did not apply to the conflict with al Qaeda.

80    Fact Sheet: Status of Detainees at Guantanamo *available at* http://www.presidency.ucsb.edu/ws/index.php?pid=79402 (last visited Mar. 9, 2009).

Yet there were significant differences. First, without prisoner of war status, the detainees would not enjoy combatant immunity, could be treated as unlawful combatants and therefore were subject to prosecution for belligerent acts against U.S. and coalition forces. Second, any favorable protection they enjoyed was driven primarily by policy, except to the extent treatment was mandated by U.S. domestic law. Thus, the president's February 7, 2002 determination stated "[a]s a matter of policy, the United States Armed Forces shall continue to treat detainees humanely and, to the extent appropriate and consistent with military necessity, in a manner consistent with the principles of [the Geneva Conventions]."[81]

The transfer of detainees to the U.S. naval station at Guantanamo Bay, Cuba (hereinafter "Guantanamo"), quickly drew petitions for writs of *habeas corpus* challenging both the detention of detainees as unlawful combatants and their possible trial by military commission, rather than prosecution in U.S. civilian courts.[82] The U.S. government opposed these petitions on the grounds that the writ of *habeas corpus* did not apply in Guantanamo because it lay outside the sovereign territory of the United States. The government relied principally on *Johnson v. Eisentrager*,[83] a U.S. Supreme Court decision handed down after World War II. In *Eisentrager*, the Court ruled that German citizens convicted by a U.S. military commission and imprisoned in an Allied-controlled prison in Landsberg, Germany for war crimes committed in China did not have the right to pursue a *habeas* claim in a U.S. court. Important to this decision were the facts that the prisoners "at no relevant time were within any territory over which the United States is sovereign, and the scenes of their offense, their capture, their trial, and their punishment were all beyond the territorial jurisdiction of any court of the United States."[84] In reaching this holding, the Court noted that granting the

---

81  *See* Memorandum, President George W. Bush, to Vice President et al., subject: Humane Treatment of al Qaeda and Taliban Detainees (Feb. 7 2002), *available at* http://www2.gwu.edu/~nsarchiv/NSAEBB/NSAEBB127/02.02.07.pdf (last visited on Mar. 9, 2009).

82  One of the first petitions was filed by a coalition of clergy, lawyers, and professors (including former Attorney General Ramsey Clark) in January 2002. *See* Coalition of Clergy v. Bush (No. CV02570AHMJTLX), 2002 WL 1377710 (C.D. Cal. 2002).

83  339 U.S. 763 (1950).

84  Johnson v. Eisentrager, 339 U.S. at 776.

writ to the prisoners would involve a considerable burden on U.S. military authorities to transport them to the United States to appear in U.S. courts. The Court also pointed out that the writ, "since it is held to be a matter of right, would be equally available to enemies during active hostilities ... and would hamper the war effort and bring aid and comfort to the enemy."[85] In the Court's view, such trials would "diminish the prestige of our commanders, not only with enemies but with wavering neutrals" and "divert his efforts and attention from the military offensive abroad to the legal defensive at home."[86]

The detailed history of the litigation of the Guantanamo *habeas corpus* cases in lower courts falls outside the scope of this chapter. Ultimately, however, conflicting outcomes in appellate courts led the U.S. Supreme Court in 2004 to grant *certiorari* in two cases involving detainees that significantly changed U.S. law and policy regarding detention of enemy combatants.

In *Rasul v. Bush*,[87] the Court held that the U.S. District Court for the District of Columbia had jurisdiction to hear *habeas corpus* petitions from twelve Kuwaitis and two Australians[88] held in Guantanamo who sought to challenge their continued detention as combatants. After examining the legal status of Guantanamo and the authority exercised by the U.S. government there, the Court found that while not technically within the sovereign territory of the United States, Guantanamo was under the "exclusive jurisdiction and control" of the United States. Therefore, the holding in *Johnson v. Eisentrager, supra*, was not controlling and the District Court could entertain *habeas* petitions from detainees, challenging the legality of their detention in Guantanamo.[89] The Court further held that "nothing in *Eisentrager* or in any of our other cases categorically excludes aliens detained in military custody outside the United States from the 'privilege of litigation' in U.S. courts."[90]

---

85   *Id.* at 779.

86   *Id.* at 779. The Court also noted that such litigation would create "a conflict between judicial and military opinion highly comforting to enemies of the United States" but without any reciprocal benefit for U.S. soldiers given the absence of the writ of *habeas corpus* in most foreign legal systems. *Id.*

87   542 U.S. 466 (2004).

88   The U.K. petitioners' appeals were rendered moot when they were released.

89   542 U.S. at 484.

90   *Id.*

Having opened the door in *Rasul* to detainees' court challenges to their detention in Guantanamo, the Court in a separate decision articulated the standards that would apply in determining whether the detention was authorized. In *Hamdi v. Rumsfeld*,[91] which was handed down on the same day as *Rasul*, Justice O'Connor, writing for a plurality of the Court, affirmed that "[t]he capture and detention of lawful combatants, and the capture, detention, and trial of unlawful combatants, by 'universal agreement and practice' are 'important incident[s] of war. . . .'"[92] The Supreme Court also found that the Congress, in authorizing the president's use of "necessary and appropriate force" under AUMF, had necessarily authorized the detention of terrorists, because "detention to prevent a combatant's return to the battlefield is a fundamental incident of waging war. . . ."[93] Thus, the Court held that detention of the petitioner, Yaser Hamdi, an American citizen who allegedly had been fighting for the Taliban in Afghanistan, was authorized if it was demonstrated that he was an enemy combatant.[94] While Hamdi challenged the fact that the indefinite duration of the GWOT meant that his detention might also be indefinite, the Court found that, because there was still active combat ongoing in Afghanistan,[95] the detention of Hamdi, as an enemy combatant, was authorized at least until active hostilities had ceased.[96]

At the same time, the Court emphasized, "a state of war is not a blank check for the president when it comes to the rights of the Nation's

---

91    542 U.S. 517 (2004).

92    *Id.* at 518.

93    *Id.* at 519.

94    *Id.* ("There is no bar to this Nation's holding one of its own as an enemy combatant.") For this purpose, the Court adopted the definition of "enemy combatant" proffered by the U.S. government, *viz*, "an individual who. . . was 'part of or supporting forces hostile to the United States or coalition partners' in Afghanistan and who 'engaged in an armed conflict against the United States.'" *Id.* at 516.

95    The petitioner in *Hamdi* was released to Saudi Arabia in 2004 on condition he relinquish his American citizenship. *Hamdi voices innocence, joy about reunion*, CNN.com, Oct. 14, 2004, *available at* http://www.cnn.com/2004/WORLD/meast/10/14/hamdi/ (last visited on Mar. 9, 2009). Active hostilities in Afghanistan are continuing as of the date of this writing and therefore, but for his early release, the petitioner could still be held today under the holding in *Hamdi*.

96    The Court noted that "indefinite detention for purposes of interrogation is not authorized." 542 U.S. at 521. Thus, the outer bounds of the period of detention, absent conviction of the detainee for a crime, would be the period of active hostilities. *Id.* at 520.

citizens."[97] Thus, Hamdi had a right to challenge his detention before a neutral decision maker under the writ of *habeas corpus*. The question was what due process standards applied to that challenge. On this issue, the government argued, among other things, that (i) any right to an individual determination of prisoner of war privileges under Article 5 of the GPW had been foreclosed by the president's conclusive determination that al Qaeda and Taliban fighters were not entitled to such privileges; (ii) a sworn affidavit presented by the government to the District Court regarding Hamdi's activities in Afghanistan, along with his acknowledged presence in the area, were sufficient to support detention; (iii) as captured enemy combatant, Hamdi did not enjoy a right to counsel to "plot a legal strategy to secure his release", particularly when a right of access to counsel would interfere with "the military's compelling interest in gathering intelligence"; and (iv) requiring further factual development regarding the enemy combatant determination would present formidable constitutional and practical difficulties, given the ongoing hostilities, and would demoralize U.S. troops called to account for their actions.[98]

Explicitly or implicitly rejecting each of the government's arguments, Justice O'Connor noted that the statute's minimum due process requirement included giving the detainee "some opportunity to present and rebut facts."[99] Accordingly, a *habeas* determination could not be made "as a matter of law, with no further hearing or fact finding necessary."[100] It also could not be made under a highly deferential "some evidence" standard, which effectively would amount to relying exclusively on the government's evidence.[101]

However, Justice O'Connor disagreed with the District Court's conclusion "the appropriate process would approach the process that accompanies a criminal trial", with the potential for "quite extensive discovery".[102] Instead, while Hamdi was entitled to "notice of the factual basis for his classification" and "a fair opportunity to rebut the factual assertions

---

97  542 U.S. at 536.

98  Government Response Brief in Hamdi, *supra* note 64, at 22–36.

99  542 U.S. at 526.

100  *Id.* at 526.

101  *Id.* at 527.

102  *Id.* at 528.

before a neutral decisionmaker,"[103] "enemy combatant proceedings could be tailored to alleviate their uncommon potential to burden the Executive at time of ongoing military conflict."[104] Thus, "hearsay may need to be accepted as the most reliable evidence," and a rebuttable presumption in favor of government evidence might be provided.[105]

As to the question of whether the petitioner had a right to counsel in *habeas corpus* proceedings, however, the Court held that he "unquestionably" had such a right.[106] The Court did not expressly decide the question of whether a detainee has a right to counsel in proceedings under Article 5 of the GPW to determine his or her status, and the Administration has interpreted the *Hamdi* decision not to require that a right to counsel be granted in military proceedings to determine the detainee's status.[107]

In *Hamdi*, the Court clearly sought to articulate a flexible approach to due process that would minimize interference with ongoing military operations in deference to the Administration's concerns about the impact of *habeas* review on its ability to prosecute the GWOT. Justice O'Connor also clarified that the procedural protections did not apply to "initial captures" on the battlefield, but rather only when a decision is being made to continue the detainee's captivity. Yet, the Court was also clear that the judiciary would play a significant role in combatant status determinations:

> While we accord the greatest respect and consideration to the judgments of military authorities in matters relating to the actual prosecution of a war, and recognize that the scope of that discretion necessarily is wide, it does not infringe on the core role of the military for the courts to exercise their own time-honored and constitutionally mandated roles of reviewing and resolving claims like those presented here.

---

103    *Id.* at 533. Justice O'Connor characterized these as "core elements" of the petitioner's rights. *Id.*

104    *Id.*

105    *Id.* at 534.

106    *Id.* at 539.

107    In the Combatant Status Review Tribunals described *infra* at notes 110–117 and accompanying text, no right to legal counsel is provided, although the detainee is assigned a commissioned officer to act as his or her personal representative.

Thus, the Administration policy on GWOT detainees, including most importantly the categorical denial of any right for enemy combatants in the GWOT to challenge their status, had to be modified.[108]

## EXECUTIVE BRANCH RESPONSE

While Justice O'Connor's plurality opinion in *Hamdi* focused upon the rights of a citizen detainee held in the United States, there was no reason to believe that procedures for non-citizen detainees at Guantanamo should be more stringent than those Justice Connor identified in *Hamdi*. Accordingly, shortly after the *Hamdi* and *Rasul* decisions were handed down, the Administration responded by adopting a process for detainees in Guantanamo that was consistent with the *Hamdi* standards. This process, which built on an administrative review board procedure that the Administration had already adopted before the *Hamdi* decision, resulted in two levels of review.

---

108   While detainees did not have a right to challenge their detention at the time *Rasul* and *Hamdi* were handed down, in early 2004, the Department of Defense (DoD) (*i.e.*, prior to the date of these decisions) had issued a fact sheet in early 2004 indicating that it had in place administrative procedures in place within the Department of Defense to review the status of detainees, including an internal DoD review panel, to assess whether a detainee should be moved to Guantanamo or released, and that further assessments were made even after arrival of the detainee at Guantanamo to determine if the detainee could be released or transferred to his government. *See* U.S. Dep't of Defense, Fact Sheet: Guantanamo Detainees *available at* www.defenselink.mil/news/Feb2004/d20040220det.pdf (last visited Mar. 9, 2009). The DoD had also announced an initiative to formalize the process and to create a review board that would consider individual detainees for release. *See* Secretary Rumsfeld Remarks to Greater Miami Chamber of Commerce, Feb. 13, 2004 *available at* http://www.defenselink.mil/transcripts/transcript.aspx?transcriptid=2075 (last visited Mar. 9, 2009). On May 18, 2004, the DoD announced that it had adopted the administrative review procedure. U.S. Dep't of Defense, Review Procedures Announced for Guantanamo Detainees, May 18, 2004 *available at* http://www.defenselink.mil/releases/release.aspx?releaseid=7386 (last visited Mar. 9, 2009). In its announcement, the DoD noted:

> The release of enemy combatants prior to the end of a war is a significant departure from past U.S. wartime practices. Enemy combatants are detained for a very practical reason: to prevent them from returning to the fight. That's why the law of war permits their detention until the end of an armed conflict. Although the global war on terror is real and ongoing, DoD has decided as a matter of policy to institute these review procedures. This process will assist DoD in fulfilling its commitment to ensure that no one is detained any longer than is warranted.

*Id.*

The first level of review was a Combatant Status Review Tribunal ("CSRT") process to determine "whether the detainee is properly detained as an enemy combatant,"[109] employing a definition of "enemy combatant" similar to the definition adopted by Justice O'Connor in *Hamdi*.[110] Justice O'Connor had mentioned in the *Hamdi* plurality opinion that "the standards we have articulated could be met by an appropriately authorized and properly constituted military tribunal" and referred to the fact that such tribunals already existed under AR 190–8. Accordingly, the CSRT was modeled after the tribunal under AR 190–8, with "three neutral commissioned officers" to hear the evidence and a recorder ("preferably a judge advocate", as stipulated under AR 190–8) to handle administrative tasks. There were significant differences from AR 190–8, however. First, the detainee was entitled to advance notice of the "unclassified factual basis" for his designation as an enemy combatant.[111] Second, in addition to the Recorder, one of the CSRT members was to be a judge advocate (*i.e.*, military lawyer).[112] Third, as noted above, the detainee was entitled to be represented by a non-lawyer military officer acting as "personal representative." The personal representative had the right to review any "reasonably available" evidence and could share any unclassified evidence with the detainee.[113] Fourth, the Convening Authority was not a commander, but rather an appointee of the Secretary of the Navy.[114] Finally, hearsay evidence was permitted "taking into account the reliability of such evidence in the circumstances."[115] Finally, there was a "rebuttable presumption" in favor of the government's evidence.[116]

---

109   2004 CSRT Order, *supra* note 22, para. (g)(12). The order makes clear that "[e]ach detainee subject to this Order has been determined to be an enemy combatant through multiple levels of review by officers of the Department of Defense." *Id.* para. a.

110   542 U.S. at 516 ("[The Government] has made clear, however, that, for purposes of this case, the 'enemy combatant' that it is seeking to detain is an individual who, it alleges, was 'part of or supporting forces hostile to the United States or coalition partners' in Afghanistan and who 'engaged in an armed conflict against the United States' there.")

111   2004 CSRT Order, *supra* note 22, para. g.(1).

112   *Id.* para. e.

113   *Id.* para. c.

114   *Id.* para. f.

115   *Id.* para. g.(9).

116   *Id.* para. g.(12).

The second level of review was the Administrative Review Board ("ARB"), which was established "to assess annually the need to continue to detain each enemy combatant during the course of the current and ongoing hostilities."[117] Like the CSRT, the ARB consisted of three officers; but, unlike the CSRT, there was no requirement for a lawyer to be a member,[118] although a lawyer would advise the ARB. As in the case of the CSRT, the detainee could be given the assistance of a non-lawyer military officer, as well as a summary of the evidence. The enemy combatant was permitted to present to the Review Board information about "why he is no longer a threat to the United States and its allies in the ongoing armed conflict against al Qaida and its affiliates and supporters, why it is otherwise appropriate that he be released, or any other relevant information." The ARB made its recommendation on retention to a designated civilian official or "DCO," who is "a presidentially appointed Senate-confirmed civilian in the Department of Defense whom the Secretary of Defense has designated to operate and oversee the administrative review process." The ARB was available for all detainees except those pending charges before military commissions and those already pending transfer/release.[119]

Taken together, these procedures far exceeded anything required by Article 5 of the GPW, Additional Protocol I, or AR 190–8. In some respects, the CSRT procedures bore a resemblance to the procedures used in Vietnam, albeit without the right to counsel. Moreover, as the procedures themselves made clear, the detainees whose cases were considered under the procedures already had been the subject of multiple reviews as they moved from the point of capture to Guantanamo. Finally, the detainees enjoyed not only an extensive review process to determine their status as enemy combatants, but even after that status had been determined, they were entitled to an annual "relook." The "relook" was

---

117 Dep'y Sec'y Defense, Order, Subject: Administrative Review Procedures for Enemy Combatants in the Control of the Department of Defense at Guantanamo Bay Naval Base, Cuba, para. 1 (May 11, 2004) *available at* http://www.defenselink. mil/news/May2004/d20040518gtmoreview.pdf (last visited on March 9, 2009). The ARB procedures were already under development in early 2004 and in fact were adopted and put in place before either *Hamdi* or *Rasul* were handed down.

118 *Id.* para. 2.B.ii. At least one member must be an officer "experienced in the field of intelligence." *Id.*

119 Both the CSRT and ARB procedures were revised and updated in 2006. In addition, a procedure for reviewing new evidence about a detainee's enemy combatant status was adopted in 2007.

more akin to the "periodical" review granted civilian detainees under Article 78 of the GCIV and was beyond anything required in applicable law of war treaties dealing with combatants.

However, there were still grounds to question whether the procedures truly met the requirements of *Hamdi* for a meaningful opportunity to challenge the basis of detention before a "neutral decision maker." First, the tribunals consisted of military officers selected to review the case for the Defense Department, which was the same organization that had decided to detain them in the first place. Second, while the Court had held that Hamdi unquestionably had a right to the assistance of counsel, none was provided in the CSRT process. Third, the procedures included presumptions in favor of the government that might be difficult to overcome, including the rule that certain evidence could be withheld from the detainee on the grounds that it was not "reasonably available."[120] Finally, there was no explicit right of appeal to a higher court.

Despite the more detailed procedures for status determinations, courts continued to accept *habeas* petitions regarding challenges to combatant status determinations, as well as to military commission procedures. In response, Congress passed the Detainee Treatment Act of 2005. Section 1005 of the DTA amended the *habeas corpus* statute to preclude courts from taking jurisdiction of petitions from or on behalf of detainees at Guantanamo, or any other action against the United States or its agents

---

120  Some of these issues were addressed in a series of decisions by the Court of Appeals for the D.C. Circuit, which held that the D.C. Circuit in reviewing a CSRT's enemy combatant determination (under a limited right granted in the DTA, *infra* note 121, to appeal CSRT determinations to the D.C. Circuit was entitled to all the information reasonably available to the Recorder in making his or her determination of the evidence to present to the CSRT. In support of a decision to deny rehearing en banc, Chief Justice Ginsburg noted various limitations of the CSRT:

> Unlike the final decision rendered in a criminal or an agency proceeding, which is the product of an open and adversarial process before an independent decisionmaker, a CSRT's status determination is the product of a necessarily closed and accusatorial process in which the detainee seeking review will have had little or no access to the evidence the Recorder presented to the Tribunal; little ability to gather his own evidence, no right to confront the witnesses against him, and no lawyer to help him prepare his case, and in which the decisionmaker is employed and chosen by the detainee's accuser.

Bismullah v. Gates, 514 F.2d 1291, 1296 (D.C. Cir. 2009) (opinion of Chief Judge Ginsburg, joined by three other judges, concurring in the denial of rehearing en banc.)

relating to any aspect of detention at Guantanamo. Instead, the U.S. Court of Appeals for the D.C. Circuit was given exclusive authority to review final decisions of the CSRTs, but only with respect to two issues:

> (i) whether the status determination of the Combatant Status Review Tribunal with regard to such alien was consistent with the standards and procedures specified by the Secretary of Defense for Combatant Status Review Tribunals (including the requirement that the conclusion of the Tribunal be supported by a preponderance of the evidence and allowing a rebuttable presumption in favor of the Government's evidence); and

> (ii) to the extent the Constitution and laws of the United States are applicable, whether the use of such standards and procedures to make the determination is consistent with the Constitution and laws of the United States.[121]

In 2006, the Supreme Court, in *Hamdan v. Rumsfeld*,[122] held, *inter alia*, that the DTA did not bar any *habeas* challenge (to a military commission's authority to try detainees) that was pending at the time the DTA was passed. In response, the president requested, and the Congress passed, the Military Commissions Act (MCA), which not only resolved legal defects in the authorization for military commissions identified by the Court, but also sought to bar all *habeas* challenges "by or on behalf of an alien detained by the United States who has been determined by the United States to have been properly detained as an enemy combatant or is awaiting such determination."[123] This provision of the MCA applied

---

121  Detainee Treatment Act, Pub. L. No. 109–148, § 1005(e)(2)(C), 119 Stat. 2680, 2742 (2005) (codified at 28 U.S.C.A. § 2241(e) (2005) [hereinafter DTA]. The DTA was amended by the MCA, *supra* note 24, § 8.

122  548 U.S. 557 (2006).

123  MCA, *supra* note 24, § 7, *codified at* 28 U.S.C. § 2241(e). The MCA also barred courts from considering "any other action against the United States or its agents relating to any aspect of the detention, transfer, treatment, trial, or conditions of confinement of an alien who is or was detained by the United States and has been determined by the United States to have been properly detained as an enemy combatant or is awaiting such determination." Although the Court in *Boumediene*, discussed *infra* notes 127–132 and accompanying text, invalidated, as an unconstitutional suspension of the writ of *habeas corpus*, the bar on *habeas* petitions to challenge the legality of detention at Guantanamo, lower courts have held that this did not affect the validity of the separate MCA provision barring other actions to challenge the conditions of detention. Khadr v. Bush, 587 F. Supp. 2d 225 (D.D.C. 2008).

not only to challenges to CSRT determinations regarding detainees at Guantanamo, but also to any enemy combatant determination made worldwide regarding persons in the custody of the United States.

In *Boumediene v. Bush*,[124] this provision of the MCA was determined to be an unconstitutional suspension of the writ of *habeas corpus*.[125] The Court reached this conclusion in two steps. First, it held that detainees at Guantanamo enjoyed a constitutional right to *habeas corpus*.[126] Even though Guantanamo was outside the sovereign territory of the United States, the reach of the constitutional right of *habeas corpus* was not determined by formal sovereignty, but rather on a case by case determination involving the examination of "at least" three factors: "(1) the detainees' citizenship and status and the adequacy of the process through which that status was determined; (2) the nature of the sites where apprehension and then detention took place; and (3) the practical obstacles inherent in resolving the prisoner's entitlement to the writ."[127] Weighing these factors in the case before it, the Court found that the constitutional right to the writ of *habeas corpus* extended to aliens held as enemy combatants at Guantanamo.

Second, the Court rejected the government's argument that the CSRT process or the right to appeal the CSRT's findings to the D.C. Circuit Court of Appeals (D.C. Circuit) provided an adequate substitute for *habeas* proceedings in a Federal court. The Court recognized that a

---

124   128 S. Ct. 2229, 2274 (2008).

125   Article I, section 9, clause 2 of the Constitution provides: "The privilege of the Writ of Habeas Corpus shall not be suspended, unless when in Cases of Rebellion or Invasion the public Safety may require it."

126   In Rasul v. Bush, 542 U.S. at 504, the Court similarly found the fact that Guantanamo was not sovereign U.S. territory did not preclude detainees from seeking a writ of habeas corpus under the habeas statute to challenge their detention in Guantanamo but Congress amended the *habeas* statute to specifically eliminate the detainee's ability to pursue a writ of *habeas* under the statute.

127   Boumediene v. Bush, 128 S. Ct. at 2259. The Court based its ruling in part on *Eisentrager v. Johnson*, discussed *supra* notes 83–86 and accompanying text. *Eisentrager* is a post-World War II decision in which the Court held that German prisoners of war tried by the U.S. military commission in China and imprisoned in occupied Germany did not have a right to pursue a writ of *habeas corpus* to challenge their detention. Previously, however, *Eisentrager* had been cited for the proposition that aliens tried and imprisoned outside the territorial limits of United States could not seek the writ, which was the formalistic approach rejected by the Court in *Boumediene*.

CSRT provided "some process," but the CSRT did not provide for "a rigorous adversarial process," including a right to counsel, did not give access to all evidence relied upon to detain, and provided for liberal use of hearsay evidence (which meant that the "opportunity to question witnesses is likely to be more theoretical than real.")[128] The opportunity to appeal CSRT decisions to the D.C. Circuit also was not a sufficient substitute for *habeas*, because of the limited scope of the D.C. Circuit's review, the fact that it did not expressly have the authority to order the release of a detainee in the event detention was found to be unauthorized, and the lack of an opportunity for the detainee to present evidence discovered after the CSRT proceedings were complete.[129]

Instead, if a detainee had the constitutional right to *habeas* review, any substitute had to provide substantively the same or better rights than the detainee would have in a traditional review by a court. In this case, however, the CSRT process and the limited appeal to the D.C. Circuit were both expressly attempts by Congress and the Administration to provide less due process than a traditional *habeas* proceeding. In the case of the CSRT process, this was a fatal flaw: "[E]ven when all the parties involved in this [CSRT] process acted with diligence and in good faith, there is considerable risk of error in the tribunal's finding of fact." As for the appeal to the D.C. Circuit, the Court might interpret away some of the defects it found in the appeals process, but that would simply restore the very right to *habeas* review that the Congress clearly intended to deny the detainee. Rather than affording the legislation an interpretation that it "cannot bear," the Court held it to be an unconstitutional suspension of the writ.

The Court qualified its opinion by adding that "[o]ur holding . . . should not be read to imply that a *habeas* court should intervene the moment an enemy combatant steps in a territory where the writ runs." The Court also did not reject the CSRT process, holding instead that "[t]he Executive is entitled to a reasonable period of time to determine a detainee's status before a court entertains that detainee's habeas corpus petition."[130] The Court also noted that "accommodations" could be made to reduce the burdens of *habeas* proceedings and to protect sources and methods of intelligence gathering.

---

128    Boumediene v. Bush, 128 S. Ct. at 2259, 2269–71.

129    *Id.* at 2271–74.

130    *Id.* at 2276.

Nonetheless, the Court was far less deferential than it had been in *Hamdi* to the Executive's concerns regarding interference with national security interests:

> Security subsists, too, in fidelity to freedom's first principles. Chief among these are freedom from arbitrary and unlawful restraint and the personal liberty that is secured by adherence to the separation of powers.[131]

The Court was clearly troubled by the fact that the Administration had held the detainees in confinement for years without any confirmation of the legality of their detention by any court. In its view, separation of powers under the Constitution required a judicial determination of legality to "vindicate[]" the exercise of the Executive's war powers in detaining these individuals. The Court ominously warned that, while short conflicts in the past had made it possible to leave the "outer boundaries" of these powers undefined, the "Court might not have this luxury" if the GWOT proved to be even more lengthy. Therefore, it invited the Administration and Congress to "engage in a genuine debate about how best to preserve constitutional values while protecting the Nation from terrorism."[132]

## OBSERVATIONS

The decision in *Boumediene* effectively put an end to the Administration's attempts to preclude full *habeas* review of detentions of enemy combatants in the GWOT. Beginning in July 2008, a massive effort was launched by the District Court for the District of Columbia to provide *habeas* review for all of the Guantanamo detainees still seeking it. In response, the Administration assembled large teams of government lawyers to devote themselves full time to the task of collecting and presenting the evidence required to respond to the *habeas* petitions, and arguing the cases in court. District Court judges in the post-*Boumediene habeas* proceedings required disclosure of an extensive amount of information to support the factual basis for the detention, as well as all statements of the detainee and any reasonably available exculpatory evidence. As of the beginning of 2009, several *habeas* petitions had been decided by the District Court, with mixed results for the Government.

---

131    *Id.* at 2277.

132    *Id.*

In January 2009, President Obama issued an Executive Order that, if not rescinded, will lead to the closure of Guantanamo by early 2010. Many detainees are now expected to be released to their home countries, or if they remain in U.S. hands, to be held in facilities within the United States where the writ of *habeas corpus* clearly applies. It is not yet clear what impact these developments will have on the continued use of the "enemy combatant" paradigm for detaining terrorists, but certainly one can expect that there will be fewer court challenges to military detention to the extent the detainee population declines substantially.

At this point, it is perhaps useful to reflect on the impact of the Supreme Court decisions discussed in this chapter on detention of enemy combatants. Certainly, none of the decisions called into question the law of war rule that captured enemy combatants may be held in captivity for the duration of hostilities, which the Court in *Hamdi* described as a "fundamental and accepted . . . incident of war."[133] This holding reaffirmed the Court's analysis in *Ex Parte Quirin*[134] and other relevant World War II era precedents—analysis fundamental to the Executive's military detention authority.

In addition, none of the Court's decisions held that any of the Geneva Conventions or other law of war treaties were self-executing, or otherwise specifically limited Executive discretion. While in *Hamdan v. Rumsfeld*, the Court held that a military commission lacked jurisdiction to try an enemy combatant because it did not comply, *inter alia*, with Common Article 3 of the Geneva Conventions,[135] the Court only cited to the Geneva Conventions because the legislative authorization for military commissions relied upon by the government[136] specifically

---

133   542 U.S. at 518.

134   317 U.S. 1 (1942)

135   548 U.S. 557, 631–632 (2006).

136   The provision relied upon in *Hamdan* was Article 21 of the UCMJ, *supra* note 57 (codified at 10 U.S.C. § 821). Article 21 provides that "[t]he jurisdiction [of] courts-martial shall not be construed as depriving military commissions . . . of concurrent jurisdiction in respect of offenders or offenses that by statute or by the law of war may be tried by such . . . commissions." Accepting that UCMJ art. 21 authorized military commissions, the Court held that "compliance with the law of war is the condition upon which the authority set forth in Article 21 is granted." 548 U.S. at 628. Since the Geneva Conventions were part of the law of war, then any applicable provision of the Geneva Conventions applied to the military commissions. *Id.* While the parties disputed whether GWOT was a type of conflict

referred to the "law of war." Absent the specific reference to the "law of war" in the statute, it is questionable whether the Court would have treated the Geneva Conventions as directly applicable. Moreover, Section 5 of the MCA specifically prohibits any use of the Geneva Conventions or any of its protocols (e.g., Additional Protocol I) as a "source of rights" in any U.S. *habeas corpus* or other civil proceeding to which the United States or its agents are a party.[137] Thus, with one important exception,[138] the Administration's position that al Qaeda and the Taliban did not enjoy any specific rights under the Geneva Convention was not significantly challenged. In all cases, the source of any detainee's right to judicially challenge the nature or condition of his or her detention will stem from U.S. domestic law, rather than international law, meaning that those challenges will only reach as far as courts are willing to apply U.S. domestic law extraterritorially.

These were small victories for the Administration, however. The principal outcome of the Supreme Court decisions is both an expanded extraterritorial reach of the constitutional right to the writ of *habeas corpus*, as well as less certainty about the further expansion of that extraterritorial reach. The *Boumediene* Court's "practical considerations and exigent circumstances" approach to determining the definition and reach of the writ of *habeas corpus* has eliminated any clear geographic bright line as to where the writ does not apply. This has strengthened the legal position of detainees held overseas by U.S. forces in areas outside of Guantanamo who are seeking to use the writ to challenge their detention.

---

falling under the Geneva Conventions, the Court found that "there is at least one provision of the Geneva Conventions that applies here even if the relevant conflict is not one between signatories," *i.e.*, Common Article 3, which provides minimum treatment standards for non-international armed conflicts. *Id*. at 629. Yet it is clear from the opinion that the Court only looked to Common Article 3 because of the reference to "the law of war" in the legislation. Indeed, while a portion of Justice Stevens' opinion (joined in this case by only three other Justices) identifies API art. 75 as potentially applicable as customary law, the applicability of such customary law would stem from the reference in the legislation to the "law of war." It is not clear that the Court would have looked to customary law if the statute had not referred to the law of war.

137   *Codified at* 28 U.S.C. § 2241 note.

138   In *Hamdan*, the Court found that Common Article 3 of the Geneva Conventions applied to the GWOT with al Qaeda. 548 U.S. at 629–632. That decision was important in securing certain humane treatment standards for the detainees, but did not limit or affect U.S. authority to hold the detainees as enemy combatants.

Where the detainee is an American citizen, the writ is certainly going to apply without regard to geographic limitations. For example, in *Munaf v. Geren*,[139] a decision handed down the same day as *Boumediene*, the Court upheld the jurisdiction of U.S. federal courts to entertain *habeas* petitions filed by two American citizens held overseas by American soldiers subject to a U.S. chain of command even though the U.S. forces held the two individuals pursuant to U.S. obligations as part of a multinational force. The Court stressed that U.S. forces were still subject to U.S. command and that the individuals were U.S. citizens. However, the Court dismissed the petitions because they were not challenges to unlawful detention by the United States, but rather an attempt to prevent transfer of the detainees to Iraqi authorities in connection with Iraqi criminal proceedings. Nevertheless, the fact the Court upheld the jurisdiction of U.S. federal courts to entertain a writ filed by detainees held by U.S. forces pursuant to operations with other countries is a potentially significant expansion of the extraterritorial application of the writ, at least as applied to American citizens.[140]

It is possible to view the Court's decisions regarding detention of enemy combatants in the GWOT as part of a larger struggle between the Bush Administration and the majority of the Court regarding the Administration's claim to a very expansive interpretation of the Executive's war power.[141] If the change of Administrations leads to a less expansive approach to the war power, future rulings may well result in clarifications that limit the burden of judicial review of the Executive's detention of enemy combatants.

Even under its expansive reading of the right of *habeas corpus* in *Boumediene*, the Court left room for deference to the Executive's initial exercise of military detention authority:

> If and when habeas corpus jurisdiction applies . . . then proper deference can be accorded to reasonable procedures for screening and initial detention

---

139    128 S. Ct. 2207 (2008).

140    At least one District Court has extended the writ to apply to non-U.S. citizens held by the U.S. military outside of the United States. *See* discussion, *infra*, notes 144–160 and accompanying text.

141    One important lesson of the GWOT is that a president seeking to use his or her war power to aggressively pursue and detain enemies would be well advised to seek the support of the Congress, for joint action is more likely to withstand judicial scrutiny than unilateral Executive action. Thus, the fact that the Congress passed the AUMF, for example, was critical to the Executive in establishing its authority to detain terrorists as enemy combatants in *Hamdi*, while the lack of

under lawful and proper conditions of confinement and treatment for a reasonable period of time. Domestic exigencies, furthermore, might also impose such onerous burdens on the Government that here, too, the Judicial Branch would be required to devise sensible rules for staying habeas corpus proceedings until the Government can comply with its requirements in a responsible way.[142]

Beyond this limited deference to initial detention, however, the Court also has fashioned a greater role for the judicial branch with respect to the exercise of a power traditionally wielded in military operations by the Executive without much judicial supervision. To the extent this power might be exercised with respect to detentions within military theaters of operation, it could become problematic for commanders in the field, who would need to pay greater attention to collection of evidence to respond to later judicial inquiries into a detention decision. The law of war has never contemplated this type of judicial scrutiny.[143]

At least one recent decision suggests that *Boumediene* will result in a wider application of the right of *habeas corpus* in overseas military theatres. In *Al Maqaleh v. Gates*,[144] the District Court for the District of Columbia, applying the *Boumediene* analysis to *habeas corpus* petitions filed by four non-citizen detainees held at the Bagram Air Field in Afghanistan, held that three of the four detainees had a constitutional right to the protection of Suspension Clause, meaning that the District Court could entertain their petitions notwithstanding the provision of the MCA that stripped the court of jurisdiction under the *habeas* statute.

Applying the analysis from *Boumediene*, the District Court followed a six factor test (derived from the three factors used in *Boumediene*) to make a determination with respect to each of the four detainees: "(1) the citizenship of the detainee; (2) the status of the detainee; (3) the adequacy of

---

Congressional authority for the military commissions convened by the president under the Military Order was fatal to the government's case in *Hamdan*.

142    Boumediene v. Bush, 128 S. Ct. at 2275. Even here, qualifiers such as "reasonable" and "responsible" with respect to the nature of Executive action leave open the possibility of further judicial review even in emergencies.

143    At this point, it does not yet appear that the courts would engage in extensive judicial inquiry into decisions to detain on the battlefield, but decisions to keep battlefield detainees in detention for extended periods has drawn scrutiny, even when the detention facility is near the battlefield. *See* discussion of *Al Maqaleh* case, *infra*, notes 144–160 and accompanying text.

144    Al Maqaleh v. Gates, 604 F.Supp.2d 205 (D.D.C.)

the process through which the status determination was made; (4) the nature of the site of apprehension; (5) the nature of the site of detention; and (6) the practical obstacles inherent in resolving the petitioner's entitlement to the writ."[145] However, noting the multiple references in the *Boumediene* decision to concern about the length of time that the detainees had been held, the court also identified a seventh factor that "tacitly informed *Boumediene's* analysis as well: the length of a petitioner's detention without adequate review."[146] Because the Supreme Court had not specifically called the length of detention a separate factor, the District Court would not consider it separately but noted that the detention's length may "shade" the six factors the District Court is required to consider under the *Boumediene* analysis.[147]

The District Court's analysis produced some interesting observations on the application of the six factors. For example, while it found the "status of the detainee" factor to provide little guidance on the question whether the Suspension Clause should apply, it noted that "the breadth of the definition of 'enemy combatant' utilized by respondents underscores the need for a meaningful process to ensure that detainees are not improperly classified as enemy combatants."[148] The Court also found it relevant that the detainees had been brought ("rendered") to the detention facility in Afghanistan, which made them "qualitatively different" than detainees captured in Afghanistan, which is "a theater of war, where the Constitution arguably may not reach."[149] For the District Court, "[s]uch rendition resurrects the same specter of limitless Executive power the Supreme Court sought to guard against in *Boumediene*—the concern that the Executive could move detainees physically beyond the reach of the Constitution and detain them indefinitely."[150]

Most relevant factors for the District Court's analysis were the factors of the site of detention, the process used to make the detention decision, and the practical obstacles inherent in resolving the petitioner's entitlement to the writ. With respect to the site of detention, the District Court asked whether the prison in Bagram Air Field was more like Guantanamo

---

145   *Id.* at 215.

146   *Id.* at 216.

147   *Id.* at 217.

148   *Id.* at 219–220.

149   *Id.* at 220.

150   *Id.*

Bay, to which the Supreme Court in *Boumediene* had held that the constitutional right to *habeas corpus* applied, or the Landsberg prison in occupied Germany, to which the Supreme Court in *Eisentrager* held that it did not. Applying an "objective degree of control" test in measuring whether the United States exercised sufficient control to apply the constitutional right to the writ, the District Court held that "Bagram lies much closer to Guantanamo than to Landsberg."[151]

More relevant to the subject of this chapter, the District Court held that the process for making "enemy combatant" determinations at Bagram Air Field was "less sophisticated and more error prone" than the CSRT procedure at Guantanamo Bay.

> Unlike a CSRT, where a petitioner has access to a "personal representative," Bagram detainees represent themselves. Obvious obstacles, including language and cultural differences, obstruct effective self-representation by petitioners such as these. Detainees cannot even *speak* for themselves; they are only permitted to submit a written statement. But in submitting that statement, detainees do not know what evidence the United States relies upon to justify an "enemy combatant" designation—so they lack a meaningful opportunity to rebut that evidence. Respondents' far-reaching and ever-changing definition of enemy combatant, coupled with the uncertain evidentiary standards, further undercut the reliability of the ... [Bagram tribunal's] review. And, unlike the CSRT process, Bagram detainees receive no review beyond ... [the Bagram tribunal] itself.[152]

Declining to state what would constitute an adequate process sufficient to "stave off the reach of the Suspension Clause to Bagram," the District Court held that the process now in use at Bagram was not adequate.[153]

In assessing the sixth factor—practical obstacles to application of the writ—the District Court was not convinced that difficulties in matters such as securing testimony from witnesses in Afghanistan constituted an obstacle that could not be overcome. Importantly, the District Court's views were colored by the lengthy detention, with the District Court noting that, the longer detention endured, the more "manageable" (and impliedly, less compelling) were any obstacles that might interfere with

---

151   *Id.* at 225.

152   *Id.* at 227.

153   *Id.*

military operations.[154] The impact of such obstacles was ameliorated by the requirement that a "reasonable amount of time" should be allowed as a buffer before "meaningful review" is required:

> Practical obstacles related to the military mission might loom large absent this buffer, but by providing a "reasonable amount of time" before meaningful review is required, those obstacles become more manageable. Such a reasonable time period elapsed for these detainees, like those at Guantanamo, many years ago.[155]

The District Court's willingness to disregard the practical obstacles that surely will exist in extending the writ, for the first time, to a detention facility in a war zone, surely highlights the overriding importance of the duration of detention to the outcome of any analysis as to whether the Suspension Clause applies.[156]

The District Court's decision marked a significant expansion of the scope of the writ to include areas overseas in which there is an ongoing armed conflict. Yet the District Court was quick to stress that the holding did not mean that the Suspension Clause applied everywhere overseas. Rather, the outcome was driven by "a rigorous application of the multi-factor test" in *Boumediene*,[157] including a grace period for the U.S. government to provide "meaningful review" of detention. Indeed, "if the Executive decides to provide greater process in determining the status of detainees, the balance of factors could shift against extension of the Suspension Clause."[158]

---

154   *Id.* at 229. The District Court was not at all persuaded that habeas proceedings would actually interfere with military operations:

> Although logistical issues have certainly been presented, the hearings and related proceedings are going forward with the burdens on the government falling mainly on the lawyers and administrative personnel involved, not on those who would otherwise be on the battlefield.

*Id.* at 228.

155   *Id.* at 229.

156   One obstacle that the District Court did consider determinative was the fact that one of the detainees was an Afghan citizen. The District Court found that the potential friction with the Afghanistan government that might results from the release of an Afghan detainee was in fact a "practical obstacle" to extending the writ to such a detainee. *Id.* at 235.

157   *Id.* at 231.

158   *Id.* at 231–232.

It is difficult to draw any firm conclusions from a single District Court case, which is likely to be challenged on appeal. However, the decision does suggest that *Boumediene* has significantly expanded the opportunity for non-citizens held by the United States in connection with an armed conflict outside the United States to challenge their detention in U.S. courts, even in areas where the U.S. government exercises less control than in Guantanamo Bay. The writ of *habeas corpus* may not apply everywhere, but it surely now is available in far more places than one would have thought prior to the GWOT. Further, while the degree of U.S. control of the place of detention is important to establishing a detainee's right to challenge his detention, the adequacy of the process used to make the determination that he or she can be detained and the length of that detention are equally important.

The District Court's analysis in *Al Maqaleh* suggests a possible opportunity for the Executive to resolve the Judiciary's concerns about military detention under the law of war. A stronger process for making the enemy combatant determination, perhaps modeled on the one used in Vietnam, could meet the requirements for an adequate process that would substitute for judicial review. A right to counsel, as well as a broader right for the detainee to examine and respond to the evidence of his or her combatant activities, certainly would be helpful in reducing the risk of error that has been a key concern with the process for making detention decisions in the GWOT. As the District Court in *Al Maqaleh* implied in its acknowledgment that the Executive should be accorded a "'reasonable amount of time' before meaningful review is required," the detainee need not be provided these rights immediately, but only after it becomes apparent that the detainee will be held for a significant period of time.[159] At that point, the detainee is likely to be in a secure detention facility, away from active combat, where, as the District Court suggested, the "practical obstacles" are more manageable. Moreover, if detention were to stretch over several years, the procedures could include an opportunity to reconsider the detainee's situation to determine whether continued detention is required.[160]

---

159   These enhanced procedures would not be needed for individuals, such as enemy soldiers, who are clearly entitled to treatment as prisoners of war under the GPW. GPW art. 5 does not require a tribunal to be held to determine the status of such individuals, if there is no doubt as to their status.

160   The points raised here bear on the factor in the *Boumediene* analysis relating to the process for making the detention determination. This factor is part of the

One issue that has yet to be fully resolved is whether alien detainees in U.S. custody outside the United States have the right to bring actions to challenge the conditions of their detention. In addition to its provisions stripping courts of jurisdiction over writs of *habeas corpus* brought by aliens challenging their detention (which the Supreme Court held to be unconstitutional as applied to writs brought by detainees at Guantanamo Bay), Section 7 of the MCA also strips U.S. courts of jurisdiction over "any other action against the United States . . . relating to any aspect of the detention, transfer, treatment, trial, or conditions of confinement" of a detained alien determined to be an enemy combatant. The Supreme Court in *Boumediene* expressly did "not discuss the reach of the writ with respect to claims of unlawful conditions of treatment or confinement."[161] Following the *Boumediene* decision, lower courts have relied on this language and refused to entertain actions regarding the conditions of confinement, under the authority of the MCA.[162] However, such decisions are likely to be challenged in the future, possibly resulting in greater scope for judicial review not only of who can be detained, but how that detention is to be conducted.

One possible lesson from the litigation over the president's authority to detain in the GWOT may be that greater attention to international law standards applicable to military detention could prove helpful to the Executive branch in arguing that a further expansion of judicial review is not required. In all the Supreme Court cases discussed in this chapter, a recurring concern for the Court was ensuring that the Executive did not exercise unchecked power with respect to the indefinite detention of

---

multi-factor analysis to determine whether a particular detainee has a constitution right to *habeas* under the Sixth Amendment. A separate part of the *Boumediene* analysis considers whether an adequate substitute for habeas has been provided to the detainee, but this only comes into play once it has been determined that the Sixth Amendment applies to the detainee. *Compare* 128 S.Ct. at 2260 *with* 128 S.Ct. at 2262–2272.

161    128 S. Ct. at 2274.

162    *See, e.g.*, Al-Adahi v. Obama, 596 F.Supp.2d 111 (D.D.C. 2009). In Kiyemba v. Obama, 561 F.3d 509 (D.C. Cir.). The D.C. Circuit limited these lower court decisions by holding that any claim that was the proper subject of a habeas petition fell within the scope of *Boumediene's* holding that the MCA provision stripping courts of *habeas* jurisdiction was unconstitutional as applied to detainees at Guantanamo Bay, but nonetheless dismissed the detainees challenge to their transfer to other countries on the grounds that it was not a proper basis for a *habeas* petition under the authority of Munaf v. Geren, 128 S.Ct. 2207 (2008).

individuals seized as enemy combatants in the GWOT.[163] While the Court did not challenge that enemy combatants captured in connection with an armed conflict could be held in indefinite detention, it did insist that judicial scrutiny of the enemy combatant classification was essential because the consequences of indefinite detention were so severe.[164] Assurances that those consequences would be no greater than those faced by prisoners of war generally could well make a difference in the Court's evaluation of the need to intervene regarding the conditions of detention. This is not to suggest that combatant immunity be given to detainees who would not otherwise qualify for it under existing treaties. Detainees could still be prosecuted for belligerent acts consistent with the rules articulated earlier in this chapter. However, to accord to all detainees to the maximum extent feasible the standards of treatment accorded to prisoners of war would seem consistent with the law of war theory, upon which military detention of detainees is based and which posits that detention (at least absent prosecution) is not punishment.[165] The Obama administration could thereby allay fears that a failure to permit judicial review of conditions of detention could result in harsh punishment for the detainees for years to come.

---

163   *See, e.g.*, Hamdi v. Rumsfeld, 542 U.S. at 530 ("[A]s critical as the Government's interest may be in detaining those who actually pose an immediate threat to the national security of the United States during ongoing international conflict, history, and common sense teach us that an unchecked system of detention carries the potential to become a means for oppression and abuse of others who do not present that sort of threat").

164   *Id.* at 536 (noting the importance of judicial review serving as "an important judicial check on the Executive's discretion in the realm of detentions.")

165   *See* notes 7–8, *supra*, and accompanying text.

# CHAPTER 4

# INTERROGATION AND TREATMENT OF DETAINEES IN THE GLOBAL WAR ON TERROR

By Dick Jackson[†]

## INTRODUCTION

Interrogation is at the core of the legal debates regarding the al Qaeda and Taliban members detained by the U.S. government after the inception of the Global War on Terror (GWOT) in October 2001. The desire to obtain timely and accurate intelligence from captured terrorists drove the discussion, from the fall of 2001 to late 2008, when Supreme Court cases, legislation, and policy developments restored specific law of war standards to the U.S. military's treatment and interrogation of detainees.[1] In the interim, the military (with substantial policy direction from the leadership of the U.S. Department of Defense, the U.S. Department of Justice's Office of Legal Counsel [OLC], and the White House) essentially abandoned its long-standing reliance on law of war treaties and principles applicable to international armed conflict as the base-line

---

[†]    Richard B. "Dick" Jackson is the Special Assistant to the U.S. Army Judge Advocate General for Law of War Matters. He is a retired Colonel, with over 30 years experience as an Infantryman and Judge Advocate in such far-flung places as Panama, Haiti, Bosnia, Kosovo, and Iraq. Dick Jackson retired from the Army in 2005, having served the previous ten years as a Staff Judge Advocate (the senior legal advisor) at the NATO Joint Forces Command in NATO, the U.S. Army, Pacific, Multinational Division North in Bosnia, the 25th Infantry Division in Hawaii, and the U.S. Army Special Operations Command, in Fort Bragg, North Carolina. He was also the Chair of the International and Operational Law Department at the U.S. Army Judge Advocate General's Legal Center and School, in Charlottesville, Virginia. Mr. Jackson has written extensively and frequently lectured on law of war matters. The views or opinions expressed in this article are not attributable to the U.S. Department of Defense or the U.S. Army, but are strictly the views and opinions of the author. All statements are based on information drawn from the public record.

1    President Obama's January 22, 2009 Executive Order applied the Army Field Manual standard, discussed *infra* at note 139 and accompanying text, which is based on an international law standard, to the Central Intelligence Agency's (CIA) interrogation action, withdrawing President Bush's Executive Order 13440. The CIA standard for interrogation is not the subject of this paper.

for the treatment of detained terrorists, in favor of a narrowly drawn legal position that allowed the U.S. government to selectively use aggressive interrogation and treatment techniques that did not comport with the time-tested law of war standards traditionally applied by the military to all of its detainees. Although the change in approach to the application of the law of war was resisted at every level by the military legal community, some of the aggressive interrogation and treatment techniques adopted for these terrorists were able to migrate to the field and resulted in mistreatment of detainees in several instances [despite the efforts of many Judge Advocates in the chain of command]. It is only in the last three years that those standards of treatment have been restored and reinforced for military personnel engaged in GWOT.

## THE HISTORICAL APPLICATION OF GENEVA CONVENTION STANDARDS

The U.S. military has been at the forefront of training and applying the law of war to detention in military operations, since well before the 1907 Hague Regulations or the 1949 Geneva Conventions. The Lieber Code, developed at the request of the Chief of Staff of the Army, General Halleck, by a Napoleonic War veteran, Francis Lieber, set the standard for treatment of captured enemy in the American Civil War.[2] Despite the potential for applying a brutal internal armed conflict standard to "rebels" who had seceded from the Union, the "Lieber Code" required Union Soldiers to treat captured enemy with respect and humility, in accordance with standards for international armed conflict:

> Art. 49. A prisoner of war is a public enemy armed or attached to the hostile army for active aid, who has fallen into the hands of the captor, either fighting or wounded, on the field or in the hospital, by individual surrender or by capitulation.
>
> All soldiers, of whatever species of arms; all men who belong to the rising en masse of the hostile country; all those who are attached to the army for its efficiency and promote directly the object of the war, except such as are hereinafter provided for; all disabled men or officers on the field or elsewhere, if captured; all enemies who have thrown away their arms and ask

---

2     Francis Lieber, Instructions for the Government of Armies of the United States in the Field (The Lieber Code, U.S. War Dep't General Orders No. 100 (Apr. 24, 1863), reprinted in Laws of Armed Conflicts: A Collection of Conventions, Resolutions & Other Documents (Dietrich Schindler & Jiri Toman eds., 4th ed. 2004) The Lieber Code is the first codification of the Law of War, prepared by a former soldier, for soldiers, to regulate armed conflict.

for quarter, are prisoners of war, and as such exposed to the inconveniences as well as entitled to the privileges of a prisoner of war. . . .

Art. 56. A prisoner of war is subject to no punishment for being a public enemy, nor is any revenge wreaked upon him by the intentional infliction of any suffering, or disgrace, by cruel imprisonment, want of food, by mutilation, death, or any other barbarity.

Neither did the code condone cruelty or torture. Instead, Lieber advised:

Art. 16. Military necessity does not admit of cruelty—that is, the infliction of suffering for the sake of suffering or for revenge, nor of maiming or wounding except in fight, nor of torture to extort confessions.

By promulgating this code as General Order 100 to the Union Armies, President Lincoln endorsed one of the basic premises of the law of war, "Men who take up arms against one another in public war do not cease on this account to be moral beings, responsible to one another and to God."[3]

The United States participated fully in the negotiation and ratification of the principal law of war treaties of the twentieth century, the Hague Regulations of 1907[4], and the Geneva Conventions of 1929 and 1949[5], which regulated the treatment of captured enemy and applied these same standards to their capture and treatment. The 1929 Geneva Convention for the Treatment of Prisoners of War (1929 Geneva Convention), which applied to many countries during World War II, mandated treatment standards for captured personnel, similar to those of the Lieber Code:

Art. 2 . . . [Prisoners of war] shall at all times be humanely treated and protected, particularly against acts of violence, from insults and from public curiosity. . . .

---

3    Lieber Code, Art. 15.

4    Regulations Respecting the Laws and Customs of War on Land, annexed to Convention Respecting the Laws and Customs of War on Land, Oct. 18, 1907, 36 Stat. 2277, 1 Bevans 631 [hereinafter Hague IV]. Article 1 of Hague IV adopted the four-part standard for defining members of the armed forces, militia, and volunteer corps entitled to be treated as prisoners of war upon capture. Hague IV art. 4 mandated that prisoners of war be "humanely treated."

5    Geneva Convention (III) Relative to the Treatment of Prisoners of War art. 4, Aug. 12, 1949, 6 U.S.T. 3316, 75 U.N.T.S. 135 [hereinafter GCIII].

Art. 3 Prisoners of war are entitled to respect for their persons and honour. . . .

Art. 5 . . . No pressure shall be exercised on prisoners to obtain information regarding the situation in their armed forces or their country. Prisoners who refuse to reply may not be threatened, insulted, or exposed to unpleasantness or disadvantages of any kind whatsoever.[6]

The U.S. Army field manuals promulgated for use during World War II and afterwards maintained the high standards of treatment proscribed by the 1929 Geneva Convention. The interrogation field manuals published in 1940 and 1945 prohibited coercion, consistent with the requirements of Article 5 of the Prisoner of War Convention of 1929.[7] The 1940 version commented on the inefficacy of coercion, recommending "recognized law enforcement" methods, instead, adding, "Resort to third degree or torture generally indicates that the examiner lacks aptitude or training or is too indifferent and lazy to apply sound methods of interrogation."[8] The U.S. Army's Prisoner of War Technical Manual from 1944 applied the "spirit as well as the letter" of the 1929 Geneva Convention, quoting directly the "humane treatment" provisions of Articles 2 and 3, while the "Enforcement of Discipline" section prohibited "cruel and inhuman" treatment.[9]

After the adoption of the Geneva Conventions of 1949, which incorporated provisions to protect partisan groups and civilians on the battlefield,[10] as well as minimum standards of humane treatment for

---

6 Convention Relative to the Treatment of Prisoners of War, July 27, 1929, 47 Stat. 2021, 118 L.N.T.S. 343.

7 U.S. WAR DEP'T, FIELD MANUAL 30-15, MILITARY INTELLIGENCE: EXAMINATION OF ENEMY PERSONNEL, REPATRIATES, DOCUMENTS, AND MATERIEL, para. 9a. (22 July 1940); U.S. WAR DEP'T, FIELD MANUAL 30-15, MILITARY INTELLIGENCE: EXAMINATION OF ENEMY PERSONNEL, REPATRIATES, DOCUMENTS, AND MATERIEL, para. 45 (June 1945);

8 U.S. WAR DEP'T, FIELD MANUAL 30-15, MILITARY INTELLIGENCE: EXAMINATION OF ENEMY PERSONNEL, REPATRIATES, DOCUMENTS, AND MATERIEL, para. 9c. (22 July 1940).

9 U.S. WAR DEP'T, TECHNICAL MANUAL 19-500, PRISONER OF WAR ADMINISTRATION para. 2. and 57c., respectively (5 October 1944).

10 COMMENTARY: III GENEVA CONVENTION RELATIVE TO THE TREATMENT OF PRISONERS OF WAR (Jean de Preux ed. 1960). According to the Commentary:

During the preparatory work for the Conference, and even during the Conference itself, two schools of thought were observed. Some delegates considered that

---

"non-international armed conflict" in Common Article 3 to all four Geneva Conventions ("GC"), the U.S. military adopted the Prisoner of War (PW) treatment standard [from GCIII] for treatment and interrogation of detainees. Civilians who were interned for reasons of security or their own safety in occupied territory were to be treated in accordance with the Civilians Convention [GCIV].[11] In a seminal 1951 academic article on the subject of "unprivileged belligerents," Major Richard Baxter (who worked for the Office of the Judge Advocate General, International Law Division, at the time) indicated that the 1949 Conventions left a gap between GCIII and GCIV, particularly for civilians who were found to be committing belligerent acts in a zone of conflict, but were not part of a "levée en mass" (a spontaneous uprising of the populace against the invaders).[12] Several years later, however, in preparing a field manual to guide U.S. soldiers in the field in implementing the 1949 Geneva Conventions (ratified by the United States in 1955), Major Baxter penned the following admonition: "... those protected by *GC[IV]* also include all persons who have engaged in hostile or belligerent

---

partisans should have to fulfill conditions even stricter than those laid down by the Hague Regulations in order to benefit by the provisions of the Convention. On the other hand, other experts or delegates held the view that resistance movements should be given more latitude. The problem was finally solved by the assimilation of resistance movements to militias and corps of volunteers "not forming part of the armed forces" of a Party to the conflict.

*Id.* at 49-50. *See generally* IIA Final Record of the Diplomatic Conference of Geneva of 1949 at 241–243 (1949). The partisan debate was informed by the delegates' recent experience in World War II, where partisans in Russia were mistreated with impunity by the German military. *See* U.S. v. von Leeb et al (The German High Command Trial), XII Law Reports of Trials of War Criminals 40 (UN War Crimes Commission 1949) (noting evidence that German policy was to summarily execute suspected partisans). The recent experience of the Spanish Civil War prompted the delegates to address the protection of civilians and others not actively participating in hostilities in civil war. *See Denise Plattner, Assistance to the Civilian Population: The Development and Present State of International Humanitarian Law* 288 Int'l Rev. Red Cross 249 (1992).

11    Geneva Convention Relative to the Protection of Civilian Persons in Time of War, Aug. 12, 1949, art. 78, 6 U.S.T. 3516, 75 U.N.T.S. 287 [hereinafter GCIV].

12    *Major Richard R. Baxter, "So-Called 'Unprivileged Belligerency': Spies, Guerillas and Saboteurs",* 28 Brit. Y.B. Int'l L. 323, 327-328 (1951). The majority of the article, however, deals with the lack of "combatant immunity" for civilians participating in hostilities, exposing them to prosecution under the domestic law of the capturing state, for their belligerent acts.

conduct but who are not entitled to treatment as prisoners of war."[13] The U.S. Army's 1951 Interrogation Field Manual adopted the 1949 GCIII standards for PW treatment, particularly with regard to coercion and "threats, insults, or unpleasant or disadvantageous treatment."[14] Thus, military doctrine contained no gap in treatment standards for detainees of any kind; all detainees were to be treated in accordance with the provisions of GCIII (if they were entitled to be treated as PWs) or GCIV (in all other cases). There was no gap.

Throughout the Cold War, even during insurgencies (internal or non-international armed conflict) with communist guerrilla groups, U.S. doctrine maintained this paradigm—treatment of captured enemy PWs under GCIII and treatment of captured belligerent civilians under GCIV. During the Vietnam War, despite the temptation to turn captured Vietcong irregulars over to the Vietnamese for summary judicial action, the U.S. military treated captured enemy combatants under the provisions of GCIII.[15] The interrogation manual used during this period, "Intelligence Interrogation," Field Manual 30–15, noted the possibility of host nation forces applying lower standards for interrogation of prisoners captured during internal armed conflict;[16] but the 1967 and 1969 manuals governing interrogation by U.S. forces applied the GCIII standards strictly to PW's in international armed conflict and suggested

---

13    U.S. Dep't of Army, Field Manual 27-10, Law of Land Warfare para. 247 (July 1956).

14    U.S. Dep't of Army, Field Manual 30-15, Examination of Personnel and Documents, para. 30 (September 1951).

15    Major General George S. Prugh, Law at War: Vietnam 1964-73 at 66 (1975) ("The MACV policy was that all combatants captured during military operations were to be accorded prisoner of war status, irrespective of the type of unit to which they belonged.") The policy did not extend, however, to those who operated as terrorists, saboteurs or spies. *Id.*

16    U.S. Dep't of Army, Field Manual 30-15, Intelligence Interrogation, para. 4–8 (July 1967) [hereinafter 1967 Interrogation FM] (Humane treatment of insurgent captives should extend far beyond compliance with Article 3...); U.S. Dep't of Army, Field Manual 30-15, Intelligence Interrogation, para. 66a. (March 1969) (...any insurgent taken into custody by host government security forces may not be protected by the Geneva Conventions, but will be subject to the internal security laws of the country concerning subversion and lawlessness. Action of U.S. Forces, however, will be governed by existing agreements with the host country and by the provisions of the Geneva Conventions in the treatment of insurgents, specifically by the provisions of Article 3 of the 1949 Geneva Conventions.).

use of a minimum humane treatment standard for insurgents in non-international armed conflict, including an appendix that referred to Common Article 3 of the Geneva Conventions and its limitations on:

(a) Violence to life and person, in particular murder of all kinds, mutilation, cruel treatment, and torture;

(b) Taking of hostages;

(c) Outrages upon personal dignity, in particular, humiliating, and degrading treatment;

(d) The passing of sentences and the carrying out of executions without previous judgment pronounced by a regularly constituted court, affording all the judicial guarantees which are recognized as indispensable by civilized peoples.[17]

The 1973, 1978, and 1987 versions of the interrogation manual again adopted the standards included in GCIII, which was based on humane treatment standards that can be traced to the Lieber Code. These manuals added general references to "international humanitarian law," the Uniform Code of Military Justice, FM 27–10, and the "prohibitions, limitations, and restrictions established by the Geneva Conventions of 1949 for the handling and treatment of personnel captured or detained by military forces."[18] The appendices of all three versions include a full version of Common Articles 2[19] and 3[20] of the Geneva Conventions, GCIII art. 4 (which defines the categories of persons who are entitled to treatment as PWs), GCIII arts 13 (on humane treatment) and 17 (prohibiting coercion in questioning PWs), and GCIV art. 31 (prohibiting coercion in questioning civilian detainees). The 1973, 1978, and 1987 versions of the field manual also expanded on the prohibition against the

---

17    See, e.g., 1967 INTERROGATION FM, *supra* note 16, Appendix D. Common Article 3 refers to an article found in all the Geneva Conventions that deals with rules applicable to "an Armed conflict not of an international character". *See, e.g.*, GCIII art. 3.

18    U.S. DEP'T OF ARMY, FIELD MANUAL 30-15, INTELLIGENCE INTERROGATION para. 1–8 (June 1973); U.S. DEP'T OF ARMY, FIELD MANUAL 30-15, INTELLIGENCE INTERROGATION para. 1–8 (September 1978); U.S. DEP'T OF ARMY, FIELD MANUAL 34-52, INTELLIGENCE INTERROGATION p. 1-1(May 1987) [hereinafter 1987 INTERROGATION FM].

19    Common Article 2 refers to an article found in all of the Geneva Conventions, which defines the types of conflicts in which the Conventions apply.

20    Common Article 3 is discussed in note 17, *supra*.

use of force against detainees and proscribed "brainwashing, mental torture, or any other form of mental coercion, to include drugs."[21] The 1987 version, modified in the face of allegations that U.S. military advisors condoned torture of prisoners during the civil war in El Salvador, added the requirement that advisors eschew "brutal methods" used by host country forces, remove themselves from the scene, and report in accordance with theater command directives.[22]

The same period of insurgency in Central America added some jurisprudence on humane treatment standards, from the *Nicaragua* case before the International Court of Justice (ICJ). The court considered whether certain advice, including coercive interrogation methods contained in manuals allegedly provided to contra rebels, was contrary to standards of customary "international humanitarian law." The ICJ noted that Common Article 3 was the "minimum yardstick" of conduct for military activities conducted during a non-international armed conflict.[23] It also found that, under general principles of humanitarian law, the United States was bound to:

> . . . refrain from encouragement of persons or groups engaged in the conflict in Nicaragua to commit violations of common Article 3 of the four Geneva Conventions of 12 August 1949. The manual on "Psychological Operations in Guerrilla Warfare", for the publication and dissemination of which the United States is responsible, advises certain acts which cannot but be regarded as contrary to that article.[24]

Although the U.S. did not consent to the jurisdiction of the ICJ in that case, and its jurisprudence is not accepted as binding on the United States, references to this case and its finding continues in military doctrine and literature, to the present day. The concept of "Civilian Protection Law," developed by then-Major (now Colonel) Richard Whitaker at the Army Judge Advocate General's School in the mid 1990s adopted this minimum standard,[25] echoing the words of Jean Pictet, the author of the

---

21   *See, e.g.*, 1987 INTERROGATION FM, *supra* note 18, p. 1-1.

22   *Id.* p. 9-5.

23   MILITARY AND PARAMILITARY ACTIVITIES IN AND AGAINST NICARAGUA (Nicar. v. U.S.), 1986 I.C.J. 114, para. 218 (June 27), *reprinted in* 25 I.L.M. 1023 (1986).

24   *Id.*, at 129-130, paras. 254-256.

25   *See, e.g., Major Richard M. Whitaker, Civilian Protection Law in Military Operations: An Essay,* ARMY LAW, Sept. 1996, at 3.

official International Committee of the Red Cross (ICRC) Commentary on Common Article 3:

> It merely demands respect for certain rules, which were already recognized as essential in all civilized countries, and enacted in the municipal law of the States in question, long before the Convention was signed. What Government would dare to claim before the world, in a case of civil disturbances which could justly be described as mere acts of banditry, that, Article 3 not being applicable, it was entitled to leave the wounded uncared for, to inflict torture and mutilations and to take hostages?... no Government can object to respecting, in its dealings with internal enemies, whatever the nature of the conflict between it and them, a few essential rules which it in fact respects daily, under its own laws, even when dealing with common criminals.[26]

The Army Regulations for treatment of captured personnel also maintained the GCIII/GCIV approach throughout this period, with a "minimum humane treatment" standard echoing many of the provisions of Common Article 3. Army Regulations 633–50 (1963) and 190–8 (1982 and 1985), all entitled "Prisoner of War Administration, Employment and Compensation," contained guidance for the treatment standards of all detainees, no matter how characterized.[27] They prohibited inhumane treatment and quoted the non-discriminatory treatment provisions of Common Article 3:

> Persons taking no active part in hostilities, including members of armed forces who have laid down their arms and those placed hors de combat by sickness, wounds, detention, or any other cause, shall in all circumstances be treated humanely, without any adverse distinction founded on race, colour, religion or faith, sex, birth or wealth, or any other similar criteria.[28]

The 1982 version required punishment of PWs to be administered under due process of law and a "legally constituted court," echoing the "regularly

---

26    COMMENTARY: I GENEVA CONVENTION FOR THE AMELIORATION OF THE CONDITION OF THE WOUNDED AND SICK IN ARMED FORCES IN THE FIELD 50 (Jean Pictet ed. 1952).

27    U.S. DEP'T OF ARMY, REG. 633-50, PRISONER OF WAR ADMINISTRATION para. 4c(3). (January 1963); U.S. DEP'T OF ARMY, REG. 190-8, PRISONER OF WAR ADMINISTRATION para. 1–5 (1 July 1982) [hereinafter 1982 AR 190-8]; U.S. DEP'T OF ARMY, REG. 190-8, PRISONER OF WAR ADMINISTRATION para. 1–5 (2 December 1985) [hereinafter 1985 AR 190-8].

28    Common Article 3 is discussed in note 17, *supra*.

constituted court" language of Common Article 3.[29] It also prohibited coercion and adopted the questioning standard from GCIII art. 17:

> No physical or mental torture, nor any other form of coercion, may be inflicted on prisoners of war to secure from them information of any kind, whatsoever. Prisoners of war who refuse to answer may not be threatened, insulted, or exposed to unpleasant or disadvantageous treatment of any kind.[30]

The "prohibited acts" language in all three regulations is very similar to paragraph 1–5 of the existing 1997 version of AR 190–8 (provided in its entirety, below), mixing Common Article 3 language with some of the specific prohibitions from GCIII.

During Operation Just Cause, in Panama in 1989, U.S. forces captured a number of "Dignity Battalion" members, irregular forces created by the Panamanian strongman, General Noriega, to supplement his military forces. These fierce fighters often wore civilian clothes and employed suicidal tactics,[31] and the conflict was described as an "internationalized" internal armed conflict, since the U.S. government was "providing a stable environment for the freely elected" government of Guillermo David Endara Galimany, the legitimately elected president of Panama.[32] Despite the potential confusion about the type of conflict and the status of the individuals, detainees were afforded treatment consistent with GCIII, and classified as civilian internees or prisoners of war.[33]

---

29    Para. 1–5b, 1982 AR 190-8.

30    GCIII, *supra* note 5, art. 17; *compare* para. 1–5d, 1985 AR 190-8.

31    THOMAS DONNELLY, MARGARET ROTH, AND CALEB BAKER, OPERATION JUST CAUSE: THE STORMING OF PANAMA 310–311. (Lexington Books: New York, 1991).

32    *Id.*, at ix. At the national level, the domestic legal authority and national policy justification for a conflict often conflicts with the law of war analysis under Common Articles 2 and 3 of the Geneva Conventions, which require, for the Geneva Conventions to apply, that there be an armed conflict, either an international conflict under Common Article 2 (i.e., an international armed conflict between states) to which all the Geneva Conventions apply, or a non-international armed conflict (including, but not limited to, a civil war) to which only one article (Common Article 3) applies under the Geneva Conventions. In the case of Panama, the national government provided numerous reasons for the intervention, including protection of nationals, protection of U.S. strategic interests in the Panama Canal, and the request of the Endara government (which was installed, on a U.S. military base, the night of the invasion). *Id.*

33    FREDERIC L. BORCH, JUDGE ADVOCATES IN COMBAT: ARMY LAWYERS IN MILITARY OPERATIONS FROM VIETNAM TO HAITI 104 (2001).

Universal application of a Prisoner of War standard continued, especially after the largely conventional "Gulf War," an international armed conflict in 1991 with Iraq over its invasion of Kuwait. The Army Regulation for detention was further strengthened in the 1990s, including introduction of provisions for an Article 5 Tribunal, mandated by GCIII art. 5 for detainees whose status was in "doubt."[34] The due process standard in the regulation, which was copied from Article 5 Tribunal standards developed in U.S. Central Command regulations during the Gulf War,[35] was later cited by Justice O'Connor in her 2004 *Hamdi* opinion, as possibly reflecting "an appropriately authorized and properly constituted military tribunal" that might have met the minimum administrative due process standards that the Supreme Court believed must be provided to U.S. citizen detainees held as enemy combatants by U.S. forces to determine if they should continue to be held under the law of war.[36]

The 1997 version of AR 190–8 adds to the list of "prohibited acts" in a section of paragraph 1–5 several of the protections afforded by Article 75 of Additional Protocol I[37] and Article 4–6 of Additional Protocol II, which provide equivalent "minimum humane treatment" standards to the humane treatment standards in Common Article 3.[38] The general protection policy contained in this regulation, still in effect today, is as follows:

**1–5. General protection policy**

*a.* U.S. policy, relative to the treatment of EPW, CI, and RP in the custody of the U.S. Armed Forces, is as follows:

(1) All persons captured, detained, interned, or otherwise held in U.S. Armed Forces custody during the course of conflict will be given humanitarian care and treatment from the moment they fall into the hands of U.S. forces until final release or repatriation.

---

34  GCIII, *supra* note 5, art. 5. *See also* U.S. DEP'T OF ARMY, REG. 190-8, ENEMY PRISONERS OF WAR, RETAINED PERSONS, CIVILIAN INTERNEES AND OTHER DETAINEES para. 1–6 (October 1997) [hereinafter AR 190-8].

35  U.S. DEP'T OF DEFENSE, CONDUCT OF THE PERSIAN GULF WAR: FINAL REPORT TO CONGRESS, Appendix L, at L-3 (1992).

36  Hamdi v. Rumsfeld, 542 U.S. 507, 538, (2004).

37  Protocol Additional to the Geneva Conventions of 12 August 1949, and Relating to the Protection of Victims of International Armed Conflicts (Protocol I), June 8, 1977, and Victims of Non-International Armed Conflicts (Protocol II), Dec. 12, 1977, arts. 4-6, 1125 U.N.T.S. 609.

38  AR 190-8, *supra* note 34, para. 1–5.

(2) All persons taken into custody by U.S. forces will be provided with the protections of the GPW until some other legal status is determined by competent authority.

(3) The punishment of EPW, CI, and RP known to have, or suspected of having, committed serious offenses will be administered IAW due process of law and under legally constituted authority per the GPW, GC, the Uniform Code of Military Justice and the Manual for Courts Martial.

(4) The inhumane treatment of EPW, CI, and RP is prohibited and is not justified by the stress of combat or with deep provocation. Inhumane treatment is a serious and punishable violation under international law and the Uniform Code of Military Justice (UCMJ).

*b.* All prisoners will receive humane treatment without regard to race, nationality, religion, political opinion, sex, or other criteria. The following acts are prohibited: murder, torture, corporal punishment, mutilation, the taking of hostages, sensory deprivation, collective punishments, execution without trial by proper authority, and all cruel and degrading treatment.

*c.* All persons will be respected as human beings. They will be protected against all acts of violence to include rape, forced prostitution, assault and theft, insults, public curiosity, bodily injury, and reprisals of any kind. They will not be subjected to medical or scientific experiments. This list is not exclusive. EPW/RP [Enemy Prisoners of War/Retained Persons] are to be protected from all threats or acts of violence.

This mosaic of regulations and binding international law was cemented by the Department of Defense policy on the Law of War, included in 1998 Department of Defense Directive 5100.77.[39] The directive, which was in effect when the GWOT begin in 2001, required military forces to:

Ensure that the members of their Components comply with the law of war during all armed conflicts, however such conflicts are characterized, and with the principles and spirit of the law of war during all other operations.[40]

The Joint Chiefs of Staff Instruction to Combatant Commanders, implementing this DoD Directive, further directed forces in the field to

---

39    U.S. Dep't of Defense, Dir. 5100.77, DoD Law of War Program (9 Dec. 1998).

40    *Id.*, at para. 5.3.1.

comply with these provisions, "unless otherwise directed by competent authorities."[41] The default position, for the U.S. military, at the beginning of the Global War on Terror, was to presumptively apply GCIII or GCIV to captured individuals, and never violate the "General Protection Policy," modeled on Common Article 3 to the Geneva Conventions, in interrogation, or any other form of treatment.

## THE DEVELOPMENT OF NEW INTERROGATION AND TREATMENT STANDARDS

The law of war interrogation and treatment paradigm adopted for GWOT was changed substantially by several legal opinions, prepared by the Justice Department's Office of Legal Counsel[42] and endorsed by the White House Legal Counsel, Alberto Gonzalez.[43] The legal discussion revolved around the "status" issue discussed in the previous chapter and the application of Article 4 to GCIII to the Taliban and al Qaeda. But there was also substantial discussion regarding the difficulty of interpreting the humane treatment standard contained in Common Article 3 and the application of the War Crimes Act (which included criminal sanctions for unspecified violations of Common Article 3) to U.S. officials.[44]

---

41   Joint Chiefs of Staff, Instr. 5810.01B, The DoD Law of War Program para. 5a (August 1999).

42   *See* Memorandum, U.S. Dep't of Justice Office of the Legal Counsel, to Counsel to the President, subject: Status of Taliban Forces Under Article 4 of the Third Geneva Convention of 1949 (February 7, 2002) (authored by Jay S. Bybee, Assistant Attorney General), *available at* http://www.usdoj.gov/olc/2002/pub-artc4potusdetermination.pdf. (The OLC is charged with developing legal positions for the Executive branch. These memoranda were prepared to establish the administration positions on the status of captured enemy combatants in the fight against the Taliban and al Qaeda, as well as their treatment.) *See also* Draft Memorandum, John Yoo, Deputy Assistant Attorney General, U.S. Department of Justice & Robert J. Delahunty, Special Counsel, U.S. Department of Justice, to General Counsel, U.S. Department of Defense, subject: Application of Treaties and Laws to al Qaeda and Taliban Detainees (Jan. 9, 2002), *available at* http://www2.gwu.edu/%7Ensarchiv/NSAEBB/NSAEBB127/02.01.09.pdf.

43   Memorandum, White House Legal Counsel to President George W. Bush, subject: Decision Re Application of the Geneva Convention on Prisoners of War to the Conflict with al Qaeda and the Taliban, at 2 (Jan 25, 2002) *available at* http://www.washingtonpost.com/wp-srv/politics/documents/cheney/gonzales_addington_memo_jan252001.pdf.

44   *Id.* at 3. *See* War Crimes Act, 18 U.S.C. § 2441.

Mr. Gonzales opined that the language of the Prisoner of War Convention is "undefined" in Common Article 3, as "it prohibits, for example 'outrages upon personal dignity' and 'inhuman treatment,'" which would possibly criminalize actions that might be needed "in the course of the war on terrorism."[45] Both the Secretary of State, Colin Powell, and his legal advisor, William Howard Taft IV, tried to persuade the president that reciprocity and our "international legal obligations" militated toward application of the Geneva Conventions to the conflict in Afghanistan.[46] Powell emphasized that applying the Geneva Conventions to the conflict "provides the strongest legal foundation for what we intend to do," while preserving "our flexibility under both domestic and international law."[47] The arguments of the State Department were rejected in favor of vague standards of "humane treatment."

The president's "Military Order of November 13, 2001" mandated the following treatment of captured al Qaeda terrorists responsible for the attacks on September 11, those who "aided and abetted," and those who "knowingly harbored" them:

Any individual subject to this order shall be–

(a) Detained at an appropriate location designated by the Secretary of Defense outside or within the United States,

(b) Treated humanely, without any adverse distinction based on race, color, religion, gender, birth, wealth, or any similar criteria,

(c) Afforded adequate food, drinking water, shelter, clothing, and medical treatment,

(d) Allowed the free exercise of religion, consistent with the requirements of such detention,

---

45    *Id.* at 3.

46    *See* Memorandum, U.S. Sec. of State to Counsel to the President and Asst. to the President for National Security Affairs, subject: Draft Decision Memorandum for the President on the Applicability of the Geneva Convention to the Conflict in Afghanistan (January 26, 2002) [hereinafter Powell Memorandum], and Memorandum, Legal Advisor, U.S. State Department to Counsel to the President, subject: Comments on Your Paper on the Geneva Convention" (Feb. 2, 2002), *reprinted in* Mark Danner, Torture and Truth 88-95 (2004) [hereinafter Danner].

47    Powell Memorandum, *supra* note 46, at 3.

THE WAR ON TERROR AND THE LAWS OF WAR

(e) And detained in accordance with such other conditions as the Secretary of Defense may prescribe.[48]

The decision to apply only a vague "humane treatment" standard essentially abandoned (as a matter of law) the minimum standards of Common Article 3 and paragraph 1–5 of Army Regulation 190–8. The president's next declaration on this subject further muddied the waters and made the job of interpreting the law to be applied to the treatment of captured al Qaeda and Taliban that much more difficult. On February 7, 2002, the president declared that the conflict with al Qaeda was not governed by the Geneva Conventions and the Taliban were not covered by GCIII, as they were found to be in violation of GCIII, art. 4, which required them to carry their arms openly, wear distinctive insignia, and comply with the law of war. He did, however, invoke the "principles of Geneva," "As a matter of policy, the United States Armed Forces shall continue to treat detainees humanely and, to the extent appropriate and consistent with military necessity, in a manner consistent with the principles of Geneva."[49]

The detailed debate over what standards did apply to interrogation of Taliban and al Qaeda detainees continued at the national policy level, however. As early as December 2001, more than a month before the president signed his memorandum, the Department of Defense (DoD) General Counsel's Office had already solicited information on detainee "exploitation" from the Joint Personnel Recovery Agency (JPRA), an agency whose expertise was in training American personnel to withstand interrogation techniques considered illegal under the Geneva Conventions.[50] These "counter-resistance techniques" were developed by instructors in the Survival, Escape, Resistance, and Evasion (SERE) Committee to condition U.S. military prisoners to resist torture and coercive techniques applied by enemy regimes in contravention of

---

48    Military Order of November 13, 2001 – Detention, Treatment and Trial of Certain Non-Citizens in the War Against Terrorism, 66 Fed. Reg. 57,833 (2001).

49    Memorandum, President George W. Bush, to Vice President et al., subject: Humane Treatment of al Qaeda and Taliban Detainees (Feb. 7 2002), *available at* http://www2.gwu.edu/~nsarchiv/NSAEBB/NSAEBB127/02.02.07.pdf.

50    STAFF OF SENATE COMM. ON ARMED SERVICES, SENATE ARMED SERVICES COMMITTEE INQUIRY INTO THE TREATMENT OF DETAINEES IN U.S. CUSTODY, xiii (2008) [hereinafter Senate Inquiry], *available at* http://armed-services.senate. gov/Publications/EXEC%20SUMMARY-CONCLUSIONS_For%20 Release_12%20December%202008.pdf.

Geneva Convention standards. JPRA officials provided copies of the SERE techniques, including "waterboarding," to Defense Intelligence Agency (DIA) personnel and the DoD Deputy General Counsel for Intelligence, Richard Shiffrin.[51] The intent of the request was to "reverse engineer" the techniques, to employ them on recalcitrant or uncooperative detainees at Guantanamo.[52]

In August of 2002, John Yoo, a Deputy Assistant Attorney General at the Office of Legal Counsel (OLC) (writing for his boss, Jay Bybee), provided an opinion on permissible interrogation techniques to the General Counsel of the Department of Defense (DoD GC), William Haynes.[53] This infamous "Torture Memorandum," later repudiated[54] by Yoo's successors, provided broad latitude for the conduct of interrogations. Yoo's opinion required "specific intent" to disobey the law, which would presumably not be present for U.S. officials that relied on his opinion.[55] In addition, he interpreted the "severe pain and suffering" provision of 10 USC 2340A to require "serious physical injury so severe that death, organ failure, or permanent damage resulting in a loss of significant body function will likely result" and "severe mental pain" will only exist if there is "lasting psychological harm, such as seen in mental disorders like post-traumatic stress disorder."[56] Finally, Yoo posited that both "necessity" and "self-defense" would be available as a legal defense

---

51    Testimony of Lieutenant Colonel Daniel Baumgartner, Congressional Transcript, Senate Armed Services Committee Hearing on Aggressive Interrogation Techniques, Part One, at 19 (June 17, 2008) [hereinafter 17 June 2008 Senate Hearing]; *see also* Memorandum, Chief of Staff, JPRA to General Counsel, Dep't of Defense, subject: Exploitation (July 25, 2002), *available at* http://levin.senate.gov/newsroom/supporting/2008/Documents.SASC.061708.pdf.

52    Senate Inquiry, *supra* note 50, at xiv.

53    *See* Memorandum, Assistant Attorney General, Office of Legal Counsel, U.S. Department of Justice, to Counsel to the President, subject: Standards of Conduct for Interrogation under 18 U.S.C. §§ 2340–2340A (Aug. 1, 2002) (authored by Jay Bybee and John Yoo) [hereafter Yoo Memorandum], *available at* http://www2.gwu.edu/~nsarchiv/NSAEBB/NSAEBB127/02.08.01.pdf.

54    Memorandum, Daniel Levin, Acting Assistant Attorney General, Office of Legal Counsel, U.S. Department of Justice, to Deputy Attorney General, subject: LEGAL STANDARDS APPLICABLE UNDER 18 U.S.C. §§ 2340-2340A (DECEMBER 30, 2004) (AUTHORED BY MR. GOLDSMITH) *available at* http://www.usdoj.gov/olc/18usc23402340a2.htm.

55    Yoo Memorandum, *supra* note 53, section 1.A.

56    *Id.*, section I.C.4.

for anyone forced to use torture to determine key details of an impending al Qaeda threat to national security.[57] This legal opinion, allegedly followed by other classified legal opinions on specified techniques,[58] laid the groundwork for a proposal for DoD personnel to employ interrogation techniques clearly banned by the Geneva Conventions and the "minimum humane treatment" provisions of Common Article 3.

Shortly after receiving these legal opinions from the Office of Legal Counsel, Mr. Haynes visited the new detention facility at Guantanamo Bay Naval Station. Haynes was concerned that the current interrogation techniques were not being used effectively.[59] He was accompanied by several senior Administration attorneys, including the CIA Counsel, Mr. John Rizzo, and the Vice President's Counsel, Mr. David Addington.[60] At a meeting one week later, the Guantanamo staff discussed aggressive interrogation techniques, including sleep deprivation, death threats, and waterboarding, with Jonathan Fredman, the chief counsel for the CIA's Counter Terrorist Center; Fredman paraphrased the Yoo/Bybee Memo, "Severe physical pain is described as anything causing permanent damage to major organs or body parts . . . It is basically subject to perception. If the detainee dies, you're doing it wrong."[61] A group of Guantanamo behavioral scientists, who had attended SERE training at Fort Bragg several weeks previously, prepared a list of new interrogation techniques a week later.[62] The request included three categories of techniques, each more aggressive: Category I included yelling at the detainee, techniques of deception, and false flag (interrogators claiming to be from a harsh allied regime); Category II included stress positions, use of false documents, and up to 30 days of isolation, deprivation of auditory stimuli, prolonged interrogations, removal of comfort items (including religious items), changing hot rations to MREs, removal of clothing, forced grooming, and exploitation of detainee phobias (e.g., fear of dogs);

---

57    *Id.*, section IV.

58    A still-classified memorandum was prepared for the DoD General Counsel on specific techniques and was also released to DoD on August 1, 2002. Senate Inquiry, *supra* note 50, at xvi.

59    Testimony of David Shiffrin, 17 June 2008 Senate Hearing, *supra* note 51, at 27.

60    Senate Inquiry, *supra* note 50, at xvi.

61    Counter Resistance Strategy Meeting Minutes (Oct. 24, 2002), *available at* http://levin.senate.gov/newsroom/supporting/2008/Documents.SASC.061708.pdf, (Tab 7, at 2–5).

62    Senate Inquiry, *supra* note 50, at xvii.

Category III would include use of scenarios threatening death to him or his family, exposure to cold weather or water, use of dripping water to induce "misperception of suffocation" (waterboarding), and use of "mild, non-injurious physical contact."[63]

Lieutenant Colonel (LTC) Diane Beaver, the Staff Judge Advocate for Joint Task Force 170 at Guantanamo, prepared a legal memorandum analyzing the "counter-resistance techniques" and the Commander, Major General Dunleavy, forwarded the memo to United States Southern Command (SOUTHCOM) for review.[64] The legal memorandum, which incorporated the analysis of OLC on the definition of "torture," also discounted the application of Geneva Convention standards, Common Article 3, all Human Rights treaties to which the U.S. is a party, the Eighth Amendment, and the Uniform Code of Military Justice.[65] She did, however, caution that several of the techniques would be "assaults" under the UCMJ and would, therefore, require "immunity, in advance, from the convening authority for military members employing those techniques."[66] She recommended the techniques be approved with caution and oversight. As she testified in a Senate hearing on these techniques:

> I have repeatedly been asked whether I was pressured to write my October 2002 legal opinion. I felt a great deal of pressure, as did all of us at the facility. I felt the pressure of knowing that thousands of innocent lives might be lost if we got it wrong. I knew that honest, decent Americans would condemn our actions if we did not balance our efforts to protect them with due respect of the rule of law. I believed at the time, and still do, that such a balance could be reached if the interrogations were strictly reviewed, controlled and monitored. My legal opinion was not a blank

---

63    Memorandum, Director, J-2 to Commander, Joint Task Force 170, subject: Request for Approval of Counter-Resistance Strategies (Oct. 11, 2002), *available at* http://levin.senate.gov/newsroom/supporting/2008/Documents.SASC.061708.pdf, (Tab 8).

64    Memorandum, Commander, Joint Task Force 170 to Commander, United States Southern Command, subject: Counter-Resistance Strategies (Oct. 11, 2002), *available at* http://levin.senate.gov/newsroom/supporting/2008/Documents. SASC.061708.pdf, (Tab 8)

65    Memorandum, Staff Judge Advocate, Joint Task Force 170, to Commander, Joint Task Force 170, subject: Legal Brief on Proposed Counter-Resistance Strategies (Oct. 11, 2002), *available at* http://levin.senate.gov/newsroom/supporting/2008/ Documents.SASC.061708.pdf, (Tab 8)

66    *Id.*, at 175.

check authorizing unlimited interrogations. Throughout the opinion, I emphasized the need for medical, psychiatric and legal reviews to be conducted prior to approval of these interrogation plans.[67]

The request and Diane Beaver's memorandum were thoroughly reviewed at higher headquarters, despite Mr. Haynes' Senate testimony that he relied on the Lieutenant Colonel's opinion for his advice to the Secretary of Defense.[68] And Colonel (now retired) Manuel Superveille, the Staff Judge Advocate at U.S. Southern Command (which was responsible for operations at Guantanamo Bay Naval Station), prepared a detailed review of the proposal, concluding: the Category I techniques were permissible, with certain controls; the Category II techniques would violate GCIII, and therefore should be sparingly used; and the Category III techniques violated Common Article 3 and various criminal statutes, including the torture statute.[69] Captain (now a retired Admiral) Jane Dalton, Legal Advisor to the Chairman of the Joints Chiefs of Staff, initiated a full "legal and policy" review of the request.[70] As a result, the service representatives, led by the International and Operational Law Divisions of the service Judge Advocate Generals, registered significant objection to the proposal. Colonel (now retired) John Ley, the Army Division Chief, indicated that the Category III techniques would violate the UCMJ and the torture statute. In addition, he noted the following:

> Regarding the Category II techniques, numbers 2 (prolonged use of stress positions), 5 (deprivation of light and auditory stimuli), and 12 (using individual phobias to induce stress), in my opinion, cross the line of "humane" treatment, would likely be considered maltreatment under Article 93 of the UCMJ, and may violate the Federal torture statute if it results in severe physical pain or suffering. Techniques 10 (removal of clothing) and 11 (forced grooming) are certainly permissible for health

---

67 Testimony of Diane Beaver, 17 June 2008 Senate Hearing, *supra* note 51, at 77.

68 Senate Inquiry, *supra* note 50, at xix.

69 Interview of Colonel Superveille by the Author, July 8, 2008. Lieutenant Colonel Beaver testified at the Senate Hearing that Colonel Superveille provided "no help" in reviewing her memorandum. Testimony of Lieutenant Colonel Diane Beaver, 17 June 2008 Senate Hearing, *supra* note 51, at 86. But according to Colonel Superveille, his detailed memorandum to General Hill, the U.S. Southern Command Commander, has never been released and was incorporated, by reference, in General Hill's memorandum forwarding the request to the Chairman, Joint Chiefs of Staff. DANNER, *supra* note 46, at 179.

70 Testimony of Jane Dalton, 17 June 2008 Senate Hearing, *supra* note 51, at 91 & 101.

reasons, but are problematic and may be considered inhumane if done for interrogation purposes.[71]

The other service inputs were similar in their opposition to Category II and III techniques.[72]

Notwithstanding the legal concerns raised by the services, Mr. Haynes stopped the "legal and policy review."[73] After consulting with the Chairman, Captain Dalton, Deputy Secretary of Defense Wolfowitz, and Under Secretary of Defense for Policy Douglas Feith, he recommended approval of the Category I and II techniques and "use of mild, non-injurious physical contact" from Category III, noting that approval of other Category II techniques was "not warranted" at the time, as our forces are "trained to a standard of interrogation that reflects a tradition of restraint."[74] Secretary Rumsfeld approved the list of interrogation techniques Mr. Haynes recommended, noting, "I stand for 8–10 hours a day. Why is standing limited to 4 hours?"[75]

The approval was transmitted to Guantanamo, where several of the techniques were used on at least one detainee, Mohammed Al Qahtani, the alleged "20th hijacker," who had been denied entry into the United States and returned to Afghanistan after the September 11, 2001 attacks.[76] Al Qahtani was subjected to sleep deprivation for weeks on end, stripped naked, subjected to military working dogs and loud music,

---

71  Memorandum. John Ley Chief, International and Operational Law Division, U.S. Army Office of The Judge Advocate General, to Office of the Army General Counsel, subject: Review – Proposed Counter Review Techniques *available at* http://levin.senate.gov/newsroom/supporting/2008/Documents.SASC.061708. pdf, (Tab 12). The Ley memorandum was attached to a November 2002 memorandum from the Assistant Deputy Chief for Operations and Plans to the Legal Counsel to the Chairman, Joint Chiefs of Staff *available at* http://levin.senate. gov/newsroom/supporting/2008/Documents.SASC.061708.pdf, (Tab 12).

72  Senate Inquiry, *supra* note 50, at xix.

73  Testimony of Jane Dalton, 17 June 2008 Senate Hearing, *supra* note 51, at 102.

74  William J. Haynes II, General Counsel, Memorandum for Secretary of Defense, Subject: Counter-Resistance Techniques (27 November 2002), *available at* http:// levin.senate.gov/newsroom/supporting/2008/SASC.documents.061708.pdf.

75  *Id.*

76  Bob Woodward, *Detainee Tortured, Says U.S. Official*, WASH. POST (January 14, 2009), *available at* http://www.washingtonpost.com/wp-dyn/content/article/ 2009/01/13/AR2009011303372.html?hpid=topnews.

made to wear a leash and told to perform dog tricks.[77] Alberto Mora, the Navy General Counsel, received "back-channel" reports in mid-December 2002 from Naval Criminal Investigative Service agents on the Criminal Investigation Task Force, who were shocked that detainees at Guantanamo were "being subjected to physical abuse and degrading treatment."[78] Mr. Mora consulted with the Army General Counsel, Steven Morello, who informed him that the Secretary of Defense had approved the techniques on December 2.[79] Mr. Mora concluded that, even if the approved techniques did not rise to the level of torture, they certainly consisted of "cruel, inhuman, and degrading treatment," a violation of Common Article 3 to the Geneva Conventions.[80] By threatening to provide a formal memorandum of non-concurrence to the action, Mora convinced the DoD GC, Mr. Haynes, to prepare a memorandum for the Secretary of Defense rescinding the 2 December 2002 approval.[81]

This exchange did not conclude the "legal and policy review" of the techniques, however. The Secretary of Defense's January 15, 2003 rescission memo also established a Legal Working Group to "assess legal, policy, and operational issues relating to the interrogations of detainees held by the U.S. Armed Forces in the war on terrorism."[82] John Yoo provided additional guidance (the "Yoo Memorandum") from OLC on March 14, 2003, which repeated much of what the first OLC memo (signed by Jay Bybee but authored by John Yoo) had said six months

---

See also Senate Inquiry, *supra* note 50, at xxii (concluding that "additional interrogation techniques," including sensory deprivation and "sleep adjustment" was approved for use on detainee Mohamedou Ould Slahi at Guantanamo).

77    Senate Inquiry, *supra* note 50, at xxi.

78    Memorandum, Navy General Counsel to Inspector General, Department of the Navy, subject: Statement for the Record – Office of General Counsel Involvement in Interrogation Issues (July 7, 2004), at 3, *available at* http://www.newyorker. com/images/pdfs/moramemo.pdf [hereinafter Mora Memorandum].

79    *Id.*, at 6.

80    Testimony of Alberto Mora, 17 June 2008 Senate Hearing, *supra* note 51, at 80.

81    Mora Memorandum, *supra* note 78, at 14.

82    Memorandum, Secretary of Defense to Commander, U.S. Southern Command, subject: Counter-Resistance Techniques (January 15, 2003), *available at* http:// levin.senate.gov/newsroom/supporting/2008/Documents.SASC.061708.pdf (Tab 20).

**THE WAR ON TERROR AND THE LAWS OF WAR**

earlier.[83] John Yoo essentially concluded that no domestic or international law constrained military interrogators:

> For the forgoing reasons, we conclude that the Fifth and Eighth Amendments do not extend to alien enemy combatants held abroad. Moreover, we conclude that different canons of construction indicate that generally applicable criminal laws do not apply to the military interrogation of alien unlawful combatants held abroad. Were it otherwise, the application of these statutes to the interrogation of enemy combatants undertaken by military personnel would conflict with the President's Commander-in-Chief power.
>
> We further conclude that [the Convention Against Torture] CAT defines U.S. international law obligations with respect to torture and other cruel, inhuman, or degrading treatment or punishment. The standard of conduct regarding torture is the same as that which is found in the torture statute, 18 U.S.C. §§ 2340–2340A. Moreover, the scope of U.S. obligations under CAT regarding cruel, inhuman, or degrading treatment or punishment is limited to conduct prohibited by the Eighth, Fifth, and Fourteenth Amendments. Customary international law does not supply any additional standards.
>
> Finally, even if the criminal prohibitions outlined above applied, and an interrogation method might violate these prohibitions, necessity or self-defense could provide justifications for any criminal liability.[84]

The Working Group, led by Air Force General Counsel Mary Walker, was severely constrained by the terms of the Yoo Memoranda; according to Mr. Mora, these memoranda "created the contours and boundaries for the working group."[85] Colonel Ley's concerns about military interrogators being prosecuted and about violations of international law's torture and "cruel, inhuman, and degrading treatment"[86] standards were

---

83   Memorandum, John Yoo, Deputy Assistant General Counsel, Department of Justice Office of Legal Counsel, Memorandum, to William J. Haynes, General Counsel, Department of Defense, subject: Military Interrogation of Alien Unlawful Enemy Combatants Held Outside the United States (March 14, 2003), *available at* http://ftp.fas.org/irp/agency/doj/olc-interrogation.pdf.

84   *Id.*, at 81.

85   Testimony of Alberto Mora, 17 June 2008 Senate Hearing, *supra* note 51, at 145.

86   Article 16, Convention against Torture and Other Cruel, Inhuman or Degrading Treatment or Punishment, Adopted and opened for signature, ratification and accession by General Assembly resolution 39/46 of 10 December 1984, *entry into force* 26 June 1987, *available at* http://www.unhchr.ch/html/menu3/b/h_cat39.htm.

completely marginalized. As a result, the conclusions were fore-ordained, despite the significant disagreement with the legal conclusions expressed by the Working Group members.[87] On April 16, 2003, less than two weeks after the Working Group completed its report,[88] the Secretary authorized the use of 24 specific interrogation techniques for use at GTMO. While the authorization included such techniques as dietary manipulation, environmental manipulation, and sleep adjustment, it was silent on many of the techniques in the Working Group report.[89] Secretary Rumsfeld's memo said, however, that "If, in your view, you require additional interrogation techniques for a particular detainee, you should provide me, via the Chairman of the Joint Chiefs of Staff, a written request describing the proposed technique, recommended safeguards, and the rationale for applying it with an identified detainee."[90]

## APPLICATION OF POLICIES IN THE FIELD

What did the president's declaration and the Secretary of Defense's interrogation memos mean for forces in the field? Was this balancing test—humane treatment, consistent with military necessity—an invocation of the "military necessity" defense that was rejected at Nuremburg?[91] Was the very constrained authorization of certain techniques a *carte blanche* for use of the techniques in the field? Most reasonable Judge Advocates, faced with uncertain guidance from the top, would stick with the clear doctrinal templates available in the Geneva Conventions, FM 27–10 (the Army manual on the Law of Land Warfare), AR 190–8 (the military's detainee regulation), and FM 34–52 (the Army's interrogation

---

Nations are bound by the treaty to prohibit and criminally sanction torture, but only required to take other measures necessary to suppress CID.

87    Mora Memorandum, *supra* note 78, at 20.

88    Working Group Report on Detainee Interrogation in the Global War on Terrorism: Assessment of Legal, Historical, Policy, and Operational Considerations (April 4, 2003), *available at* http://www.defenselink.mil/news/Jun2004/d20040622doc8. pdf.

89    Memorandum, Secretary of Defense to Commander, U.S. Southern Command, subject: Counter-Resistance Techniques in the War on Terrorism (April 16, 2003) *available at* http://levin.senate.gov/newsroom/supporting/2008/Documents.SASC. 061708.pdf (Tab 23).

90    *Id.*

91    *See* U.S. v. List, 11 T.W.C. 759 (1950) (Hostage Case), XI Law Reports of Trials of War Criminals 40 (U.N. War Crimes Commission 1949).

field manual). And most did, only changing the approach when directed to do so by "competent authority," per the regulatory guidance. For example, when faced with the prospect of receiving Taliban and al Qaeda detainees in Guantanamo Bay Naval Base, in Cuba, in the first week of January 2002, the U.S. Southern Command Staff Judge Advocate consulted with the International Committee of the Red Cross (ICRC) and recommended application of the GCIII standards to the development of the camp.[92] And the Commander of Joint Task Force 160 (the Task Force in Guantanamo responsible for care of the prisoners, as opposed to their interrogation, which was the responsibility of Joint Task Force 170), U.S. Marine Corps Brigadier General Michael Lehnert, made a valiant effort to apply those portions of the conventions that ensured the "prisoners' safety and dignity." One of his attorneys, Lieutenant Colonel Timothy Miller, considered GCIII his "working manual." And Lehnert directed his attorneys to study the 143 articles of the Prisoner of War Convention, "paying particular attention to Common Article 3," which resulted in an initial standard of care for the Guantanamo detainees that included ICRC oversight and, as far as practicable, GCIII standards of treatment. These standards of treatment, with reasonable accommodations for imperative reasons of security, guided the housing of detainees at Guantanamo from the early days; but the treatment standards changed with Lehnert's departure in March of 2002 and the initiation of interrogation-focused detention at Guantanamo.[93]

Some Judge Advocates in the field, when confronted with the "new paradigm" of a conflict that did not strictly apply either the higher standards of the Geneva Conventions or the more limited standards of Common Article 3, concluded that some of the aggressive techniques considered at the DoD level did not violate the Geneva "principle" of humane treatment invoked by the president. So the techniques approved at the Department of Defense level for limited application at Guantanamo migrated to Afghanistan, and later to Iraq, without adequate legal oversight.[94] These amorphous standards were susceptible to abuse, resulting

---

92    Interview with Colonel Manuel Superveille, in Karen J. Greenberg, *When Gitmo Was (Relatively) Good*, WASH. POST (Jan. 25, 2009), at B1.

93    *Id.*

94    FINAL REPORT OF THE INDEPENDENT PANEL TO REVIEW DoD DETENTION OPERATIONS 36 (Aug. 24, 2004) [hereinafter Schlesinger Report] ("In the initial development of these Secretary of Defense policies, the legal resources of the Services' Judge Advocates and General Counsels were not utilized to their fullest

in numerous subsequent investigations of misconduct toward detainees in Afghanistan and, later, Iraq.[95]

Shortly after Mr. Rumsfeld approved aggressive interrogation techniques, in December of 2002, the techniques became known in Afghanistan. Captain Carolyn Wood, the Officer-in-Charge of the Intelligence Section at Bagram Airfield in Afghanistan, said that she saw a PowerPoint presentation listing the aggressive techniques authorized by the Secretary in January of 2003.[96] Despite the Secretary's January 15, 2003 rescission of authority for the use of the techniques at Guantanamo, his approval of the techniques six weeks earlier continued to influence the interrogation policies in the field.[97] Nine days after that rescission memorandum, on January 24, 2003, the Staff Judge Advocate for Combined Joint Task Force 180 (CJTF-180, which was the command then responsible for military operations in Afghanistan) produced an "interrogation techniques" memorandum that authorized certain techniques approved in the earlier Secretary of Defense memorandum, including "removal of clothing" and "exploiting the Arab fear of dogs."[98] Soldiers who conducted interrogations at Bagram Air Base, north of Kabul, the capital of Afghanistan, also claimed that they had been authorized to provide "punishment blows" to detainees who were not cooperating with the interrogation.[99] When their abusive interrogation resulted in the death of the taxi driver, Nabibullah, and others, their

---

potential.") *available at* http://fl1.findlaw.com/news.findlaw.com/wp/docs/dod/ abughraibrpt.pdf. *See also* Major General Fay, Investigating Officer, *AR 15-6 Investigation of the Abu Ghraib Prison and 205th Military Intelligence Brigade*, at 20 (Aug. 25, 2004) [hereinafter Fay Report] *available at* http://www.dod.gov/news/ Aug2004/d20040825fay.pdf.

95 See Tom Lasseter, "Day 2: U.S. Abuse of Detainees Was Routine at Afghanistan Base," McClatchy Newspapers (June 16, 2008) [hereinafter Lasseter], *available at* http://www.mcclatchydc.com/detainees/story/38775.html; *see also* Fay Report, *supra* note 94, at 22.

96 Senate Inquiry, *supra* note 50, at xxii.

97 *Id.*

98 Although the memorandum remains classified, portions of the memorandum were discussed in unclassified versions of the Fay Report, *supra* note 94. Senate Inquiry, *supra* note 50, at xxiii.

99 Lasseter, *supra* note 95; *see also* the documentary film by Alex Gibney, Taxi to the Dark Side (released 18 January 2008).

conduct was punished by military court martial, however.[100] The misconduct of soldiers, in using unauthorized interrogation techniques or committing aggravated assault or murder, cannot be directly traced to the policy changes in Washington; but the abuse resulted, at least in part, "from misinterpretation of law or policy" and "confusion about what techniques were permitted."[101]

All of the investigations of the abuses at Abu Ghraib, including the overarching Schlesinger Report, which evaluated the involvement of the chain of command in the scandal, came to the same conclusion.[102] The first investigation, regarding alleged military police misconduct and conducted by Major General Antonio Taguba, concluded that there were numerous incidents of "sadistic, blatant, and wanton criminal abuses intentionally inflicted on several detainees from October to December 2003;"[103] he recommended criminal liability for those Soldiers. Major General George Fay, who investigated the involvement of military intelligence interrogators, concluded that "most of the violent or sexual abuse occurred separately from interrogations and was not caused by uncertainty about law or policy. Soldiers knew they were violating approved techniques and procedures."[104] He also found that the Joint Intelligence Center (JIC) Commander, Colonel Thomas Pappas [assisted by the same Captain Wood who had been in Bagram], consented to "clothing removal and the use of dogs" without proper authorization from higher headquarters; but those actions did not cause the violent or sexual abuse at Abu Ghraib.[105]

In addition, the investigators made several critical conclusions about the involvement of Judge Advocates and the application of Geneva Convention treatment standards to the military police and interrogation functions. Major General Taguba concluded that the Military Police Brigade Judge Advocate "lacked initiative and was not willing to accept

---

100   *Id.*

101   Fay Report, *supra* note 94, at 22.

102   *See* Schlesinger Report and Fay Report, *supra* note 94; *see also* Major General Taguba, Investigation of the 800th Military Police Brigade (March 2004), *available at* http://news.findlaw.com/hdocs/docs/iraq/tagubarpt.html [hereinafter Taguba Report].

103   Taguba Report, *supra* note 102, at 16.

104   Fay Report, *supra* note 94, at 11.

105   *Id.*, at 22.

any responsibility."[106] In his look at systemic issues, he concluded that it was "[c]ritical to have a dedicated senior Judge Advocate, with specialized knowledge and training in international and operational law to assist in the administration of detainee operations."[107] The Commander of Combined Joint Task Force 7 Lieutenant General Sanchez (CJTF-7 was responsible for U.S. military operations in Iraq in 2003–2004) had mandated GCIV treatment with advice from his attorney, the CJTF-7 Staff Judge Advocate Colonel Marc Warren, but Warren had authorized (for Sanchez's personal approval) some of the techniques mentioned in the Secretary of Defense's approval memorandum.[108] The approval and oversight mechanism created at CJTF-7 was never exercised, as subordinate commands never requested to use the techniques;[109] Major General Fay's investigation concluded, much like Major General Taguba, that the abuses in interrogations would not have occurred if the directives in place had been followed and mission training was conducted.[110] But he cautioned that the clear application of Geneva Convention standards to

---

106  Taguba Report, *supra* note 102, at 40.

107  *Id.*, at 21.

108  *Id.*, at 20. See also Coalition Provisional Authority Memorandum 3, "Detention Procedures" (June 27, 2004), ("The operation, condition and standards of any internment facility established by the MNF [Multi-National Force] shall be in accordance with Section IV of the Fourth Geneva Convention."), *available at* http://www.ictj.org/static/MENA/Iraq/iraq.cpamemo3.062704.eng.pdf. The CJTF-7 efforts to provide guidance on interrogation standards was also frustrated by the mixed messages emanating from the continuing efforts from the Secretary of Defense to improve interrogation (intelligence) output; Major General Miler's visit to Iraq at the end of August 2003 included a message to "get tough on detainees;" and the SERE instructors were, once again, involved in transferring SERE techniques to Iraq, at the request of an in-theater commander, in September of 2003. Senate Inquiry, *supra* note 50, at xxiii. *But see* Memorandum, U.S. Department of Justice Office of Legal Counsel, to the Counsel to the President, subject: "Protected Person" Status in Occupied Iraq Under the Fourth Geneva Convention (March 18, 2004), *available at* http://www.usdoj.gov/olc/2004/gc4mar18.pdf (concluding there is no GCIV protection for al Qaeda operatives detained in Iraq).

109  Colonel Pappas was reprimanded and fined, under Art. 15, Non-Judicial Punishment, of the Uniform Code of Military Justice, for failure to seek permission for the use of dogs as an interrogation technique. Jeffrey Smith, *Abu Ghraib Officer Gets Reprimand*, WASH. POST (May 12, 2005), A16, *available at* http://www.washingtonpost.com/wp-dyn/content/article/2005/05/11/AR2005051101818.html.

110  Fay Report, *supra* note 94, at 5.

detainee interrogation was essential; "Soldiers should never again be put in a position that potentially puts them at risk for non-compliance with the Geneva Conventions or the Laws of Land Warfare."[111]

## RESTORATION OF STANDARDS

The development of policy and law continued, inexorably, "in the wake of the public disclosure of detainee abuse at Abu Ghraib."[112] It is undeniable that the investigations into detainee abuse in Guantanamo, Afghanistan, and Iraq resulted in considerable policy discussion and, eventually, reaffirmation of the Common Article 3, GCIII, and GCIV standards of treatment. For example, the involvement of the Joint Personnel Recovery Agency, with their SERE techniques, abruptly stopped after the Abu Ghraib news broke and the JPRA issued policy guidance limiting support to interrogations.[113] The Army provided detailed guidance to interrogators on the application of Common Article 3 and GC's III and IV to the interrogation function, filling the specific "legal void" created by the DoD interrogation policy by providing Training Support Packages to the field and emphasizing the use of AR 190–8 and FM 34–52 as guidance, in the absence of specific combatant command direction to the contrary.[114] In messages intended to reinforce Major General Taguba's and Major General Fay's conclusions, the Army emphasized compliance with the "humane treatment" provisions of Common Article 3 and the prohibitions on coercion in GCIII art. 17, and GCIV art. 31, respectively.[115] In lieu of substantive changes in policy at the DoD level, through doctrine, literature, and training guidance, the Army reinforced the Judge Advocate's role in training interrogators and military policemen, as well as the exercise of judgment in providing advice to the operational commander.[116]

---

111   *Id.*, at 6.

112   Senate Inquiry, *supra* note 50, at xxv.

113   *Id.*

114   *See, generally,* Lieutenant Colonel Paul F. Kantwill, Captain Jon D. Holdway, and Geoffrey S. Corn, *Improving the Fighting Position: A Practitioner's Guide to Operational Law Support to the Interrogation Process,* Army Law, July 2005, at 12.

115   *Id.*, at 22.

116   *Id.*, at 26.

Congress proposed the Detainee Treatment Act (DTA) to establish minimum standards of treatment for detainees.[117] But the DTA adopted the same "cruel, inhumane, or degrading" ("torture light") treatment standard John Yoo discussed in his 2002 and 2003 memos, adopting the 5th, 8th, and 14th Amendments' jurisprudence on cruel, unusual, and inhumane treatment or punishment. Since the "cruel and unusual punishment" standard was only applicable to sentenced criminals, and the 14th Amendment only applied the law to the States, it added nothing to the equation. The resulting interpretation of policy relied on the 5th Amendment "substantive due process" standard, which analyzed the importance of the governmental interest involved and balanced that with interrogators' conduct that must "shock the conscience," in the context of a dire threat to national security.[118] In the final analysis, the DTA had no effect on detainee treatment or interrogation policy.

DoD policy began to change, significantly, in the fall of 2005. The DoD GC, Mr. Haynes, led a working group to determine the standards for "humane treatment," to be integrated in a revised DoD directive on the treatment of detainees. Its initial policy recommendation for adoption of Common Article 3 as the minimum standard of treatment was rejected by the White House.[119] While the Judge Advocate Generals of the military services supported the application of Common Article 3,[120] the department adopted paragraph 1–5 of AR 190–8 as the standard of treatment in DoD Directive 2310.01E, "DoD Detainee Program."[121] In the meantime, the Department of Defense published its directive for the Law of War, DoD Directive 2311.01A, which reiterated that, as a matter

---

117   Detainee Treatment Act of 2005, Pub. L. No. 109-148, § 1005(e), 119 Stat. 2680, 2742-44 [hereinafter, DTA].

118   Michael Garcia, *U.N. Convention Against Torture (CAT): Overview and Application to Interrogation Techniques*, CONGRESSIONAL RESEARCH SERVICE (January 26, 2009), at 6, *available at* http://www.fas.org/sgp/crs/intel/RL32438.pdf.

119   Jane Mayer, *The Memo: How an Internal Effort to Ban the Abuse and Torture of Detainees Was Thwarted*, THE NEWW YORKER (February 27, 2006), at 10.

120   *See, e.g., Hearing on the Future of Military Commissions to Try Enemy Combatants Before the Senate Armed Services Committee*, 109th Cong. (2006) (statement of Major General Scott C. Black, The Judge Advocate General, U.S. Army, regarding application of Common Article 3 standards to military operations).

121   *Compare* para. 1-5, AR 190-8, *supra* note 34, with U.S. DEP'T OF DEFENSE, DIRECTIVE 2310.01E, DoD DETAINEE PROGRAM, Enclosure A (Sept. 5, 2006) [hereinafter DoD DIR. 2310.01E].

of DoD policy, the law of war was applicable to military operations, "during all armed conflicts, however such conflicts are characterized, and in all other military operations."[122] It seemed to indicate that the default standard was the Geneva Convention standard of treatment, rather than the "minimum humane treatment standard" of Common Article 3.[123]

Just prior to the approval of the detainee directive, the Supreme Court issued its opinion in *Hamdan*,[124] affirming the value of Common Article 3 in establishing norms of conduct in the GWOT:

> The Court of Appeals thought, and the Government asserts, that Common Article 3 does not apply to Hamdan because the conflict with al Qaeda, being "international in scope," does not qualify as a "'conflict not of an international character.'" 415 F.3d at 41. That reasoning is erroneous. The term "conflict not of an international character" is used here in contradistinction to a conflict between nations. So much is demonstrated by the "fundamental logic [of] the Convention's provisions on its application." *Id.*, at 44 (Williams, J., concurring). Common Article 2 provides that "the present Convention shall apply to all cases of declared war or of any other armed conflict which may arise between two or more of the High Contracting Parties." 6 U.S.T., at 3318 (art. 2, P 1). High Contracting Parties (signatories) also must abide by all terms of the Conventions vis-à-vis one another even if one party to the conflict is a nonsignatory "Power," and must so abide vis-à-vis the nonsignatory if "the latter accepts and applies" those terms. *Ibid.* (art. 2, P 3). Common Article 3, by contrast, affords some minimal protection, falling short of full protection under the Conventions, to individuals associated with neither a signatory nor even a nonsignatory "Power" who are involved in a conflict "in the territory of" a signatory. The latter kind of conflict is distinguishable from the conflict described in Common Article 2 chiefly because it does not involve a clash between nations (whether signatories or not). In context, then, the phrase "not of an international character" bears its literal meaning.

---

122 U.S. Dep't of Defense, Dir. 2311.01E, DoD Law of War Program (May 9, 2006) [hereinafter DoD Dir. 2311.01E].

123 *Compare Dick Jackson, Lieutenant Colonel Eric T. Jensen and Robert Matsuishi, The Law of War After the DTA, Hamdan, and the MCA*, Army Law, Sept. 2007, at 19, *with Major John T. Rawcliffe, Changes to the Department of Defense Law of War Program*, ARMY LAW, Aug. 2006, at 23. The authors of the former article endorsed Major Rawcliffe's conclusion that practitioners should "assume that Common Article 2 and similar triggers have been satisfied, to apply the law of war broadly, and to seek active involvement and consent from higher echelons of command when appropriate." *Id.* at 32.

124 Hamdan v. Rumsfeld, 126 S. Ct. 2749 (2006).

See, *e.g.*, J. Bentham, Introduction to the Principles of Morals and Legislation 6, 296 (J. Burns & H. Hart eds. 1970) (using the term "international law" as a "new though not inexpressive appellation" meaning "betwixt nation and nation"; defining "international" to include "mutual transactions between sovereigns as such"); Commentary on the Additional Protocols to the Geneva Conventions of 12 August 1949, p. 1351 (1987) ("[A] non-international armed conflict is distinct from an international armed conflict because of the legal status of the entities opposing each other").[125]

The Deputy Secretary of Defense immediately issued a memorandum to the services and the forces in the field to ensure that the minimum standards of Common Article 3 applied to all policies and directives.[126]

In September 2006, the DoD published DoD Directive 2310.01E, *The Department of Defense Detainee Program*, its long-awaited directive on detainee treatment. This directive provided the overarching DoD policy with respect to detainee operations. The revision set out policy guidance not only for detention operations in traditional conflicts, but also included treatment standards for individuals detained in the GWOT by incorporating the numerous lessons learned and taking into account the recommendations in the twelve major investigations of its detention operations conducted by the DoD.[127] The directive specifically incorporated references to Common Article 3 and provided that all detainees would be treated humanely and in accordance with U.S. law and the laws of war. Paragraph 4.2 of the directive specifically provided:

> All persons subject to this Directive shall observe the requirements of the law of war, and shall apply, without regard to a detainee's legal status, at a minimum the standards articulated in Common Article 3 to the Geneva Conventions of 1949 [. . .], as construed and applied by U.S. law, and those found in Enclosure 4, in the treatment of detainees, until their final release, transfer out of DOD control, or repatriation. Note that certain categories of detainees, such as enemy prisoners of war, enjoy protections

---

125    *Id.*, at 2795-2796.

126    Memorandum, Deputy Sec'y of Defense to Sec'ys of Military Dep'ts et al., subject: Application of Common Article 3 of the Geneva Conventions to the Treatment of Detainees in the Department of Defense (July 7, 2006), *available at* http://www.fas.org/sgp/othergov/dod/geneva070606.pdf.

127    Briefing by Charles "Cully" Stimson et al., *Department of Defense Directive on Detainee Operations, the Release of the Army Field Manual for Human Intelligence Collection and an Update on Military Commissions*, Sept. 7, 2006, *available at* http://2002-2009-fpc.state.gov/71958.htm.

under the law of war in addition to the minimum standards prescribed in Common Article 3....[128]

In addition to the treatment standards of Common Article 3, Enclosure 4 of the directive contained many other requirements, some of which exceeded the standards articulated in Common Article 3, that the DOD considered essential to ensure the humane care and treatment of detainees. For example, detainees were also entitled to "adequate food, drinking water, shelter, clothing, and medical treatment."[129] They will also be free to "exercise their religion, consistent with the requirements of detention."[130] Finally, paragraph E4.1.1.3 provided:

> All detainees will be respected as human beings. They will be protected against threats or acts of violence including rape, forced prostitution, assault and theft, public curiosity, bodily injury, and reprisals. They will not be subjected to medical or scientific experiments. They will not be subjected to sensory deprivation. This list is not exclusive.[131]

The release of this directive was an important step in ensuring that DoD detention policies complied with Common Article 3. It provided a baseline standard of treatment for all detainees. Its release, especially in combination with the subsequent issue of a new manual on interrogation, was widely perceived as a repudiation of the harsh interrogation tactics and treatment standards approved subsequent to the attacks of September 11.[132]

The Army, which was designated Executive Agent for policy development and training of military police and military interrogators, next provided an updated version of the field manual for Internment and Resettlement Operations, FM 3–19.40, which relied on GCIII and GCIV for the treatment standards of detainees, both prisoners of war and civilian internees.[133] The succeeding development in policy was the issuance of the substantially revised "Interrogation Manual," Field

---

128  DoD Dir. 2310.01E, *supra* note 121, para 4.2, at 2.

129  DoD Dir. 2310.01E, *supra* note 121, para. E4.1.1.3, at 11.

130  *Id.*

131  *Id.*

132  Josh White, *New Rules of Interrogation Forbid Use of Harsh Tactics*, Wash. Post, Sept. 7, 2006, at A1.

133  U.S. Dep't of Army, Field Manual 3-19.40, Internment and Resettlement Operations (July 21, 2006), Appendix C.

Manual 2–22.3, "Human Intelligence Collector Operations,"[134] which the DTA had mandated to control interrogation standards.[135] The DTA mandate was a curious one, from a legal perspective, as it required military interrogators to comply with a doctrinal publication that was fungible and could be modified by the responsible service at any time. But the high profile of the manual and the requirement to consult with Congress made the publication of a revised FM 2–22.3 a significant event in the development of policy regarding interrogations.

The Field Manual included accumulated requirements, in law and policy, to maintain a minimum "humane treatment" standard, incorporating many of the lessons learned from the GWOT. The Manual prohibits torture and cruel, inhuman, or degrading treatment, referencing the DTA and Common Article 3 for the minimum standard. But the manual also incorporates a single standard of treatment, based on GCIII, for all detainees regardless of their status. It authorizes eighteen interrogation techniques which, consistent with the Detainee Treatment Act of 2005, are the only interrogation techniques authorized for any detainee, whether lawful or unlawful combatants. Applying the standards of Article 17 of GCIII, the manual bans coercive interrogation, the denial of basic rights and the use of disparate treatment intended for the purpose of persuading a detainee to talk.[136] The only exception to the GCIII standard is the use of isolation as an interrogation technique; but this technique is limited to "unlawful combatants," carefully controlled by the first General Officer in the chain of command and limited to 30 days at a time.[137] With that one exception, the Field Manual restores the full Geneva Convention standard to interrogation.

An unfortunate coincidence over-shadowed the publication of FM 2–22.3. The president announced that 16 "high-value detainees," kept in CIA custody to that point, were to be transferred to Guantanamo on the same day the FM was published. In addition, the president announced his intent to continue the use of "aggressive interrogation techniques" for

---

134  U.S. Dep't of Army, Field Manual 2-22.3 (FM 34-52), Human Intelligence Collector Operations (Sept. 6, 2006) [hereinafter FM 2-22.3]. The new field manual replaced FM 34-52, but is much broader than FM 34-52 in its scope and application.

135  DTA, §1002(a).

136  FM 2-22.3, *supra* note 134, para. 5–73.

137  FM 2-22.3, *supra* note 134, Appendix M.

**THE WAR ON TERROR AND THE LAWS OF WAR**

"unlawful combatants" in CIA custody. On July 20, 2007, the president issued Executive Order 13440, which purported to apply Common Article 3 standards to those techniques, when used by the CIA. The Army quickly announced that the Executive Order did not apply to its interrogation techniques; the Judge Advocate General took the unusual step, in a message to the field, of emphasizing that the treatment and interrogation standards detailed in DoD Directive 2310.01E and both Army field manuals for military police internment operations and inter-rogation operations were controlling.[138] The newly inaugurated presi-dent's recent Executive Order reversed that decision by President Bush and eliminated all doubt about the standard of treatment to be applied to detainees in military or CIA custody; he required future CIA inter-rogations to employ the techniques of interrogation outlined in Field Manual 2–22.3.[139]

## CONCLUSION

The treatment and interrogation standards to be applied in the Global War on Terror have come full circle. Beginning with the first set of policy discussions over interrogation techniques, prior to the president's Memorandum of February 7, 2002, the State Department and Defense Department attorneys with the experience in applying the law of war to military operations (and the judgment to see the consequences of apply-ing a new standard) opposed limiting the application of the standards embodied in GCIII and GCIV to detainees picked up on this "new battlefield." Even when these standards were not available, as a matter of law (largely due to legal interpretations made by OLC or the White House), the GCIII or GC IV standards were applied as a matter of policy in the field manuals developed and promulgated in the last several years. As the discussion above indicates, the available evidence suggests that, in policy discussions and battlefield application of the interrogation and treatment standards, Judge Advocates usually took the "high road" in offering advice to commanders, applying GCIII or GCIV standards to the problems they encountered, and counseling caution in applying techniques that were close to the lines on torture and "cruel, inhumane, and degrading treatment."

---

138    Dick Jackson and LTC Eric Jensen, *Common Article 3 and its Application to Detention and Interrogation*, THE ARMY LAWYER (May 2007), at 69.

139    *Ensuring Lawful Interrogations*, EXECUTIVE ORDER (January 22, 2009), *available at* http://www.whitehouse.gov/the_press_office/Ensuring_Lawful_Interrogations/.

In the policy discussions and field application of the law, three attempts by Army Judge Advocates to stop the inevitable slide of standards stand out. The first is Colonel John Ley's memorandum, in November 2002, opposing the Category II and III techniques for Guantanamo. The second is Colonel Manuel Superveille's assistance to General Lehnart, the CJTF-160 Commander at Guantanamo, to apply GCIII standards to the new camp, with ICRC help. And the third is the decision, advised by Colonel Marc Warren to LTG Sanchez, the Commander of CJTF-7, to apply GCIV standards, protecting security detainees captured during the occupation of Iraq, as if they were "protected persons" and "civilian internees," under the Fourth (Civilians) Convention. The policy battles in Washington pale in comparison to the tough decisions made by soldiers in the field to stick to the moral high ground, except for a few isolated instances. The advice of each of these senior legal advisors, involved in both policy development and application of the policy on the battlefield, was essential to establish and maintain a Geneva Convention-based humane treatment approach that was consistent in most circumstances and resulted in a high standard of treatment across the GWOT battlefield.

But it was those isolated instances of criminal conduct that caused the light of day to shine on the deficiencies in military interrogation and treatment of detainees. Without the conclusions of investigating officers and the force of public opinion, the policy, which was limited in its formal application but insidious in its influence, could not have been changed. Thanks to the judgment of those senior officers, Major General Taguba and Major General Fay, and the Schlesinger Report, the reaffirmation of Geneva Convention-based treatment and interrogation standards was not long delayed.

The U.S. Army is left with the standards it began the War on Terror with—the minimum humane treatment standards of Common Article 3 as a legal baseline in all conflicts, supplemented, as a matter of policy, with the protections afforded by GCIII and GCIV, to treat all those that are hors de combat (no longer taking an active part in hostilities) as decently and humanely as the conscience of our individual soldiers and the dictates of the public conscience demand.[140]

---

140    Preamble, Hague IV (Martens Clause – "in cases not included in the regulations
       . . . the inhabitants and the belligerents remain under the protection and the rule
       of the principles of the law of nations, as they result from the usages established
       among civilized peoples, from the laws of humanity, and the dictates of the public
       conscience.")

# CHAPTER 5

# TRIAL AND PUNISHMENT FOR BATTLEFIELD MISCONDUCT

By Geoffrey S. Corn[†] and Eric T. Jensen[‡]

The terms war crime and terrorism share common connections: they both refer to the unjustified infliction of suffering, they both connote the victimization of the innocent, and they both trigger criminal sanction. But these two terms also differ in certain legally substantial ways. Perhaps the most important difference is the source of law that operates to condemn these crimes. War crimes are quintessential international law violations—crimes that are defined by international law and subject to criminal sanction either through international tribunals or domestic tribunals invoking the substance of international law. Terrorism, in contrast, although ostensibly universally condemned, is primarily the subject of domestic law, subject to criminal sanction as the result of domestic criminal prohibition.

[†]    Associate Professor of Law at South Texas College of Law in Houston Texas, where he has been on the faculty since 2005. He is a graduate of Hartwick College and the U.S. Army Command and General Staff College, and the U.S. Army Officer Candidate School. He earned his J.D., *highest honors* at George Washington University and his LL.M., *distinguished graduate*, at the Judge Advocate General's School. Prior to joining the faculty, Professor Corn served in the U.S. Army for 21 years, retiring as a Lieutenant Colonel in the Judge Advocate General's Corps. He earned his commission in 1984 from Officer Candidate School and served five years as a tactical intelligence officer before attending law school and joining the JAG Corps. As a Judge Advocate, Professor Corn's experience focused primarily on criminal and international law, including service as a supervisory defense counsel for the Western United States; Chief of International Law for U.S. Army Europe; and Professor of International and National Security Law at the U.S. Army Judge Advocate General's School, and Chief Prosecutor for the 101st Airborne Division.

[‡]    Chief, International Law Branch, Office of The Judge Advocate General, U.S. Army. LTC Jensen holds an LL.M. from Yale Law School, and LL.M. from The Judge Advocate General's Legal Center and School and a Juris Doctor degree from University of Notre Dame Law School. He has served for twenty years in the U.S. Army and was deployed as a legal advisor to operations in Bosnia, Macedonia, and Iraq. He was also an assistant professor at The Judge Advocate General's Legal Center and School where he taught international law and law of war topics.

Prior to September 11, these distinctions had virtually no practical significance: war crimes and terrorism were distinctly defined and prosecuted as distinct classes of crime. This changed, however, when President Bush issued his now infamous Military Order Number 1 establishing Military Commissions to try certain individuals captured in the context of the newly proclaimed war on terror.[1] By subjecting acts of terrorism to the jurisdiction of what had to that time been understood as a "law of war" court, the president initiated one of the most controversial debates related to the U.S. struggle against transnational terrorism.[2] Could the conduct of terrorists violate the laws and customs of war? Could terrorism itself be characterized as a war crime? Could the jurisdiction of a "war court" be extended to acts of terrorism? If terrorists were to be tried by such courts, would they be entitled to invoke the fundamental trial rights guaranteed by the law of armed conflict[3] to challenge procedures of the court? Did these defendants have a right to judicial review of their challenges?

The debate related to all of these questions unfolded in the months and years following the creation of the military commissions. As a result, the commissions themselves went through a fairly radical transformation—at least procedurally. Substantively, however, the basic proposition that provided the impetus for the president's initial order—that acts of transnational terrorism could be designated either as war crimes or in the alternative be subjected to the jurisdiction of a military commission—remained essentially unaltered. Accordingly, at the time of the writing of this text, members of al Qaeda are being tried by the military commission for terrorism type offenses, such as the provision of material support to terrorism.[4]

There is nothing fundamentally irrational about the use of military courts to try war crimes. The very notion of the war crime is derived

---

1    See generally Military Commission Order No. 1, available at http://www. defenselink.mil/news/Mar2002/d20020321ord.pdf.

2    See generally Geoffrey S. Corn, Hamdan, Lebanon, and the Regulation of Armed Hostilities: The Need to Recognize a Hybrid Category of Armed Conflict, 40 Vand. J. Transnat'l L. 295, 299–300 (2007) (defining transnational armed conflict as "a term used to represent the extraterritorial application of military combat power by the regular armed forces of a state against a transnational non-state armed enemy").

3    Hereinafter LOAC.

4    Military Commissions Order No. 1, supra note 1 (providing jurisdiction for military commissions over violations of the laws of war).

from a history of "warriors judging warriors" in military courts vested with such jurisdiction. Indeed, the advent of civilian international tribunals vested with jurisdiction over such crimes is a relatively new phenomenon. What is unclear, however, is how this historically valid use of military "war courts" can be reconciled with the designation of the struggle against terrorism as an armed conflict. When the uncertainty associated with designating the struggle against international terrorism as an armed conflict is added into this equation, this lack of clarity becomes particularly profound. For the United States, procedural obligations related to the use of military tribunals to try terrorism offenses have been defined by a combination of the Supreme Court decision in *Hamdan v. Rumsfeld*[5] and the subsequent statutory framework for military commissions passed by Congress: the Military Commission Act of 2006.[6] Substantive clarity, however, has remained elusive. Although this same statute purports to define with precision those offenses validly subject to the jurisdiction of military commissions, internal inconsistencies in the statute coupled with the continuing judicial challenges to the subject-matter jurisdiction of these tribunals have contradicted this congressional purpose.

This chapter will explore the issues surrounding the use of courts whose jurisdiction is derived from the Law of Armed Conflict ("LOAC") for the trial of operatives captured in the course of the armed struggle against transnational terrorism. It will assert why such use can and should be considered legitimate, but also how this legitimacy is contingent on respecting substantive and procedural limitations. While the debate on the legitimate use of such tribunals will no doubt continue for some time, it seems increasingly apparent that if the characterization of armed conflict applied to this struggle is valid, there is no logical reason why individuals who transgress certain fundamental LOAC norms should be immune from such jurisdiction simply because their misconduct is subject to the concurrent jurisdiction of civilian courts.

## THE JURISDICTION CREATED BY "ANY" ARMED CONFLICT

Application of LOAC principles as a matter of policy may provide regulatory solutions to many operational issues, but it does not provide a legal basis for the war crimes prosecution of individuals captured during

---

5    *Hamdan v. Rumsfeld*, 548 U.S. 557 (2006).

6    Military Commissions, 10 U.S.C. §§948a -950w (2006).

these operations. War crimes prosecutions are based on a legally simple but factually complex jurisdictional predicate: a violation of proscriptions established by the international law of armed conflict.[7] Accordingly, any war crimes allegation must rest on a two-prong foundation: first, that the LOAC applied at the time of the alleged misconduct; second, that the defendant's acts or omissions violated a proscription established by that law.

The president's decision in November of 2001 to order the establishment of a military commission for the trial and punishment of captured terrorist operatives was a clear indication that the United States considered the struggle against al Qaeda an "armed conflict" sufficient to trigger LOAC application. In his Order, the president explicitly asserted this conclusion when he determined:

> International terrorists, including members of al Qaida, have carried out attacks on United States diplomatic and military personnel and facilities abroad and on citizens and property within the United States on a scale that has created a state of armed conflict that requires the use of the United States Armed Forces.[8]

And that:

> To protect the United States and its citizens, and for the effective conduct of military operations and prevention of terrorist attacks, it is necessary for individuals subject to this order pursuant to section 2 hereof to be detained, and, when tried, to be tried for violations of the laws of war and other applicable laws by military tribunals.[9]

While this Order and the trials it generated would ultimately lead the Supreme Court to rule that the trial structure created by the president violated both domestic and international law, nothing in that decision challenged the basic jurisdictional premise reflected in these excerpts.[10] Indeed, by focusing on the procedural defects of the military commission instead of any jurisdictional defect, *Hamdan v. Rumsfeld* was, if anything, an implicit endorsement of these conclusions.[11] There may be

---

7    10 U.S.C. § 948d (2006).

8    Military Order of November 13, 2001: Detention, Treatment, and Trial of Certain Non-Citizens in the War Against Terrorism, 66 Fed. Reg. 57,833 §1(a) (2001).

9    *Id.* at § 1(e).

10    *See Hamdan*, 548 U.S. 557.

11    *Id.*

rational explanations for why the Court seemed to avoid any meaningful critique of the jurisdictional foundation of trial of al Qaeda terrorists as war criminals—first among these the apparent concession of jurisdiction by Hamdan's lawyers. In its opinion, the Court noted that "[Petitioner] concedes that a court-martial constituted in accordance with the Uniform Code of Military Justice (UCMJ) . . . would have authority to try him."[12] Because such court-martial jurisdiction could be based only on applicability of the law of war to Hamdan, this one sentence reveals that the jurisdiction for trying Hamdan as a war criminal was never challenged by his lawyers. Nonetheless, the Court's focus was not lost on Congress, which almost immediately following the decision adopted the president's initial jurisdictional determinations in the form of the Military Commission Act of 2006. According to this statute:

> This chapter establishes procedures governing the use of military commissions to try alien unlawful enemy combatants engaged in hostilities against the United States for violations of the law of war and other offenses triable by military commission.[13]

In a subsequent provision of the MCA, Congress emphasized that the offenses created by the statute were not new and had always been subject to trial by military commission—clearly implying that the MCA has merely codified existing war crimes.[14]

Thus, from the outset of the Global War on Terror, the struggle against transnational terrorism has been treated by the United States as an armed conflict triggering LOAC obligations. This determination is critical, for it provides the jurisdictional basis for designating acts and omissions of terrorist operatives as "war crimes". This treatment of terrorism as a war crime is no less controversial today than it was on the day the president issued his military order, and only time will tell if such an approach to both the LOAC applicability and individual responsibility will gain wider acceptance in the international community. At a more immediate level, however, must be a critique of the subordinate issues created by this invocation of the LOAC: what is the legitimate scope of criminal jurisdiction derived from a transnational armed conflict, and what, if any, procedural protections does the LOAC demand for any person subject to trial for violating this law?

---

12    *Id.* at 567.

13    10 U.S.C. § 948b(a) (2006).

14    10 U.S.C. §950p.

This Chapter will focus on these two issues as they relate to the trial of non-state actors captured by the United States in the struggle against terrorism. It is based on the assumption that the acts or omissions forming the basis for war crimes charges leveled against these detainees did in fact occur within the context of a non-international "transnational" armed conflict. Any other assumption would totally invalidate such charges. And, while most of the alleged misconduct subject to characterization as war crimes addressed in this chapter is also subject to domestic (and perhaps international) criminal jurisdiction, in keeping with the focus of this text, treatment of these venues is left to other scholars. Our focus is therefore clear: If the military component of the struggle against transnational terrorism is an armed conflict, what war crimes liability does this fact legitimately create, and what minimum procedural protections must be respected in such trials?

## JURISDICTION DERIVED FROM TRANSNATIONAL ARMED CONFLICT

The law of armed conflict is and has always been inherently responsive to the changing realities of warfare. In a very real sense, rules developed for the regulation of armed hostilities are never truly validated or discredited until they are tested in the "battle laboratory."[15] It is therefore unsurprising that some of the most significant developments in the law have occurred in the aftermath of wars. Most experts—indeed many laymen—could identify the post-World War II war crimes trials as marking one of these landmark developments. It was not, however, until the end of the Cold War that the concept of individual criminal responsibility for violations of the laws and customs of war came to full fruition. In response to the brutal internal conflict that broke out in the former Yugoslav republic of Bosnia-Herzegovina, the United Nations established the first *ad hoc* international war crime tribunal since the end of World War II.[16] Like its predecessors from that war, the International Criminal Tribunal for the Former Yugoslavia, or ICTY, was tasked with holding accountable individuals who had committed, among other offenses, serious violations of the laws and customs of war. Unlike its predecessor, however, the ICTY would ultimately conclude that its

---

15    *See generally* Leslie C. Green, The Contemporary Law of Armed Conflict 59–61 (2d ed. 2000); *see also* Int'l & Operational Law Dep't, The Judge Advocate Gen.'s Sch., Law of War Workshop Deskbook (Bill J. Brian et al. eds., 2004).

16    S.C. Res. 827, U.N. Doc. S/RES/827 (May 25, 1993), *available at* http://www. icty.org/x/file/Legal%20Library/Statute/statute_827_1993_en.pdf.

jurisdiction was not limited to offenses committed in the context of an inter-state armed conflict. Instead, for the first time in history, the concept of individual criminal responsibility for violating the laws of war would extend into the realm of intra-state, or non-international armed conflict.[17]

In light of the brutality historically associated with internal armed conflicts, this extension seemed pragmatic and justified. Nonetheless, it was regarded then and remains today a landmark development in the law of armed conflict. Added to this extension of jurisdiction was an expanded scope of norms applicable to this realm of armed conflict. In its first opinion, the ICTY determined that many norms of the law that had been developed to regulate the methods and means of warfare in international armed conflicts had "migrated" into the realm of non-international armed conflicts.[18] This new development established both enhanced accountability for individuals participating in these internal armed conflicts and significantly expanded regulation of non-international armed conflicts in general.

The jurisprudence of the ICTY and its sister tribunal the International Criminal Tribunal for Rwanda unleashed a new wave of LOAC development that finally addressed the reality that the regulation of hostilities and the protection of victims of hostilities must be driven first and foremost by the existence of armed conflict, irrespective of its characterization.[19] In fact, in the years following the ICTY's first decision of *Prosecutor v. Tadic*,[20] a remarkable shift in the law occurred. Prior to that decision, the law of non-international armed conflict was understood as a minor offshoot of the law of international armed conflict, focused almost exclusively on the most fundamental protections of individuals who were not participating in hostilities.[21] Today, the understanding is inversed: The

---

17    Updated Statute of the International Criminal Tribunal for the Former Yugoslavia art. 5, Sept. 29, 2008, *available at* http://www.icty.org/x/file/Legal%20Library/Statute/statute_sept08_en.pdf.

18    *See* Prosecutor v. Tadic, Case No. IT-94-1-AR72, Appeal on Jurisdiction (Oct. 2, 1995), at par. 70, *reprinted in* 35 I.L.M. 32 (1996).

19    *See generally* S.C. Res. 955, U.N. Doc. S/RES/955 (Nov. 8, 1994), *available at* http://69.94.11.53/ENGLISH/Resolutions/955e.htm.

20    *Prosecutor v. Tadic*, Case No. IT-94-1, Appeals Chamber Judgment, (July 15, 1999).

21    *See* Commentary: I Geneva Convention for the Amelioration of the Condition of the Wounded and Sick in Armed Forces in the Field 19–23 (Jean S. Pictet ed., 1960). A similar Commentary was published for each of the four Geneva

fundamental norms applicable to both types of armed conflict have become in large measure synonymous, and it is the disparities between applicable law that have become minor.[22] The operative word is of course norms, for the applicability of treaty rules established to regulate international armed conflicts, such as the bulk of the Geneva Conventions, cannot simply be extended to the realm of non-international armed conflict by fiat. But because so many of these rules and those of other LOAC treaties reflect underlying norms of operational conduct, the difference between the two types of armed conflict have become virtually transparent at the operational level.[23]

These developments of the law also planted the seed for another step forward in the realm of individual responsibility: extending war crimes liability to transnational terrorist operatives. Once the president determined that the United States was engaged in an armed conflict, the extension of international criminal responsibility to non-international armed conflict became the logical focal point for a new approach for prosecuting terrorists. This intersection of war crimes jurisdiction and a revised assessment of the nature of the struggle against transnational terrorism is manifested first in the president's Military Order establishing the military commissions, when he determined it was necessary:

> for individuals subject to this order pursuant to section 2 hereof to be detained, and, when tried, to be tried for violations of the laws of war and other applicable laws by military tribunals.[24]

---

Conventions. Because Articles 2 and 3 are identical—or common—to each Convention, however, the Commentary for these articles is also identical in each of the four Commentaries.

22  *See* MICHAEL N. SCHMITT, CHARLES H.B. GARRAWAY & YORAM DINSTEIN, THE MANUAL ON THE LAW OF NON-INTERNATIONAL ARMED CONFLICT WITH COMMENTARY (San Remo-International Institute of Humanitarian Law 2006); *see also* Geoffrey S. Corn and Eric T. Jensen, Transnational Armed Conflict: A 'Principled' Approach to the Regulation of Counter-Terror Combat Operations, (Israel Law Review, forthcoming), *available at* http://papers.ssrn.com/sol3/papers. cfm?abstract_id=1256380.

23  The most significant exception to this trend is qualification for status as a prisoner of war and the accordant combatant immunity derived from that status. This status is and will almost certainly continue to be restricted to belligerents involved in international armed conflicts. *See* Major Geoffrey S. Corn and Major Michael L. Smidt, *"To Be or Not To Be, That Is the Question"*, Contemporary Military Operations and the Status of Captured Personnel, 1999 Army Lawyer 1 (1999).

24  Military Order of November 13, 2001, *supra* note 9.

An analogous invocation of liability derived from the law of armed conflict also lies at the core of the Military Commission Act of 2006, and has already been the basis for several trials and convictions of al Qaeda operatives.[25]

If, as the president and the Congress have concluded, the armed component of the struggle against transnational terrorism is an armed conflict, then there does seem to be a legitimate basis to subject terrorist operatives to war crimes jurisdiction. Once this extension of war crimes jurisdiction to transnational armed conflict is understood as the foundation for trying terrorists for war crimes (a proposition rejected by many experts in the field), it becomes necessary to determine what range of offenses can be legitimately derived from this "internationalized" non-international armed conflict. In addition, if the LOAC is the source of jurisdiction upon which trial and punishment of terrorist operatives are derived, then it becomes equally essential to determine whether and to what extent the LOAC provides procedural protections that must be respected in this adjudication process.

The scope of criminal prohibition derived from the law of non-international armed conflict is not unlimited. International law does not countenance bringing charges before a military tribunal for any crime selected or created by the president or his subordinate officers. Even Congress is arguably limited in the range of offenses it may properly designate as war crimes under the jurisdiction of military tribunals. Instead, international law provides a basis for establishing jurisdiction only for violations of the law of armed conflict applicable to the conflict in which the alleged misconduct occurred. While this may seem axiomatic, the nature of offenses established for trial by military commission—both by the president pursuant to his original order and by Congress in the Military Commission Act—was not necessarily consistent with this jurisdictional limit. Instead, the range of offenses reflected a combination of proscriptions derived from the law of international armed conflict, non-international armed conflict, and domestic prohibitions against terrorism.

This limitation on the exercise of war crimes jurisdiction by U.S. military tribunals (to include commissions) is reflected in the U.S. military

---

25    10 U.S.C. §§948a -950w; *see generally* U.S. v. Mohammed, U.S. v. Binalshibh, U.S. v. Ali, U.S. v. al Hawsawi, U.S. v. Hicks, *available at* http://www.defenselink.mil/ news/commissions.html.

code: the Uniform Code of Military Justice.[26] While the Code allows for the use of military tribunals to try captured enemy personnel for pre-capture misconduct, it explicitly limits that jurisdiction to violations of the laws and customs of war.[27] This authorization for the use of military tribunals as venues for the trial and punishment of alleged war crimes committed by *any* person is consistent with the historic interrelationship between military tribunals and the law of armed conflict. As the U.S. Supreme Court recognized in its *Hamdan* decision, this history provides a solid foundation for the use of military courts to try war crimes. However, by implication this historical rule also limits the jurisdiction of such tribunals to acts or omissions that violate the laws and customs of war, a conclusion that was equally central to an earlier Supreme Court decision endorsing the use of military tribunals for war crimes prosecutions, *Ex parte Quirin*.[28] As the Court noted in that opinion:

> We have no occasion now to define with meticulous care the ultimate boundaries of the jurisdiction of military tribunals to try persons according to the law of war ... *We hold only that those particular acts constitute an offense against the law of war which the Constitution authorizes to be tried by military commission.*[29]

Accordingly, in relation to individuals associated with al Qaeda, this source of jurisdiction may be legitimately asserted only for a very narrow category of offenses derived from violations of the LOAC rules and norms applicable to non-international armed conflict in which al Qaeda operatives participate. The most significant source of liability would be violations of the principle of humanity as reflected in Common Article 3[30]

---

26    10 U.S.C. §§ 801–950 (2000) [hereinafter UCMJ].

27    10 U.S.C. §818.

28    *Ex parte Quirin*, 317 U.S. 1 (1942).

29    *Id.* at 45–46 (emphasis added).

30    *See* Geneva Convention for the Amelioration of the Condition of the Wounded and Sick in Armed Forces in the Field, August 12, 1949, art. 3, T.I.A.S. 3362 [hereinafter GWS], *reprinted in* Department of the Army Pamphlet 27–1, TREATIES GOVERNING LAND WARFARE, (December 1956); Geneva Convention for the Amelioration of the Condition of Wounded, Sick, and Shipwrecked Members at Sea, August 12, 1949, art. 3, T.I.A.S. 3363 [hereinafter GWS Sea], *reprinted in* Department of the Army Pamphlet 27–1, TREATIES GOVERNING LAND WARFARE, (December 1956); Geneva Convention Relative to the Treatment of Prisoners of War, August 12, 1949, art. 3, T.I.A.S. 3364 [hereinafter GPW], *reprinted in* Department of the Army Pamphlet 27–1, TREATIES GOVERNING LAND WARFARE, (December 1956); Geneva Convention Relative to the Treatment

and Additional Protocol II.[31] These treaty provisions impose the universal obligation that all participants in armed conflict treat individuals not actively participating in hostilities humanely. The provisions therefore provide a basis for establishing criminality that is broad enough in scope to sanction almost all conduct that would fall under the broad definition of terrorism for the simple reason that acts of terror are presumptively directed against non-combatants. These treaty provisions would certainly provide a legitimate basis for holding individuals associated with the attacks of September 11 accountable for their actions. As reflected in both Common Article 3[32] and Additional Protocol II,[33] this principle prohibits murder, torture, or other cruel, inhumane, or degrading treatment.

The principles reflected in Common Article 3, therefore, provide a sufficient legal basis for prosecution before any forum empowered by international law to enforce the law of armed conflict, including military tribunals. Common Article 3's humane treatment mandate represents a "compulsory minimum"[34] standard of conduct for any and all participants in any armed conflict—not necessarily as a matter of treaty

---

of Civilian Persons in Time of War, August 12, 1949, art. 3, T.I.A.S. 3365 [hereinafter GC], *reprinted in* Department of the Army Pamphlet 27–1, TREATIES GOVERNING LAND WARFARE, (December 1956).

31   The 1977 Protocol II Additional to the Geneva Conventions, December 12, 1977, *reprinted in* 16 I.L.M. 1391 [hereinafter Additional Protocol II].

32   The provision is referred to as "common" article 3 because it is found identically in each of the four Geneva Conventions. *See* Convention (I) for the Amelioration of the Condition of the Wounded and Sick in Armed Forces in the Field, Article 3 *opened for signature* Aug. 12, 1949, 6 U.S.T. 3114, 75 U.N.T.S. 31, *reprinted in* DIETRICH SCHINDLER & JIRI TOMAN, THE LAWS OF ARMED CONFLICTS 373, 376 (3d ed. 1988) (hereinafter GWS); Convention (II) for the Amelioration of the Condition of Wounded, Sick, and Shipwrecked Members of Armed Forces at Sea, *opened for signature* Aug. 12, 1949, 6 U.S.T. 3217, 75 U.N.T.S. 85, *reprinted in* SCHINDLER & TOMAN, *supra*, at 404 (hereinafter GSW); Convention (III) Relative to the Treatment of Prisoners of War, *opened for signature* Aug. 12, 1949, 6 U.S.T. 3316, 75 U.N.T.S. 135, *reprinted in* SCHINDLER & TOMAN, *supra*, at 429–30 (hereinafter GPW); and Convention (IV) Relative to the Protection of Civilian Persons in Time of War, *opened for signature* Aug. 12, 1949, 6 U.S.T. 3516, 75 U.N.T.S 287, *reprinted in* SCHINDLER & TOMAN, *supra*, at 501 (hereinafter GCC).

33   *Supra* note 31.

34   *Prosecutor v. Tadic*, Case No. IT-94-1-AR72, Appeal on Jurisdiction, ¶ 94 (Oct. 2, 1995), *reprinted in* 35 I.L.M. 32, 62 (1996) at 37.

obligation,[35] but as a principle of customary international law. This conclusion is only reinforced by the fact that humane treatment represents the very purpose of the Geneva Conventions.[36] Violations of the law of armed conflict based on the principles reflected in this Article could therefore encompass the taking of the airline passengers as hostages; the targeting of structures filled with civilians, or, in the language of the law, the targeting of "persons taking no active part in hostilities"; the terrorizing of the civilian population; and the killing of the thousands of innocent civilians on September 11. No additional "positive legislation" is required. International law proscribes the conduct of the September 11 terrorists; and those who planned, encouraged, and supported them, violated these minimum standards of conduct that must be respected to during any armed conflict.[37]

---

35    It is certainly plausible to assert the applicability of Common Article 3, and not merely the principles reflected therein, to any armed conflict not of an international character, even if not occurring in the territory of a High Contracting Party. *See* Derek Jinks, *September 11 and the Laws of War*, 28 Yale J. Int'l L. 1 (2003) (citing Harold Hongju Koh, *The Spirit of the Laws*, 43 Harv. Int'l L. J. 23, 26 (2002)).

    In this regard, it is also worth noting that the subject of the binding nature of Common Article 3 has been a significant issue for the ICRC. In fact, in the September-October, 1978 edition of the *International Review of the Red Cross*, the International Committee for the Red Cross along with the League of Red Cross Societies published the *Fundamental Rules of Humanitarian Law Applicable In Armed Conflicts*, 206 INTERNATIONAL REVIEW OF THE RED CROSS 246 (September—October 1978), *reprinted in* Adam Roberts and Richard Guelff, DOCUMENTS ON THE LAWS OF WAR, 469–470 (1989). The International Committee for the Red Cross and the League of Red Cross Societies, while emphasizing the informal nature of the rules, noted the rules "express in useful condensed form some of the most fundamental principles of international humanitarian law governing armed conflicts." The rules are based on the four Geneva Conventions of 1949, the two Protocols Additional to the Geneva Conventions of 1977, the Hague Regulations, and customary international law.

36    Common Article 3, *supra* note 32.

37    It is the opinion of these authors that the offense of "unlawful belligerency" would be both much more difficult to sustain, and unnecessary to charge due to the clear applicability of Common Article 3 as a basis for criminal prosecution. The essence of a charge of "unlawful belligerency" is that individuals engaged in armed conflict without satisfying the international law standard for identifying themselves as members of a combatant force. In support of this offense, there has been much said and much written about the "four criteria" from the Geneva Prisoner of War Convention's Article 4 that must be satisfied by conflict participants. However, the criteria relied upon to assert that members of al Qaeda and the Taliban

Additional Protocol II[38] is an equally significant source of definition for the principles applicable to non-international armed conflicts.[39] As of the date of this article, 159 States were parties to this treaty.[40] Although this treaty is by its terms applicable only to internal armed conflicts, it also can be viewed as a reflection of underlying principles applicable to any non-international armed conflict. It therefore seems reasonable to refer to the definition of the principle of humanity contained in this treaty as an additional indication of the scope of this obligation.

---

engaged in unlawful belligerency—that they failed to carry arms openly, wear fixed insignia recognizable from a distance, operate under effective command, and comply with the law of war—are requirements that apply, by the terms of the Convention, only to conflicts of an international (state versus state) character, and not to internal armed conflicts.

This is illustrated by the fact that these criteria are used to determine when a member of an insurgent or militia group becomes entitled to status as an enemy prisoner of war. However, by the terms of both treaty and customary international law, warriors who engage in non-international armed conflicts are not now, nor have they ever been, legally entitled to prisoner of war status (and the accompanying combatant immunity) upon capture, regardless of their uniform or conduct. It is a simple fact of international law that such warriors receive no immunity for their warlike acts, and therefore are fully susceptible to prosecution for violation of domestic law based on the actions they engaged in while involved in conflict. Based on this, it is difficult to understand how engaging in warlike activities while in civilian clothes during a non-international armed conflict amounts to an offense under international law. There simply is no requirement to be in uniform because there is no benefit of combatant immunity for wearing a uniform.

It seems that the true objection to the conduct of al Qaeda and their Taliban sponsors was not so much who they were, but what they did. Their attacks on non-combatants were certainly unlawful. While they may have therefore been "unlawful belligerents" in the pragmatic sense of the term, they were not in the legal sense of the term. Instead, their crimes were violations of Common Article 3, and it is this provision of the law of war, which should form the basis for any subsequent prosecution.

38   *Supra* note 31.

39   *See* Geoffrey S. Corn, Hamdan, Fundamental Fairness, and the Significance of Additional Protocol II, The Army Lawyer (August 2006).

40   *See* International Committee of the Red Cross International Humanitarian Law database: States Party and Signatories by Treaty, *available at* http://www.icrc.org/ihl.nsf/WebNORM?OpenView&Start=1&Count=150&Expand=53.1#53.1.

Like Common Article 3[41], Article 4 of Additional Protocol II[42] imposes upon participants in a non-international armed conflict the general obligation to treat humanely individuals affected by the armed conflict who are not actively participating in hostilities. And, like Common Article 3, Article 4 of the treaty expressly defines activities that are *per se* inconsistent with this obligation. However, Article 4 is more extensive in this respect than Common Article 3.[43] This additional illumination of the scope and content of the humane treatment obligation adds several potentially viable sources of criminal liability derived from violations of this basic principle. Among these are pillage, slavery, sexual assaults, and remarkably, acts of terrorism. While terrorism is not defined, the ICRC Commentary indicates that Article 4's intent was to prohibit attacks directed against civilians. Attacks intended to spread terror among the civilian population are also prohibited by Art. 13 of AP II:

> Article 13—Protection of the civilian population
>
> 1. The civilian population and individual civilians shall enjoy general protection against the dangers arising from military operations. To give effect to this protection, the following rules shall be observed in all circumstances.
>
> 2. The civilian population as such, as well as individual civilians, shall not be the object of attack. *Acts or threats of violence the primary purpose of which is to spread terror among the civilian population are prohibited.*[44]

The ICRC Commentary provides the following explanation of the emphasis of this prohibition:

> Acts or threats of violence the primary purpose of which is to spread terror among the civilian population are prohibited." Attacks aimed at terrorizing are just one type of attack, but they are particularly reprehensible . . .
>
> Any attack is likely to intimidate the civilian population. The attacks or threats concerned here are therefore those, the primary purpose of which is to spread terror, as one delegate stated during the debates at the Conference.[45]

---

41    *Supra* note 32.

42    *Supra* note 31, at art. 4.

43    *Id.*

44    Additional Protocol II, *supra* note 31, at art. 13 (emphasis added).

45    *Commentary on the Additional Protocols of 8 June 1977 to the Geneva Conventions of 12 August 1949* at 1453, *available at* http://www.icrc.org/ihl.nsf/COM/475–760019?OpenDocument [hereinafter ICRC Commentary—Protocol II].

The collective effect of these treaty provisions is to offer more precise meaning to the principle of humanity as it relates to all armed conflicts. These provisions, including the substance of Common Article 3,[46] if not applicable to such armed conflicts as a matter of treaty obligation, nonetheless serve as reflections of the LOAC principles applicable to all conflicts as a matter of custom. They offer a viable source of obligation for all individuals engaged in armed conflict—to include members of transnational armed entities like al Qaeda. Accordingly, they provide a source of jurisdiction that is broad enough if scope to allow for the prosecution of members of al Qaeda without resort to principles of criminal responsibility derived from the law of international armed conflict or domestic law. Thus, the most appropriate charge available for the military prosecution of a terrorist operative could generally follow this example:

*The Charge: Violation of the Laws of War*

*The Specification: In that, (name of individual), a member of an armed organization engaged in armed conflict against the United States, did, at or near (location) on or about (date), engage in conduct in violation of the principle of (humanity, distinction, prohibition against the use of specially weapons), to wit: participating in an attack directed against civilians (and) (or) civilian objects (with the intent of terrorizing the population).*

Simple, clear, and supported by the law of armed conflict, charges alleging violations of the basic principles of this law offer the most legitimate jurisdictional basis for trial of al Qaeda operatives before a military tribunal, including the Military Commission.

Another source of proscription ostensibly applicable to non-international armed conflict are those fundamental LOAC norms that have, in the language of the ICTY, "migrated" from the realm of international to non-international armed conflicts. These norms extend beyond the humane treatment obligation to regulate methods and means of warfare. Prohibitions against deliberate targeting of civilians or civilian property, launching attacks expected to produce excessive incidental injury to civilians, use of indiscriminate weapons, and use of weapons calculated to cause unnecessary suffering would all fall into this category.[47] In addition, LOAC prohibitions against perfidy and treachery, such as feigning

---

46    *Supra* note 32.

47    *See generally* Protocol Additional to the Geneva Conventions of 12 August 1949, and Relating to the Protection of Victims of International Armed Conflicts (Protocol I) arts. 35, 51–52.

surrender or misuse of a protected emblem, are also applicable to non-international armed conflicts.[48] Accordingly, violation of these norms in the context of non-international armed conflict provides an equally legitimate basis for war crimes accountability of transnational terrorist operatives.

If the subject-matter jurisdiction of the military commission established first by President Bush and subsequently by Congress through the MCA had been limited to the offenses discussed above, much of the criticism of the commissions would have been averted. This is because objections to jurisdiction would have been focused on the debate over the legitimacy of characterizing the struggle against terrorism as an armed conflict. However, this was not the case. Instead, expanding the range of offenses available to military prosecutors beyond this limited source of international proscription exacerbated the criticism of the commission's jurisdiction. The questionable nature of this expansion is exemplified by two offenses that have been central to the military commission process: murder in violation of the laws of war and material support to terrorism.[49]

Few would debate that murder in violation of the laws of war should be subject to criminal sanction. In fact, any deliberate killing that is not justified by the LOAC should be considered murder. In this regard, the title of the offense is misleading, for it suggests that it is the law of war that renders a killing unlawful. In reality, all killing is unlawful unless authorized pursuant to the LOAC, even when committed by belligerents in an armed conflict. But this incongruity reveals what is so troubling about this offense. This offense is a derivative of an offense originally established by Department of Defense Instruction for the original military commission: Murder by an Unprivileged Belligerent.[50] The thread that connects these offenses is the asserted legal predicate for the crime: any killing by a belligerent who does not qualify for prisoner of war status is a violation of the LOAC, *per se* unlawful, and therefore murder. This is reflected in the following explanation for this offense contained in the Manual for Military Commissions, the regulatory implementation

---

48 *Id.* at art. 37.

49 *See generally* 10 U.S.C. §950v(15),(25) (2006).

50 U.S. Dep't of Defense, Military Commission Instruction No. 2 §6(B)(3) (April 30, 2003), *available at* http://www.defenselink.mil/news/May2003/ d20030430milcominstno2.pdf.

of the MCA: "A 'violation of the law of war,' may be established by proof of the status of the accused as an unlawful combatant . . ."[51] This critical foundation for the prosecution of individuals for war crimes alleged to have occurred in the context of the transnational armed conflict against al Qaeda is also reflected in this excerpt from the Manual:

> It is generally accepted international practice that unlawful enemy combatants may be prosecuted for offenses associated with armed conflicts, such as murder; such unlawful enemy combatants do not enjoy combatant immunity because they have failed to meet the requirements of lawful combatancy under the law of war.[52]

The flaw in this theory of war crimes liability in the context of a non-international armed conflict is revealed by this excerpt, which is over-broad and imprecise. Contrary to the assertion, there is no such "general acceptance" in the context of non-international armed conflict. Instead, the assertion that operating without privilege renders the belligerent conduct of an individual a violation of *international* law has only been asserted in the context of international armed conflict (this theory is ostensibly derived from the U.S. Supreme Court's *Quirin*[53] decision, which upheld the trial of German saboteurs for the war crime of "unlawful belligerency" during the Second World War). Even in this context that assertion of liability has never been universally or even widely endorsed. But even assuming *arguendo* the legitimacy of this theory of war crimes liability in the context of international armed conflict, there is simply no precedent for extending the theory to non-international armed conflict. Indeed, such an extension produces an anomaly: in the context of an international armed conflict, the offense provides an international sanction for failing to comply with the requirements for gaining the benefit of international law—combatant immunity. However, because nothing a non-state belligerent can do can ever result in "lawful" belligerent status, it imposes *international* legal sanction without a complimentary *international* legal reward. In this regard, the underlying rationale for endorsing the Supreme Court's endorsement of this offense—to "incentivize" operating as a lawful belligerent—is nullified when the theory is extended to non-international armed conflicts.

---

51    U.S. Dep't of Defense, The Manual for Military Commissions §6(a)(16)(c) (Jan. 18, 2007), *available at* http://www.defenselink.mil/pubs/pdfs/The%20Manual%20for%20Military%20Commissions.pdf.

52    *Id*. at §6(a)(13)(d).

53    *Ex parte Quirin*, 317 U.S. 1 (1942).

This does not, of course, mean that the Manual was incorrect to suggest that the unlawful enemy combatants do not enjoy combatant immunity. But by mixing the benefits of status with the consequence of participation in non-international armed conflicts, the Manual distorts the impact of failing to qualify for combatant immunity. Non-state belligerents cannot qualify for this immunity, a privilege reserved for state armed forces engaged in international armed conflicts. But this does not result in the conclusion that acting as a belligerent without qualification for combatant immunity is *ipso facto* a war crime. Instead, it simply permits the application of domestic criminal jurisdiction to the acts and omissions of the belligerent. In short, the lack of qualification deprives the belligerent of combatant immunity, subjecting him to the criminal jurisdiction of the state in which his conduct occurs, which for a warrior could include murder, assault, arson, kidnapping, etc.

In order to qualify as a war crime, those acts or omissions must violate not only applicable domestic law (such as prohibitions against murder, assault, arson, kidnapping, mayhem, etc.), but also *international* law, or more specifically the LOAC. And here the over-breadth of the theory is exposed, for there is simply no basis to assert that the mere participation in a non-international armed conflict by a non-state actor violates international law. Instead, those individuals become *internationally* liable for their acts or omissions only when those acts or omissions violate norms of conduct applicable to this type of armed conflict. Why would the ICTY and the ICTR have ever even bothered to assess which norms of conduct had migrated from international to non-international armed conflict if participation in the conflict by a non-state actor was itself a "war crime"? The answer is clear: operating without the privilege of combatant immunity does not automatically result in international criminal responsibility for belligerent actions.

Because the MCA applies to both al Qaeda and Taliban personnel, and because the U.S. treated the armed conflict with Afghanistan as "international," it is possible that this offense was intended to apply only to international armed conflicts. Such a limited application would at least preserve symmetry between international benefit and international sanction. This has not, however, been confirmed by practice. Instead, military prosecutors have used this offense to charge captured al Qaeda operatives, reflecting a particularly problematic but central theory to the extension of war crimes liability to transnational armed conflict.

Perhaps even more problematic is the designation as a war crime "material support to terrorism," another offense central to the U.S. military trial of captured terrorist operatives. Unlike murder in violation of the law of war, there is not even an international armed conflict precedent for this offense. Instead, including material support to terrorism (and other terrorism offenses) within the subject-matter jurisdiction of the Military Commission, a tribunal the Supreme Court recognized in its *Hamdan* opinion exists for the sole purpose of adjudicating war crimes allegations, seems motivated by the desire to avoid bringing such cases to trial in civilian courts. While this may be both logical and even legitimate from a national security policy perspective, it does not comport with the subject-matter limitations historically associated with military war crimes tribunals.

Defendants have challenged both these offenses, but to no avail. Unsurprisingly, the judges who have ruled on these challenges have concluded that so long as Congress includes an offense within the commission's jurisdiction, the exercise of jurisdiction is valid. These rulings may ultimately be scrutinized by appellate courts, and the outcome of defense efforts to challenge this expansive jurisdiction will be important for the development of war crimes jurisprudence. A plurality of the Supreme Court has already demonstrated it is willing to question assertions of war crimes jurisdiction by the president (concluding conspiracy to violate the law of war is not a valid offense); whether they will be willing to do so when the offense is defined by Congress seems less likely. Nonetheless, it would be unfortunate if the relatively simplistic analysis relied on to sustain jurisdiction at the Commission level were to avoid appellate scrutiny.

The role of Congress in defining these offenses raises one additional consideration. Congress is expressly vested by the Constitution with the authority to "define and punish offenses in violation of the law of nations."[54] Because of this, there is a plausible argument that Congress is justified in including within the category of war crimes offenses that lie in the proverbial twilight zone between armed conflict and transnational terrorism. This argument certainly seems to have persuaded the military judges who have rejected challenges to the subject-matter jurisdiction of the commission. While such an exercise of constitutional authority does not, of course, automatically produce legitimacy at the international level, the reaction of reviewing courts and future political leaders to this trend may impact both international acceptance of this theory and its adoption in the future by other states. As a result, in spite of the intense criticism

---

54    U.S. Const. art. 1, § 8, cl. 10.

the jurisdiction of the military commission has generated, it may be the first step in a reassessment of the scope of war crimes liability in relation to terrorism.

The transnational armed conflict chapter in the history of war crimes has only just begun to be written. In fact, only time will tell whether the experience of the military commission is a draft that will be relegated to the international law trash bin, or the initiation of a further extension of individual criminal responsibility in the realm of armed conflict. If it is to be the latter, then precision in the application of the doctrine and caution in its extension must be the defining characteristics of national invocation of this international source of criminal liability. In this regard, the U.S. experiment has been both a success and a failure, but it ultimately does suggest that the continuing trend towards characterizing the armed component of the struggle against transnational terrorism as armed conflict will require the international community to come to terms with the difficult challenges that have been confronted by the participants in the military commission process.

## PROCEDURAL ASPECTS OF TRIAL OF TERRORISTS BY MILITARY COURTS

Unlike substantive jurisdiction, discussed above, where clarity is lacking for LOAC prosecutions of transnational terrorists, procedural limitations affecting the exercise of jurisdiction are clearer. Prior to the U.S. Supreme Court's ruling in *Hamdan v. Rumsfeld*[55] and the subsequent passage of the Military Commissions Act (MCA),[56] the military commissions process was insufficient to guarantee the basic necessary procedures to ensure fair trials. In fact, the Court in *Hamdan* stated quite clearly that "The procedures that the Government has decreed will govern Hamdan's trial by commission violate [fundamental guarantees]." However, in response to *Hamdan*, Congress's passage of the MCA provides a commissions process containing the necessary procedural limitations to provide fair trials.

Establishing procedures that provide for a legitimate tribunal under international law is a component of the principle of humane treatment,

---

55    *See* Hamdam v. Rumsfeld, 548 U.S. 557 (2006).

56    Military Commissions Act of 2006 § 3, 10 U.S.C. § 948b(a) (2006) [hereinafter MCA].

a principle reflected in several significant treaty provisions related to punishing violations of the law of armed conflict. Common Article 3 is the starting point of these treaty articles. Among its basic protections, it prohibits "the passing of sentences and the carrying out of executions without previous judgment pronounced by a regularly constituted court affording all the judicial guarantees which are recognized by civilized peoples."[57] In *Hamdan*, the Supreme Court embraced this standard and specifically stated, "Common Article 3, then, is applicable here and, as indicated above, requires that Hamdan be tried by a 'regularly constituted court affording all the judicial guarantees which are recognized as indispensable by civilized peoples.'"[58]

Common Article 3's "non-exclusive" enunciation of humane treatment requires only a "regularly constituted" tribunal but does not expressly clarify the elements of one. However, both Additional Protocol I and Additional Protocol II have provisions that clarify Common Article 3's requirement. Article 75 of Additional Protocol I was drafted for the specific purpose of supplementing the explanation of humane treatment provided in Common Article 3.[59] According to Article 75:

> No sentence may be passed and no penalty may be executed on a person found guilty of a penal offence related to the armed conflict except pursuant to a conviction pronounced by an impartial and regularly constituted court respecting the generally recognized principles of regular judicial procedure . . .[60]

---

57    *See supra* note 32.

58    *See* Hamdam v. Rumsfeld, 548 U.S. 557, 631–32 (2006).

59    The ICRC Commentary to Article 75 states:

> The wording of this introductory sentence is based on Common Article 3. However, Article 3 refers to a "regularly constituted court", while this paragraph uses the expression "impartial and regularly constituted court". The difference is slight, but it emphasizes the need for administering justice as impartially as possible, even in the extreme circumstances of armed conflict, when the value of human life is sometimes small. Article 3 relies on the "judicial guarantees which are recognized as indispensable by civilized peoples", while Article 75 rightly spells out these guarantees. Thus this article, and to an even greater extent, Article 6 of Additional Protocol II '(Penal prosecutions),' gives valuable indications to help explain the terms of Article 3 on guarantees.

> *See* Protocol Commentary, *supra* note 45, at 878.

60    *See* Protocol I, *supra* note 47, at art. 75(4).

The *Hamdan* court spoke approvingly of Article 75 as a standard for further enunciation of Common Article 3's standard.

> Inextricably intertwined with the question of regular constitution is the evaluation of the procedures governing the tribunal and whether they afford 'all the judicial guarantees which are recognized as indispensable by civilized peoples." Like the phrase "regularly constituted court," this phrase is not defined in the text of the Geneva Conventions. But it must be understood to incorporate at least the barest of those trial protections that have been recognized by customary international law. Many of these are described in Article 75 of Protocol I to the Geneva Conventions of 1949, adopted in 1977. Although the United States declined to ratify Protocol I, its objections were not to Article 75 thereof. Indeed, it appears that the Government "regards the provisions of Article 75 as an articulation of safeguards to which all persons in the hands of an enemy are entitled."[61]

Analogous language was also included in Additional Protocol II, the treaty developed to supplement the law applicable to conflicts not of an international character. According to Article 6 of that treaty, "No sentence shall be passed and no penalty shall be executed on a person found guilty of an offence except pursuant to a conviction pronounced by a court offering the essential guarantees of independence and impartiality."[62] As with Protocol I, there is no evidence to support the conclusion that these provisions were considered objectionable.

Specifically, the Court held that the military commissions as then constituted "dispense[d] with the principles, articulated in Article 75 and indisputably part of the customary international law, that an accused must, absent disruptive conduct or consent, be present for his trial and must be privy to the evidence against him."[63] The Court was also very concerned about the wholesale disregard for evidentiary protections in the military commissions order. These three failings of the military commissions were sufficient to make them violative of the international standard and an unacceptable procedural method for trying transnational terrorists for war crimes. To remedy this failing, the Supreme Court announced that the procedural requirements of a fair trial would be met by reference to the Uniform Code of Military Justice and provisions for

---

61    *See* Hamdam v. Rumsfeld, 548 U.S. 557, 633 (2006) (citations omitted).

62    *See* Protocol II, *supra* note 31, at art. 6 (2).

63    *See* Hamdam v. Rumsfeld, 548 U.S. 557, 634 (2006).

THE WAR ON TERROR AND THE LAWS OF WAR

court-martial. As the Court states, "At a minimum, a military commission 'can be "regularly constituted" by the standards of our military justice system only if some practical need explains deviations from court-martial practice."[64] Where following such standards was impracticable, evidence to support that assertion would need to be presented.[65]

Given that guidance by the Supreme Court, the president and Congress went to work to produce an amended tribunal process that would comport with customary international law. The result was the Military Commissions Act. This Act was passed to amend the military commissions process and to overcome the problems highlighted by the Supreme Court in the prior commissions process. The MCA takes into account many of the criticisms of the Supreme Court and establishes the procedures, in compliance with international law, to try those under its jurisdiction.

In response to the Supreme Court's comment on regularly constituted courts and the UCMJ, the MCA states: "The procedures for military commissions set forth in this chapter are based upon the procedures for trial by general court-martial under chapter 47 of this title (Uniform Code of Military Justice)."[66] The Statute further asserts "A military commission established under this chapter is a regularly constituted court affording all the necessary 'judicial guarantees which are recognized as indispensable by civilized peoples' for purposes of common Article 3 of the Geneva Conventions."[67] While this assertion is not necessarily accepted, particularly by those facing military commissions, and will likely be tested in the U.S. judicial process, the statement's presence in the statute makes clear that the United States accepts the standard of Common Article 3 as the basis for procedural fairness in the trials of transnational terrorists.

The MCA responds to the three specific objections to the military commissions process in *Hamdan*, though again with varying acceptance by academics and practitioners. In responding to the requirement that the accused be present at trial, section 949d(b) of the MCA states: "Except as provided in subsections (c) and (e), all proceedings of a military

---

64  *See* Hamdam v. Rumsfeld, 548 U.S. 557, 632–33 (2006).

65  *See* Hamdam v. Rumsfeld, 548 U.S. 557, 622–24 (2006).

66  MCA section 948b.(c).

67  MCA section 948b.(f).

commission under this chapter, including any consultation of the members with the military judge or counsel shall (A) be in the presence of the accused, defense counsel, and trial counsel, and (B) be made part of the record."[68] Subsection (c) exempts the deliberations on guilt or innocence by the members of the commission (the jury), and subsection (e) allows the judge to "exclude the accused from any portion of a proceeding upon a determination that, after being warned by the military judge, the accused persists in conduct that justifies exclusion from the courtroom, (1) to ensure the physical safety of individuals; or (2) to prevent disruption of the proceedings by the accused."[69] These provisions represent a significant reversal from prior commissions practice.

An accused's access to the evidence against him was also one of the failings of the previous commissions' process noted by the Supreme Court. The MCA attempts to strike a balance between the need for the United States to maintain its national security information and the principle of providing legitimate information to the accused to allow him to prepare his defense. Again, the final resolution of these provisions will likely be the subject of further litigation, but the statute's language is an important insight into what the United States Government views as the limits of what it can withhold from the accused. For example, MCA section 949(f) contains the provisions on protection of classified information and allows the government to protect the disclosure of "sources, methods, or activities by which the United States acquired the evidence if the military judge finds that (i) the sources methods, or activities by which the United States acquired the evidence are classified, and (ii) the evidence is reliable."[70] The judge may require the trial counsel to produce an unclassified summary if practicable.

Finally, in dealing with the Supreme Court's concern about evidentiary protections in general, and the issue of coerced evidence in specific, the MCA again tries to strike a balance. The MCA excludes all evidence obtained by torture, but allows coerced statements made prior to December 30, 2005 (the date the Detainee Treatment Act[71] came into force) if the military judge finds that "(1) the totality of the circumstances

---

68    MCA section 949d(b).

69    MCA section 949d(e).

70    MCA section 949d.(f)(2)(B).

71    Detainee Treatment Act of 2005, Pub. L. No. 109–148, § 1005(e), 119 Stat. 2680 [hereinafter DTA].

renders the statement reliable and possessing sufficient probative value; and (2) the interests of justice would best be served by admission of the statement into evidence."[72] For evidence obtained by coercion after that date, a third element is also required—"the interrogation methods used to obtain the statement do not amount to cruel, inhuman, or degrading treatment prohibited by section 1003 of the Detainee Treatment Act of 2005."[73]

This was one of the most hotly debated provisions in the MCA ratification process and continues to draw the focus of experts in the field. While all questioning has some degree of coercion inherent to it, potentially allowing evidence that was obtained by cruel, inhuman, or degrading treatment has not found much support among those most vocal about the MCA. The requirement that a military judge make that determination will likely play an important role in the survivability of that provision, as various cases make their way through the commissions' process.

Despite these ongoing debates as to the specific procedural limitations on military commissions, the process in the United States has made clear that the legal standards for such tribunals rest with Common Article 3, Article 75 of API and Article 6 of APII. Though there may still be differences as to the specific application of those standards, the standard is clear and the detail will likely become further refined as the commissions process continues.

## CONCLUSION

In the wake of current U.S. practice since 2001, it seems clear that since the fight against transnational terrorism is an armed conflict, transnational terrorists detained in the conduct of that fight are legitimately subject to military commissions. Once detained, they accrue customary and treaty law rights, including those found in Common Article 3 and its companion provisions in API and APII. These provisions provide not only procedural but substantive limitations to jurisdiction and determine the basic rights that all such detainees gain. The United States practice in this area is instructional, especially with regard to procedural limitations, where there is little doubt that the current commissions' process will refine those rights with significant clarity.

---

72    MCA section 948r(c).

73    MCA section 948r(d).

Where substantive jurisdiction is the issue, it is still unclear how the United States practice will resolve. It seems clear that the MCA is prosecuting terrorists for crimes that are not traditional international law crimes, though they are domestic crimes. The resolution of the interconnection between these two sources of law and their application to the armed conflict against transnational terrorists undoubtedly deserve continuing observation and analysis.

# CHAPTER 6

# COMMAND RESPONSIBILITY AND ACCOUNTABILITY

By Victor M. Hansen[†]

## INTRODUCTION

The doctrine of command responsibility is the cornerstone Law of Armed Conflict ("LOAC") compliance mechanism. It is derived from the expectation that the LOAC is only as effective as the military commanders entrusted with the responsibility to ensure that their subordinates understand and respect this law. By imposing liability on commanders for subordinates' misconduct that the commanders were capable of preventing, suppressing, and punishing, the law incentivizes the discharge of command responsibility in a manner that fosters a climate of respect and compliance with the LOAC.

The essence of this doctrine lies in its scope of liability. Based on the lessons of history, international law evolved to expand a commander's liability beyond the traditional notions of principal and accomplice liability to a broader theory of derivative liability. As a result, commanders may be responsible not only for the LOAC violations they committed or ordered, but also for violations that could have been averted if they had discharged their responsibilities effectively by preventing violations they knew or should have known would occur. While this scope of liability may be expansive when compared to those applicable in peacetime, it has

† Associate Professor, New England Law | Boston. Professor Hansen has a Juris Doctor (magna cum laude) from Lewis and Clark Law School, an L.L.M. from the Judge Advocate General's School and a Bachelor of Arts degree from Brigham Young University. Professor Hansen teaches Criminal Law, Criminal Procedure, Evidence, and Professional Responsibility. Before joining the New England Law faculty, he was a lieutenant colonel in the United States Army JAG Corps. His duty assignments included service as a regional defense counsel for the United States Army Trial Defense Service, military prosecutor and supervising prosecutor, and he has been involved in military capital litigation as a prosecutor and as a defense attorney. He also served as an associate professor of law at The Judge Advocate General's School in Charlottesville, Virginia. He is the author and co-author of several articles and books on criminal and military law, and national security issues.

become increasingly accepted that only through such an expansion will the law establish symmetry between the obligations of a battlefield commander and his authority.

Over time, the centrality of this doctrine to the effective regulation of armed conflict has led to its extension to individuals in positions of *de jure* and *de facto* command. It has also been extended into the realm of internal armed conflict, reflecting its customary international law character. With each step in this evolutionary process, the expectation of LOAC compliance has been enhanced by ensuring that commanders at all levels and in all conflicts understand their obligations so as to ensure that their subordinates comply with the law.

If this doctrine provides the foundation for LOAC compliance, the invocation of LOAC authority, either expressly or implicitly, would seem to mandate its applicability to the emerging realm of transnational armed conflict. In fact, the very nature of military operations directed against transnational terrorism—operations that involve tremendous uncertainty related to target identification and an enemy that ignores the most fundamental humanitarian obligations of the law—enhances the danger of non-compliance produced by anger, frustration, and uncertainty. Nonetheless, because this doctrine of criminal responsibility is derived from the LOAC, its application to these operations is rendered uncertain by the same factors that create uncertainty as to the legal characterization of these operations.

What is necessary, therefore, is to consider whether this doctrine could extend into the realm of transnational armed conflicts and whether such an extension is logically and pragmatically justified. Perhaps more importantly, if such an evolution of the law is considered the logical next step in the development of the doctrine, it is also necessary to consider how the effect of the doctrine can be ensured until such a time when transnational armed conflicts move from the realm of emerging reality to accepted law. Finally, it is also essential to consider the logic, or perhaps illogic, of applying this doctrine not only to the regular armed forces of states engaged in this struggle, but also to their terrorist non-state enemies.

This chapter will explore these issues. It will first review the origins, evolution, and rationale of the doctrine of command responsibility. It will then examine why this evolution justifies the conclusion that the application of this doctrine to military operations directed against transnational terrorism is an essential component of the LOAC compliance equation. This chapter will explain why the current military disciplinary practices of the U.S. armed forces fail to effectively implement this doctrine, and how an amendment to the military justice code can cure this defect, ensure that the purpose of the doctrine is fulfilled during any military operation, and eliminate the jurisdictional uncertainty inherent in relation to military operations occurring in this emerging realm of transnational armed conflict. Finally, the chapter will examine why application of this doctrine to transnational counter-terror operations must inevitably be understood as a unilateral undertaking.

## THE DOCTRINAL UNDERPINNINGS OF COMMAND RESPONSIBILITY

To better understand the doctrine of command responsibility, it is important to begin with a discussion of the meaning of the doctrine in the context of substantive criminal law principles. Much of the discussion within legal literature is unclear on exactly this point, and the term "command responsibility" has been applied to a broad range of conduct.[1] It is important to make clear what the doctrine of command responsibility is by explaining what it is not. Command responsibility does not refer to instances of direct liability. For example, a commander who *orders* his forces to attack a protected target; a commander who *encourages* his forces to kill or otherwise mistreat prisoners of war; or a commander who *assists* his subordinates in covering up evidence of a war crime are all

---

1    Scholars have associated the term "command responsibility" with concepts of direct liability, liability as a principal, and derivative liability. *See* Yuval Shany & Keren R. Michaeli, *The Case Against Ariel Sharon: Revisiting the Doctrine of Command Responsibility*, 34 N.Y.U. J. INT'L L. & POL. 797, 883 (2002) (stating that Article 43 of the Hague Relations should be construed as a direct liability form of command responsibility); Allison Martson Danner & Jenny S. Martinez, *Guilty Associations: Joint Criminal Enterprises, Command Responsibility, and the Development of International Criminal Law*, 93 CAL. L. REV. 75, 120 (2005). For use of the term 'command responsibility' when discussing liability as a principal (Conspiracy), see Richard P. Barrett & Laura E. Little, *Lessons of Yugoslavia Rape Trials: A Role of Conspiracy Law in International Tribunals*, 88 MINN. L. REV. 30 (2003).

Using derivative liability as a basis of 'command responsibility' see David Marcus, *Famine Crimes in International Law*, 97 AM. J. INT'L L. 245, 276 (2003); *see also* Alexander K.A. Greenawalt, *Rethinking Genocidal Intent: The Case for a Knowledge-Based Interpretation*, 99 COLUM. L. REV. 2259, 2283 (1999); Timothy Wu & Yong-Sung Kang, *Recent Development: Criminal Liability for the Actions of Subordinates—The Doctrine of Command Responsibility and its Analogues in United States Law*, 38 HARV. INT'L L.J. 272, 279 (1997).

cases where the military commander may not have been the person actually committing the offense. Nevertheless, in each case the commander shares in the criminal intent of his subordinates to either commit war crimes or prevent their detection by outside authorities. Furthermore, in each of these examples, the commander has taken some affirmative action or refrained from fulfilling a legal duty, in order to assist his subordinates in the commission of a war crime.[2] Because in these situations the liability of the commander is based on criminal law doctrines of accomplice liability and accessory liability, they do not implicate the more complicated doctrinal issues of command responsibility.

Nor does command responsibility refer to situations involving strict vicarious liability. Strict vicarious liability denotes instances where the defendant is held liable for an offense committed by another even though the defendant lacked the culpability required for the offense and did not satisfy the objective elements of the offense. Such liability would exist if a commander is held liable for the conduct of his subordinates merely because of his position of authority as their commander. Under such a theory, no proof that the commander was in any way derelict in his duties is required to impose criminal sanctions.[3] Likewise, no evidence is required to show that the commander knew or even could have known of the crimes being committed by his subordinates.[4] Liability would exist solely by virtue of the position of command. Strict liability is liability

---

2      Cases involving this type of direct liability of senior officers are fairly rare in American military history, but examples do exist. One of the most blatant examples involves the court-martial of Army Brigadier General Jacob A. Smith, commander of U.S. forces in the Philippines during the Philippine insurrection in 1901. *See* ELIHU ROOT, TRIALS OR COURTS-MARTIAL IN THE PHILIPPINE ISLANDS IN CONSEQUENCE OF CERTAIN INSTRUCTIONS, S. Doc. No. 213, at 1 -17 (2nd Session 1903). During the insurrection, Brigadier General Smith ordered his subordinate officer, Major L.W.T. Waller, as follows, "I want no prisoners and I wish you to kill and burn. The more you kill and burn, the more you will please me, and the interior of Samar must be made a howling wilderness." *Id*. at 2. Because of this order, Brigadier General Smith was convicted of conduct prejudice to the good order and discipline of the military. *Id* at 2-3.

3      Prosecutor v. Akayesu, Case No. ICTR-96-4-I, ¶ 488 (Sept. 2, 1998), *reprinted in* 1B GLOBAL WAR CRIMES TRIBUNAL COLLECTION at 316 (S. De. Haardt & W. Van Der Wolf eds., 2000) (One view is that command responsibility derives from strict liability).

4      *Id.*

without fault[5] and has been rejected as a doctrinal basis for imposing criminal liability on military commanders for the law of war violations committed by their forces.[6]

Command responsibility is therefore neither direct liability nor strict vicarious liability. Command responsibility is instead based on the principle of derivative imputed liability. The term derivative liability refers to liability that is derived by a causal link between the actor and the independent process for which the actor is held accountable.[7] The commander's liability is derived from his relationship to his subordinates and the link between the commander's act or omission and the crimes committed by his subordinates. If such a causal relationship can be established, the criminal liability of the subordinate can be imputed to the commander, and the commander can be punished as if he had committed the actual crime.

Command responsibility has both a *mens rea* and an *actus reus* component.[8] The *mens rea* component focuses on what the commander was aware of, or failed to be aware of, regarding the crimes about to be committed, being committed, or that had been committed by forces under his command. The *actus reus* component focuses on the commander's complete failure to act or his failure to adequately act, where he had the duty to act, and an ability to either prevent forces from committing war crimes, stop his forces from committing on-going war crimes, or punish his forces for their commission of past war crimes.[9] Under this doctrine,

---

5     George Fletcher, Rethinking Criminal Law 469 (1978).

6     *See Diplomatic Conference on Reaffirmation and Development of International Humanitarian Law Applicable in Armed Conflicts, Protocol additional to the Geneva Conventions of 12 August 1949, and Relating to the Protection of Victims of International Armed Conflicts (Protocol 1)*, 72 Am. J. Int'l L. 457 (1978) [hereinafter *Diplomatic Conference*]; S.C. Res. 995, U.N. Doc. S./RES/995 (Nov. 8, 1994) [hereinafter S.C. Res. 995], *reprinted in* 2 The International Criminal Tribunal For Rwanda at 3 (Virginia Morris & Michael P. Scharf eds., 1998); S.C. Res. 808, U.N. Doc. S./RES/808 (May 3, 1993) [hereinafter S.C. Res. 808], *reprinted in* 2 The International Criminal Tribunal For Rwanda at 504 (Virginia Morris & Michael P. Scharf eds., 1998); The Rome Statute of the International Criminal Court (Jul. 17, 1998), *reprinted in* The Rome Statute of the International Criminal Court: Materials at 3 (Antonio Cassese, Paola Gaeta, and John R.W.D. Jones eds., 2002) [hereinafter The Rome Statute].

7     Fletcher, *supra* at 583.

8     *See* Danner & Martinez, *supra* note 1, at 122.

9     *Id.*

---

**THE WAR ON TERROR AND THE LAWS OF WAR**       

the commander does not have to share a common criminal purpose with the subordinates who actually engaged in the commission of the war crimes.[10] What is required is that the commander had some level of awareness or failed to become aware of the criminal conduct of his subordinates, that he had a duty to act, and failed to fulfill that legal duty.[11]

If these *mens rea* and *actus reus* components can be established, then the law will impute liability on the commander for the war crimes committed by his soldiers, and the commander can be punished as if he had committed the underlying offenses, even though the commander would not have shared in the criminal purpose, or indeed had any *mens rea* with respect to the underlying offense. In a sense, command responsibility can be viewed as a hybrid between omissions liability and strict liability. The relevant *mens rea* focus for the commander is on his awareness or failure to be aware of the LOAC violations committed by his forces. If the requisite *mens rea* can be established along with a duty and a failure to act, then we look to the *mens rea* of the subordinate committing the LOAC offense and connect that *mens rea* to the commander and hold him accountable for the underlying offense. This is the doctrine of command responsibility that developed as part of customary international law and as a central component of ensuring responsible command and compliance with LOAC.

## HISTORICAL DEVELOPMENT

The principle of holding a commander responsible for the LOAC violations of his subordinates has early historical origins. Recognition of the special role and responsibilities of a military commander gives a commander both the legal authority and the legal obligation to control the conduct of forces under his command. Placing this authority and responsibility on the military commander helps to minimize the risk of subordinate LOAC violations.[12] As a corollary, giving this responsibility and authority to the military commander also suggests that a commander can be held accountable for the LOAC violations of his forces if he was either directly involved in those violations, or even if the commander

---

10   *See* Marcus, *supra* note 1, at 275-76.

11   *Id.* at 276.

12   *See* Hague Convention Respecting the Laws and Customs of War on Land, Annex art. 1, sec. 1, Oct. 18, 1907, 36 Stat. 2277, 1 Bevans 631 [hereinafter Fourth Hague Convention] ("The law of war . . . [requires that armies] . . . be commanded by a person responsible for his subordinates.").

failed to adequately control the forces under his command. These underlying objectives of the doctrine were highlighted in perhaps one of the most well-known war crimes trials following World War II.

In the first post-World War II tribunal to address the doctrine of command responsibility, the trial of General Yamashita, the United States asserted that Yamashita could be held liable for the LOAC violations committed by his forces in Manila and throughout the Philippines.[13] This theory of liability was based on the assertion that these violations were so flagrant and wide ranging that General Yamashita must have known about them if he had made any effort to fulfill his responsibilities as a commander. If General Yamashita did not know of these acts, it was because he "took affirmative action not to know."[14] In claiming that General Yamashita was willfully blind to these atrocities, the prosecution's theory relied, at least in part, on the idea that General Yamashita's liability may be predicated on the concept of command responsibility because he failed to take adequate steps to determine what his forces were doing and to prevent them from committing war crimes.

In response to the evidence presented by the prosecution to establish this theory, the military commission charged with determining General Yamashita's fate concluded that there was a complete failure by the higher echelons of command to detect and prevent cruel and inhuman treatment accorded by local commanders and guards.[15] Accordingly, the commission found that General Yamashita failed to provide effective control of his forces and that he was criminally responsible for their

---

13    The trial of General Yamashita was not an international military tribunal. U.N.
      WAR CRIMES COMMISSION, LAW REPORTS OF TRIALS OF WAR CRIMINALS,
      (William S. Hein & Co. 1997) (1948) [hereinafter U.N. WAR CRIMES, *Yamashita*]
      at 1. General Yamashita was tried by a United States military commission established under the provisions of the Pacific Regulations of September 24, 1945,
      governing the trial of war criminals. *Id.* at 2. The commission acted under the
      authority of General MacArthur, Commander-in-Chief, United States Army
      Forces, Pacific Theatre and, General Styer, Commanding General, United States
      Army Forces, Western Pacific. The commission was convened on October 8, 1945.
      *Id.* at 3. The members of the tribunal were American military general officers,
      none of whom were judges or lawyers. *Id.* at 2–3, 40.

14    *Id.* The evidence brought before the Commission established that hundreds of atrocities had occurred. *Id.* at 18. These offences were widespread in both space and time. All
      of these acts were committed by members of the Japanese forces under the command
      of General Yamashita. *Id.*

15    *Id.*

conduct. The decision of the commission was ultimately upheld by a bitterly divided Supreme Court.[16]

The theory of command responsibility was important to the commission's decision to hold General Yamashita criminally liable. As a result, the Yamashita case elevated the doctrine into the mainstream of the law of war. And while the elements of the doctrine were not crystallized in Yamashita, some contours began to emerge.

The Yamashita case makes clear that the law of war imposes a duty on a commander to take actions to prevent war crimes.[17] A commander cannot claim failure to act as a defense in cases where some action is required.[18] Another contour of the doctrine that emerged from Yamashita is the *actus reus* of command responsibility. Yamashita made clear that once a duty to act is triggered, the commander must do something to prevent or suppress war crimes from being committed by his forces. But, contrary to common misconception, this case did not create a standard of strict liability; instead it held that a commander cannot remain willfully blind to the conduct of his troops and then claim that he had no duty to act or that the duty to act had not yet been triggered. Between these extremes there remained a significant grey area that was left unanswered by Yamashita. Later cases, statutes, and treaties have attempted to address some of these questions.

While many questions followed from the Yamashita decision, the case did make clear that if liability can be established for not only aiding or abetting a war crime, but also for failing to discharge the duty of care associated with responsible command, the commander can be punished as if he actually committed the crimes. In the case of General Yamashita, the commission found him guilty and sentenced him to death by hanging.

## CODIFICATION OF THE DOCTRINE

From Yamashita to the International Criminal Court, the modern contours of the command responsibility doctrine have emerged. The first formal codification of the doctrine in the international context came

---

16    *In re* Yamashita, 327 U.S. 1 (1946).

17    *See* U.N. War Crimes, *Yamashita, supra* note 13, at 22, 35.

18    Matthew Lippman, *Humanitarian Law: The Uncertain Contours of Command Responsibility*, 9 TULSA J. COMP. & INT'L L. 1, 12–14 (2001).

several decades after Yamashita, with the promulgation of the 1977 Additional Protocol I to the 1949 Geneva Convention (Protocol I).[19] Articles 86 and 87 of this treaty codified the command responsibility doctrine under Protocol I and provide:

Article 86—Failure to Act

1. The High Contracting Parties and the Parties to the conflict shall repress grave breaches, and take measures necessary to suppress all other breaches, of the Conventions or of this Protocol which result from a failure to act when under a duty to do so.

2. The fact that a breach of the Conventions or of this Protocol was committed by a subordinate does not absolve his superiors from penal or disciplinary responsibility, as the case may be, if they knew, or had information which should have enabled them to conclude in the circumstances at the time, that he was committing or was going to commit such a breach and if they did not take all feasible measures within their power to prevent or repress the breach.

Article 87—Duty of Commanders

1. The High Contracting Parties and the Parties to the conflict shall require military commanders, with respect to members of the armed forces under their command and other persons under their control, to prevent and, where necessary, to suppress and to report to competent authorities breaches of the Conventions and of this Protocol.

2. In order to prevent and suppress breaches, High Contracting Parties and Parties to the conflict shall require that, commensurate with their level of responsibility, commanders ensure that members of the armed forces under their command are aware of their obligations under the Conventions and this Protocol.

3. The High Contracting Parties and Parties to the conflict shall require any commander who is aware that subordinates or other persons under his control are going to commit or have committed a breach of the Conventions or of this Protocol, to initiate such steps as are necessary to prevent such violations of the Conventions or this Protocol, and, where appropriate, to initiate disciplinary or penal action against violators thereof.[20]

These two articles must be read together in order to best understand their full import. Article 86 codifies the doctrine of command responsibility by

---

19    Diplomatic Conference, *supra* note 6.

20    *Id.* at 496-497.

recognizing that violations of the law of war can occur through a failure to act when a duty to act exists. This article further recognizes that a commander has a special responsibility and can be criminally responsible for war crimes committed by his subordinates. Understanding that commanders have unique responsibilities to ensure their troops' observance of the law of war, Article 87 sets out in general terms what a commander must do to meet those obligations.

In addition to Protocol I there have been other, more recent efforts to codify the doctrine of command responsibility in various contexts. Of particular interest are the statutes of the International Court for the Former Yugoslavia (ICTY) and the International Court for Rwanda (ICTR). These charters for international criminal responsibility are virtually identical and are similar in many respects to Articles 86 and 87 in Protocol I. Article 7(3) of the ICTY states:

> The fact that any of the acts referred to in articles 2 and 5 of the present Statute [Grave Breaches of the Geneva Conventions of 1949 and Crimes Against Humanity] was committed by a subordinate does not relieve his superior of criminal liability if he knew or had reason to know that the subordinate was about to commit such acts or had done so and the superior failed to take the necessary and reasonable measures to prevent such acts or to punish the perpetrators thereof.[21]

Article 6(3) of the ICTR states:

> The fact that any of the acts referred to in articles 2 and 4 of the present Statute [Genocide and Violations of Article 3 Common to the Geneva Conventions and Additional Protocol II] was committed by a subordinate does not relieve his or her superior of criminal liability if he or she knew or had reason to know that the subordinate was about to commit such acts or had done so and the superior failed to take the necessary and reasonable measures to prevent such acts or to punish the perpetrators thereof.[22]

The most significant difference between these statutes and Protocol I is the language used in the statutes to establish the *mens rea* of command responsibility. Instead of adopting the language found in Protocol I, both the ICTY and the ICTR use the term "know or had reason to know" to reflect the *mens rea* standard.[23] Nonetheless, the effect is clear: international

---

21    S.C. Res. 808, *supra* note 6, at art. 7(3).

22    S.C. Res. 995, *supra* note 6, at art. 6(3).

23    S.C. Res. 808, *supra* note 21; S.C. Res. 995, *supra* note 22.

law unquestionably imposes criminal responsibility on commanders for LOAC violations committed by subordinates for a commander's failure to do his duty.

An even more recent codification of the command responsibility doctrine is found in the International Criminal Court (ICC). This court has jurisdiction to hear cases involving genocide, crimes against humanity, war crimes, and the crime of aggression.[24] The Rome Statute sets forth the ICC's authority. Article 28 of the Rome Statute entitled "Responsibility of Commanders and Other Superiors" states:

> In addition to other grounds of criminal responsibility under this Statute for crimes within the jurisdiction of the Court:
>
> (a) A military commander or person effectively acting as a military commander shall be criminally responsible for crimes within the jurisdiction of the Court committed by forces under his or her effective command and control, or effective authority and control as the case may be, as a result of his or her failure to exercise control properly over such forces, where:
>
> > (i) That military commander or person either knew or, owing to the circumstances at the time, should have known that the forces were committing or about to commit such crimes; and
> >
> > (ii) That military commander or person failed to take all necessary and reasonable measures within his or her power to prevent or repress their commission or to submit the matter to the competent authorities for investigation and prosecution.
>
> (b) With respect to superior and subordinate relationships not described in paragraph (a), a superior shall be criminally responsible for crimes within the jurisdiction of the Court committed by subordinates under his or her effective authority and control, as a result of his or her failure to exercise control properly over such subordinates, where:
>
> > (i) The superior either knew, or consciously disregarded information which clearly indicated that the subordinates were committing or about to commit such crimes;
> >
> > (ii) The crimes concerned activities that were within the effective responsibility and control of the superior; and
> >
> > (iii) The superior failed to take all necessary and reasonable measures within his or her power to prevent or repress their commission or to

---

24  THE ROME STATUTE, *supra* note 6.

submit the matter to the competent authorities for investigation and prosecution.[25]

The Rome Statute differs from Protocol I and the ICTY and ICTR in some areas while maintaining a generally consistent approach to the codification of the command responsibility doctrine.

Unlike any of the previous statutes, the Rome Statute explicitly establishes that pursuant to this theory of criminal responsibility a commander can be punished as if he had actually committed the war crimes. The statute provides that a commander "shall be criminally responsible for crimes within the jurisdiction of the Court committed by forces under his or her effective command and control . . . ."[26]

## APPLICATION OF THE DOCTRINE OF COMMAND RESPONSIBILITY

Since the doctrine of command responsibility was first enunciated in 1945, it has been used to hold numerous commanders accountable for the war crimes of their subordinates. Many of these cases came at the end of World War II. These cases, and subsequent application of the doctrine to military and civilian leaders, established the doctrine as a cornerstone of LOAC compliance in the realm of international armed conflicts. Although there have been disagreements related to the precise contours of the doctrine—as is reflected in the disparities among the examples extracted above—the doctrine evolved the status of customary international law. It was not, however, until the end of the Cold War and the subsequent outbreak of civil war in the Balkans that the evolution of the doctrine penetrated the realm of non-international armed conflict.

## INTERNAL ARMED CONFLICTS

Until the end of the twentieth century there was little legal precedent to suggest that the law of war applied to internal armed conflicts. Matters began to change first with Additional Protocol II to the 1949 Geneva Conventions. The provisions of Protocol II were to apply in situations where

> an armed conflict which takes place in the territory if a high contracting party between its armed forces and dissident armed forces or other organized groups, which, under responsible command, exercise such control

25   Id.

26   Id.

over a part of its territory as to enable them to carry out sustained and concerted military operations and to implement this Protocol.[27]

This represented a formal recognition that in some internal conflicts, at least certain aspects of international humanitarian law regarding such things as humane treatment, protection of the wounded and sick, and the protection of civilian populations from attack now applied. While Protocol II in its entirety is not regarded as customary international law, it is generally agreed that the core of Protocol II forms part of customary international law.

Additionally, in the latter half of the twentieth century, state practice enabled the creation of a body of legal principles that have evolved into customary international law.[28] These principles include, at a minimum, the protections afforded by Common Article 3. So, while the exact extent and scope of the international humanitarian law applicable to internal armed conflicts has not been delineated, the general principles of the LOAC applicable in international armed conflicts are also now applicable to internal armed conflicts.[29] As the LOAC gradually evolved to inject regulation into non-international armed conflicts, it led almost invariably to the question of whether the doctrine of command responsibility also applied in this realm.

## ICTY & ICTR

The internal armed conflict in Bosnia generated the seminal treatment of command responsibility in the context of non-international armed conflict. In its Celebici decision, the ICTY for the first time addressed the application of the doctrine to this realm of armed conflict.[30] In its *Tadic* opinion, the ICTY extended individual criminal responsibility to the realm of non-international armed conflict. That court built upon that extension in *Celebici*, which involved the prosecution of four individuals for various serious violations of international humanitarian law relating to the mistreatment and killing of prisoners of war at the Celebici

---

27     Protocol Additional to the Geneva Conventions of 12 August 1949, and Relating to the Protection of Victims of Non-International Armed Conflicts (Protocol II), 8 June 1977, Part 1, Article 1.

28     EVE LAHAYE, WAR CRIMES IN INTERNAL ARMED CONFLICTS 74 (2008).

29     *Id.*

30     *See* Prosecutor v. Delalic *et al.*, Case No. IT-96-21-T (Nov. 16, 1998), *available at* http://www.un.org/icty/celebici/trialc2/judgement/cel-tj981116e.pdf.

prison camp.[31] Two of the defendants, Zdravko Mucic and Zenjnil Delali, were responsible for the operation the prison camp, and they held positions of authority over the guards at the camp.

In assessing their liability, the ICTY was required to determine if command responsibility applied in the context of non-international armed conflict, and if so, whether liability could be imposed on both civilian and military leaders based on both *de facto* as well as *de jure* command relationships between the superior and the subordinates. The tribunal ultimately determined that the principle of superior responsibility could be applicable so long as the superior has effective control over the persons committing the underlying violations of international law.[32] If the predicate is established that the subordinates were engaged in violations of international humanitarian law and if all of the elements of command responsibility are met, military and civilian leaders can be held criminally liable for those offenses. In this case, the tribunal ultimately found both of these officers criminally liable for violations committed by forces under their supervision and control.

The tribunal's holding was a clear application of the command responsibility doctrine to an internal armed conflict. Several other cases heard by the ICTY have followed the *Celebici* approach, imposing criminal liability on both civilian and military officials. Likewise, in the ICTR, the tribunal was required on a number if occasions to apply the doctrine of command responsibility.

This extension of command responsibility to non-international armed conflicts was subsequently adopted by the ICTR. Unlike the former Yugoslavia, the conflict in Rwanda that spawned the ICTR was unquestionably purely internal. The government and rebel forces engaged in a vicious armed struggle largely along ethnic lines that raged for several months. After the end of the hostilities, an international tribunal was established to prosecute those who engaged in serious violations of the law of war. As noted above, the authorizing statute codified the doctrine of command responsibility in language identical to the ICTY statute. And like the ICTY, the ICTR has had occasion to adjudicate cases that involved this doctrine.

---

31     *Id.* at ¶ 3.

32     *Id.* at ¶ 378.

One such example is the case against Jean Paul Akayesu. Akayesu was a bourgmestre, responsible for maintaining law and public order in his commune. At least 2000 Tutsis were killed in Taba between April 7 and the end of June 1994, while he was still in power. Although he had the authority and responsibility to do so, Jean Paul Akayesu never attempted to prevent the killing of Tutsis in the commune, nor did he call for assistance from regional or national authorities to quell the violence.[33] Akayesu was charged with genocide, crimes against humanity, and violations of Article 3 common to the Geneva Conventions.

In its judgment against Akayesu, the Chamber analyzed his criminal liability under both a theory of individual responsibility and command responsibility. The Chamber was particularly cautious about applying this doctrine against a civilian. Nevertheless, the Chamber did not reject the possibility that this doctrine could be applied to a civilian for crimes committed by his subordinates in an internal armed conflict. The Chamber stated:

> that in the case of civilians, the application of the principle of individual criminal responsibility, enshrined in Article 6 (3), to civilians remains contentious. Against this background, the Chamber holds that it is appropriate to assess on a case by case basis the power of authority actually devolved upon the Accused in order to determine whether or not he had the power to take all necessary and reasonable measures to prevent the commission of the alleged crimes or to punish the perpetrators thereof.[34]

These examples of applying the doctrine of command responsibility to the realm of non-international armed conflict ("NIAC") are clear indicators that the doctrine is a recognized form of criminal liability applicable as a matter of custom to both international and non-international armed conflicts. This evolution of the doctrine, when coupled with the emerging reality of "internationalized" non-international armed conflict, now raises the question of whether these developments in the law support an extension of the doctrine to this emerging realm of transnational armed conflict. The answer to this question, and the potential scope of liability such an extension would create, must be based on a commitment to the underlying objectives inherent in the doctrine that have animated its development to date.

---

33    Akayesu, *supra* note 3, at ¶ 12.

34    *Id.* at ¶ 491.

## CONFLICTS BETWEEN NATION-STATES AND NON-STATE ACTORS (TRANSNATIONAL ARMED CONFLICT)

If armed hostilities between states and transnational non-state entities are characterized as armed conflicts, then consideration of the applicability of the doctrine of command responsibility to this realm seems not only justified, but necessary. Such an analysis must consider as a possibility the gradual extension of this doctrine from the realm of international armed conflict to the realm of internal armed conflict. This analysis of the doctrine's possible extension must also closely look at the rationale for such an extension. Such a focus reveals that the doctrine of command responsibility is a critical LOAC compliance mechanism, thereby making it an essential component in enhancing the probability of effective application of this law. Like other LOAC principles addressed in this text, it is the *de facto* existence of armed conflict, or perhaps more importantly the *de facto* invocation of authorities derived from this law, that makes it imperative that this doctrine operate to incentivize effective and responsible command decision-making. Indeed, the effective application of other principles in this realm of legal uncertainty may be dependent on commanders understanding that this doctrine of command responsibility is as relevant in this context as it is in the realm of traditional inter-state armed conflicts.

Failure to extend the doctrine of command responsibility to transnational armed conflicts can have serious consequences. In this area of legal uncertainty, commanders may be tempted to let their guard down and either allow their subordinates to act in ways inconsistent with the LOAC or turn a blind eye when they suspect their soldiers will engage in violations of the LOAC. This temptation can come not only from the legal uncertainty in which the forces are operating, but also out of a sense of frustration, anger, and hatred of their terrorist foes and from the fact that terrorists are unlikely to respect LOAC norms. If the doctrine of command responsibility is not applied in this context, there will be little incentive for commanders to control the forces under their command, and the temptation and likelihood of LOAC violations and cover-ups will therefore be great.

In addition, failings at higher levels of command often stem from the commander failing to properly prioritize LOAC compliance, respond appropriately to allegations of LOAC violations, properly train subordinates on LOAC obligations, and adequately resource forces to accomplish their assigned tasks in a manner that minimizes the risk of violations. If the standard that commanders will be held to for these failings is unclear, and the consequences commanders will suffer as a result of these failings is unknown or non-existent, it is unlikely that commanders will place appropriate emphasis on LOAC compliance.

Finally, the lack of a clear standard of command responsibility cuts at the very essence of a military organization. The key characteristic of any military organization is the establishment of a command system. This command system invests the military commander with significant authority and responsibility to command and control his forces and ensure their compliance with the law of war. If a nation's military force has no clear mechanism by which to hold commanders responsible for their leadership failings when those failings cause or contribute to law of war violations by their soldiers, then the force has, in essence, recognized only half of the equation of what it means to be a commander. The force has given its commanders the authority to execute their duties without affixing any of the responsibility on them when their failings contribute to violations of the law of war. It is here that the current U.S. legal structure is deficient.

In spite of the apparent imperative of ensuring that this doctrine of responsibility is fully embraced and implemented, the reality for the U.S. armed forces is inexplicably the exact opposite. Understanding this disparity between what the LOAC has established as a critical compliance mechanism and the current state of affairs in the U.S. armed forces requires an understanding of the disciplinary tradition of this force: the Uniform Code of Military Justice (UCMJ). It is and has been U.S. policy for the last fifty years to rely exclusively on the punitive articles of this military criminal code as the exclusive basis for addressing misconduct within the armed forces, whether such misconduct occurs in the garrison or on the battlefield. While these articles provide effective criminal proscription for commanders when evidence establishes that they acted as principals or accomplices to subordinate war crimes, the articles fail to provide for liability coextensive with the doctrine of command responsibility. As a result, because this doctrine has not been codified in the UCMJ, the United States has in effect nullified the command responsibility doctrine. Understanding this disparity requires an understanding of the extent and limits of the current doctrines of principal and accessory liability as codified under the UCMJ.

Article 77 of the UCMJ, entitled "Principles," sets out the well-recognized criminal law doctrine of accomplice liability.[35] This article serves

---

35    Unif. Code of Military Justice § 877 art. 77, *reprinted in* Manual for Courts-Martial United States at A2-24 (2005).

an umbrella-like function, applying the doctrine of accomplice liability to other punitive articles within the code. In order for liability to attach under this theory, the accomplice must share in the criminal purpose or design of the perpetrator and take some action or fail to perform some legal duty that aids, abets, counsels, or commands the perpetrator to commit the act. Because a commander would have to share in the criminal purpose of his subordinates for liability to attach, Article 77 is a narrow concept that does not adequately capture the doctrine of command responsibility.

Article 78 establishes the elements for an accessory to a crime. As in the case of Article 77's rule, under Article 78, to be guilty an accessory must know that the perpetrator committed a criminal offense under the UCMJ and must assist the perpetrator for the purpose of hindering or preventing the apprehension, trial, or punishment of the perpetrator.[36] Because the offender must know of the offense and assist the perpetrator in avoiding detection or punishment, Article 78 is not an adequate incorporation of the doctrine.

There are several punitive articles within the UCMJ that recognize offenses that are comparable to LOAC violations; however, none of these punitive articles incorporate the doctrine of command responsibility. Thus, there is no adequate standard that applies to a commander who fails to prevent, suppress, or punish his troops when they commit these offenses during military operations, including military operations designed to combat terrorist organizations.

This gap in U.S. domestic law must be filled and the doctrine of command responsibility must be made part of the UCMJ. This could be accomplished by including within the punitive articles a provision that clearly sets forth a commander's duty, and the consequences and punishments that can result from failing to prevent or punish LOAC violations committed by subordinate forces. Codification of this doctrine will incentivize commanders to allocate the necessary resources and attention to LOAC compliance. Most importantly in the realm of transnational armed conflict, a clear codification and application of the doctrine will eliminate some of the legal and operational uncertainty that surrounds this type of conflict. Military forces trained to one consistent standard, and military commanders who are held accountable for their leadership obligations across the entire spectrum of military operations,

---

36  Manual for Courts-Martial United States ¶ 2b at IV – 2 (2005).

including transnational armed conflict, are more likely to conduct those operations consistent with LOAC norms. History and recent experience have shown the operational value of abiding by LOAC principles, even, or perhaps especially in an uncertain environment.

A far more difficult question is whether it makes logical and practical sense to apply the doctrine of command responsibility to leaders and members of a terrorist organization. As discussed above, command responsibility is based on derivative imputed liability and is applicable in situations where the commander was not otherwise complicit in the LOAC violations. Terrorist organizations by their very nature engage in conduct that violates most recognized legal norms. The targeting of civilians, the disproportionate use of force, attacks that lack any military necessity, and the illegality of means and methods, characterize the tactics of terrorist organizations such as al Qaeda.

If that is so, any actions by any leader in a terrorist organization promote or encourage the actions of their subordinates to violate the LOAC. The doctrines of accomplice liability and accessory liability are sufficiently broad to account for most of these situations and provide an adequate basis to impose criminal liability. In addition to these familiar criminal law doctrines, under the Military Commissions Act (MCA), the United States crafted the offenses of material support to terrorism and conspiracy.[37] The MCA created the legal mechanism for trying enemy combatants by means of military commissions. The MCA was created by Congress after the Supreme Court struck down President Bush's military commission system as unconstitutional. According to the United States, the delineation of these and other offenses under the MCA are simply an effort to codify offenses that already exist under the law of war. There are many who disagree with this position, particularly regarding the offenses of material support and conspiracy. Assuming for argument's sake that material support and conspiracy are established features of the LOAC, these offenses seem broad enough to encompass just about any conduct that leaders of terrorist organizations may engage in. If this is so, why then do we even need to concern ourselves with the doctrine of command responsibility when fighting terrorists?

---

37    Military Commissions Act, Pub. L. No. 109-366, §8, 120 Stat. 2600 (Oct. 17, 2006).

Interestingly, the United States thought it was important enough to codify the doctrine under the MCA.[38] Perhaps this codification was intended to give the United States yet one more tool that it can use in prosecuting captured terrorists. The codification of the doctrine under the MCA may also be recognition of the way many terrorist cells often function. Because these cells can operate autonomously or semi-autonomously, there may be a danger that unless the doctrine of command responsibility is available, terrorist leaders may escape criminal liability by claiming that they were neither aware nor involved in the actions of a particular terrorist cell. This could be a more difficult defense to assert if liability can be imposed as broadly as the terms suggest under the MCA.

It is also possible that this codification of command responsibility into the law or principles under the MCA was intended for use against members of the Taliban and other quasi-military organizations. These organizations to some extent represent a hybrid between a pure terrorist organization like al Qaeda and more traditional military organizations. To the extent that the Taliban and similar entities operate under some

---

38 Even though the United States has yet to codify the doctrine of command responsibility as it applies to its own forces, it did codify the doctrine as it applies to "enemy combatants" it intends to prosecute under the MCA. *Id.* Subchapter VII of the act sets forth the substantive offenses to be tried by military commissions. According to section 950p, the purpose of this subsection is to "codify offenses that have traditionally been triable by military commissions." *Id.* at §950p. One of the most interesting aspects of this codification effort is the MCA's definition of "principals." Along with the traditional definition, section 950q states:

> Any person is punishable as a principal . . . who—(3) is a superior commander who, with regard to acts punishable under this chapter, knew, or had reason to know, or should have known, that a subordinate was about to commit such acts or had done so and who failed to take the necessary and reasonable measures to prevent such acts or to punish the perpetrators thereof.

*Id.* at §950q. This provision is an effort to codify the doctrine of command responsibility into the law of principals. An interesting point to note about this codification of the doctrine is the MCA's treatment of the *mens rea* of command responsibility. The MCA adopts a broad *mens rea* standard that includes actual knowledge, imputed knowledge using the term "had reason to know," as well as a negligent standard in use of the term "should have known." *Id.* This approach extends liability as broadly as possible short of strict liability. Another interesting point with the MCA's codification of this doctrine is that a superior can be liable as a principal even if his failure was nothing more than a failure to punish past violations committed by forces that are currently under his command. *Id.*

THE WAR ON TERROR AND THE LAWS OF WAR

type of military structure, applying the doctrine of command responsibility to the organization's military leaders is arguably an effective way to hold these "military leaders" responsible for the conduct of their "forces."

Nevertheless, imposing criminal liability by means of command responsibility to hold leaders of terrorist organizations accountable distorts the traditional interpretations and application of the doctrine in the LOAC. Command responsibility was created in large part to incentivize compliance with the LOAC through criminal sanctions. Commanders are more likely to prevent and suppress LOAC violations if they could be held criminally liable for their subordinates' violations. That is not the case with leaders of terrorist organizations because the very nature of the organization and the means and methods that define terrorism itself violate established legal norms. It makes little sense to impose a legal duty on a terrorist leader, which requires him to make sure that when his forces engage in terrorist activities they comply with the LOAC. By their very nature, terrorist operations violate the LOAC. Because the terrorist leader will face criminal sanctions no matter what he does, he gets no benefit from exercising the type of care that is expected of a responsible commander of a conventional military force—whether operating in an international or non-international armed conflict. With respect to that leader, command responsibility is simply another means of imposing sanctions and does not provide any concomitant incentives to abide by the LOAC. Logically it makes little sense to apply this doctrine to terrorist leaders engaged in a transnational armed conflict. More problematic is the reality that application in this context distorts the underlying purposes of the doctrine and essentially transforms a theory of liability based on the failure to comply with expected standards of conduct to one of strict liability. While it may be tempting to seek to condemn a terrorist leader as an "irresponsible" commander, the doctrine is simply inapposite to this context.

The inexorable outcome of a careful analysis of the intersection of transnational armed conflict and the doctrine of command responsibility reveals an ironic reality: the U.S. has neglected to ensure effective implementation of the doctrine where its application is most imperative while applying it where it is simply illogical. This analysis also reveals an inevitable consequence of treating the struggle against terrorism as an armed conflict: the need to accept a unilateral application of this doctrine. For some, this may be a difficult and seemingly unfair result. Why should forces and commanders of those forces be held to a standard of responsibility and duty which their foes are not? This result, however, is not unusual once it is recognized that reciprocal treatment by an opposing force is only one possible justification for LOAC compliance.

Many of the benefits that come from compliance with the established legal norms contained in the LOAC are in large part independent of whether the opposing force also complies with the law. Providing certainty and predictability in a conflict where the legal requirements are unclear is a significant benefit, as is erring on the side of compliance with LOAC. Imposing or accepting a unilateral obligation to comply with LOAC norms also enhances a force's moral authority, both within the military organization and as viewed externally. Unilateral compliance also ensures that the forces called to fight in conflicts that occur across the entire operational spectrum will be trained to one clear standard and will be less likely to contextualize LOAC compliance. Thus, the unilateral application of the command responsibility doctrine to a force called upon to fight against a transnational terrorist organization is both a logical and necessary extension of this doctrine into an uncertain realm.

The one person in this system who has the greatest ability and responsibility to control the conduct of these forces and prevent them from engaging in criminal behavior is the military commander. This unique position that the commander holds has long been recognized under the LOAC. Since World War II, the doctrine of command responsibility has developed and evolved as a way to recognize the special position that a military commander holds and places on the commander the legal obligation to fulfill this most important responsibility. It is long past the time when the United States should provide similar legal incentives for its own forces.

# CHAPTER 7

# BATTLEFIELD PERSPECTIVES ON THE LAWS OF WAR

By Michael W. Lewis[†]

## INTRODUCTION

Any genuine understanding of the role of the law of war in the struggle against transnational terrorism begins with an appreciation of the unique context in which the law of war operates. The previous chapters have focused primarily on the strategic level of war. At that level, time, space, and the nature of operational challenges allow for a robust role for both law and lawyers. As my co-authors have illustrated, while fidelity to the core principles of the law is a universal element of disciplined military operations, application of the principles in these contexts involves a high degree of complexity.

The student of the law must, however, always be aware of the reality that the strategic and operational complexity of law must somehow effectively translate into practical application. At the tactical "point of execution" level, military personnel risk their lives and take the lives of others, based upon instantaneous decisions that seldom allow for reflection or consideration, let alone the benefit of timely legal advice. For the law of war to be meaningful, it must function effectively at this level. To make it effective at this level, the process of translating the complex legal mandates from the strategic level into practical parameters is critical. This process involves a distillation of the complex and comprehensive legal regimes described in previous chapters into workable operational

---

[†] Michael W. Lewis is an Associate Professor of Law at Ohio Northern University's Pettit College of Law where he teaches International Law and the Law of War. Before graduating *cum laude* from Harvard Law School in 1998 he spent over seven years flying F-14s for the U.S. Navy. He was stationed in San Diego, California and Atsugi, Japan. He flew missions in support of Operation Desert Shield in 1991, conducted strike planning for Desert Storm and flew missions over Iraq in support of the no-fly zone in 1992. He graduated from Navy Fighter Weapons School (Topgun) in 1992. He has published several articles on the law of war and has lectured on the subject at numerous law schools and universities including Oxford, Harvard, NYU, Cornell, Duke, Notre Dame, William & Mary, Ohio State and Rutgers.

principles. Making this process work is one of the great challenges facing the law of war.

This chapter will examine some of the complex challenges facing international humanitarian law ("IHL") and its tactical implementation and how those challenges are overcome in the current environment. It is understandably difficult for rules drafted almost 60 years ago and last amended over 30 years ago to keep pace with the changes in both the means and methods of warfare that have occurred since then. While the Bush Administration's characterization of the Geneva Conventions as "quaint" was both politically misguided and improperly demeaning of the importance that IHL has in the current international order, an appreciation of the challenges associated with tactical execution will reveal that there was a kernel of truth to the statement that bears examination. The aspirational nature of many of Geneva's provisions (for example, the requirement that the detaining State pay prisoners of war and provide them with a canteen at which they can spend their money) have always required the exercise of judgment in their interpretation and enforcement. And it is the soundness of that judgment that has always been at the core of whether IHL is operationally, rather than merely notionally, effective.

The nature of warfare means that IHL can only be effective if it is instilled in the combatants involved in armed conflict. If the goal is to protect civilians, for example, then for the combatant, the 159 articles and 19,899 words of the Fourth Geneva Convention must be distilled into a few core principles. These principles must be basic enough to be easily understood by young men and women who may have limited educational backgrounds. More importantly, the principles must be clear enough to meaningfully influence their actions. The challenge for military commanders and their legal advisors has been to agree on what those core principles must be, and to frame them in a way that they effectively constrain behavior in an environment that is peculiarly unsuited to restraint.

It must always be remembered that at the ultimate point of execution, law is competing with a number of other priorities in the minds of each combatant. As one special forces officer put it when discussing the role of law of war issues in combat preparation and planning: "There are things that can get you killed, and there are things that can end your career. We spent a lot more time worrying about the former."[1] This is not

---

1    Interview with former Navy SEAL Lieutenant J. D. Denney.

to say that the things that can end your career, like failing to comply with the law of war, are not a concern for combatants. But compliance with the laws of war does not come from a fear of the professional consequences for failing to comply; rather it comes from a belief that the rules established to ensure compliance are beneficial for the combatant.

When one remains mindful of this important truth, one can ask important questions about how to ensure that law is effective at the ultimate point of execution where the available "bandwidth" that is open to law of war concerns is at its narrowest. How is law most effectively injected into combat? What external factors predictably influence this effectiveness? And how should this process of operationalization inform conclusions about law's likely successes and limitations in the war on terror?

As this chapter will illustrate, the answer to these questions depends upon the type of combat forces involved, the tactics they employ and perhaps most importantly the type of support they receive. The level of interaction between combat units and their support units, not only legal support but also the reliance upon other support units such as intelligence, is critical to effectively bringing law to the battlefield, particularly in as disaggregated a conflict as the war on terror. This chapter will also illustrate why combatants are simultaneously both more and less susceptible to changes in "senior direction" with regard to law of war issues than other parts of the military, such as interrogators or prison guards, involved in the war on terror. In some ways, executive claims of legal exceptionalism and the continual emphasis on the "unique" nature of the conflict and the enemy may have undermined the culture of compliance that had come to define the armed forces. But in other ways, the insular nature of the combat arms, which in some ways may have impeded the process of bringing law to the battlefield in the past, also served to insulate from such Executive Branch action the gains that law had made.

What should also be taken from this narrative are the two critical elements in the analysis of the role of law in this struggle. The first is how the applicability of core law of war principles through all phases of tactical execution—often through the conduit of rules of engagement (ROE)—reinforces the base premise of this text: that warriors need rules. The second is how this process reflects an essential aspect of tactical application of the law of war: the requirement for simplicity, confidence, and clarity. This chapter will address these issues by examining law's application to both aviation and ground forces in the war on terror. While each group faces unique challenges in how to most effectively inject law into the combat environment, they also display some common characteristics which are critical to the success of this endeavor.

A common thread that runs through combatant groups is the importance of what can be described as "understanding gaps" and the "influence hierarchy." The success of injecting law into the combat environment is tied to bridging these gaps and getting the buy-in of the most influential members of these groups. This begins by understanding the lack of understanding that is an inevitable part of human nature. It is impossible for an expert in one area (such as law) to truly understand the perspective of an expert in another field (such as combat). As the individual's area of expertise approaches the battlefield, the consequences for misunderstandings between groups become increasingly dire for the combatant. As a result, there are certain key individuals that combatants turn to when they have questions about direction from experts outside of their field.[2] Those at the top of this influence hierarchy for combatants have a tremendous influence on what that group values and how that group behaves. While rank is a somewhat reliable proxy for "influence hierarchy" in a strongly hierarchical organization like the military, it is not a definitive measure of influence. As result, the key to influencing combatants' behavior lies in identifying those at the top of their influence hierarchy and then bridging the understanding gap between legal experts and those influential individuals. Moreover, once the influencers have bought in, it becomes difficult for changes of direction at the highest level to quickly alter the combatant's mindset favoring compliance.

## AVIATION

### Pre-9/11 Developments

An understanding of aviation's role in the war on terror must begin with the strategic changes that occurred in the 1991 Persian Gulf War, and the technological developments that have happened since. Strategy and technology complemented each other in a way that moved law closer to the battlefield than at any other time in history. Although it should be

---

2   After my squadron received a 1990 pre-war ROE briefing during Operation Desert Shield that prohibited us from firing unless we perceived "hostile intent" or witnessed a "hostile act", the lawyers left the room and the junior officers awaited further guidance. A senior Lieutenant Commander (O-4) stood up and said quite simply, "You don't have to wait until they actually shoot at you. Don't let anyone get behind you under any circumstances and if you feel threatened don't stop shooting until they are all down." That was our ROE.

acknowledged that the practical value of law's ascendancy has not been without its critics, there can be little question that law is now more integrated into aerial bombardment than ever before.

In late 1990 and early 1991, during the run-up to the Persian Gulf War, there were competing strategic views of airpower's optimum employment. On one side were the advocates of the Air-Land Battle strategy, which viewed airpower in a critical supporting role for ground operations. For them, victory was achieved when "a 19-year-old with a rifle" was standing on the ground that needed to be occupied. On the other side were advocates of "effects-based targeting" who believed that a modern war could be won almost exclusively from the air.[3]

This idea was not new. Strategic airpower advocates from Douhet and Mitchell to Goering, Harris, and LeMay had all believed that airpower could apply decisive, conflict-terminating pressure on the civilian population, the military command structure and the political leadership. Not only had these older airpower advocates seemingly been proven wrong by the Second World War, their attempts at proving their strategy killed hundreds of thousands of civilians in Rotterdam, London, Coventry, Hamburg, Dresden, Berlin, Tokyo, and dozens of other cities around the globe. As a result, airpower advocacy seemed almost antithetical to the law of war.

But 1991 changed that. The development of precision-guided munitions and aircraft that could deliver them accurately from relatively safe altitudes allowed airpower to apply intense pressure to infrastructure, communications, and the military and political command structure without risking the lives of a substantial number of aircrew, or killing large numbers of civilians. This was significant for the law of war because the nature of the targets selected by "effects-based targeting" invited a much higher level of legal and political scrutiny. Most of the targets were "dual use" targets that had both military and civilian applications. Electrical power grids, radio and telecommunication networks, oil and gasoline storage and processing facilities, and transportation infrastructure were all targeted in order to degrade the cohesion and operating capacity of the Iraqi Army in Kuwait. Such targets required much greater legal oversight than more traditional Air-Land Battle targets such as troop

---

3    *See* Michael W. Lewis, *The Law of Aerial Bombardment in the 1991 Gulf War*, 97 AJIL 481, 484–87 (2003).

concentrations, military supply depots, military airfields, anti-aircraft batteries, prepared defensive positions, etc.

While the doctrine of proportionality, previously discussed in detail in chapter 2, applies to all attacks, most Air-Land Battle targets did not require an extensive proportionality analysis. Unless the targets were located in or near a civilian population center, in which case the likelihood of civilian casualties was based upon the accuracy and payload of the weapon, their exclusively military nature made it unnecessary to balance the military advantage gained against the cost to civilians of destroying the target. However, the "dual use" nature of so many targets in the Persian Gulf War meant that a system had to be developed for a large number of targets to receive proportionality consideration on a daily basis.[4] This process, and the way it was implemented, had a profound effect on the long-term consolidation of law's place in air operations and it began in the targeting cell.

The targeting cell is a group of officers, mostly pilots but also some intelligence officers and legal officers, tasked with implementing the air commander's broad strategic goals. During Desert Storm the cell produced the Master Attack Plan for each day's air operations, which included the targets, the aircraft, and weapons to be used to strike those targets. These targets and weapons systems were reviewed by the legal officer before the daily Air Tasking Order—which assigned each of the missions to various squadrons—was approved. As the war unfolded, the targeteers relied upon intelligence assessments to update, revise, and reprioritize their target lists. The regular interaction between targeteers, legal officers, and intelligence officers resulted in a mutual understanding of each group's goals and concerns, which stretched far beyond the month-and-a-half long conflict in 1991. As this mutual understanding and cooperation between the legal, intelligence, and targeting communities became institutionalized in the following years, they created a self-reinforcing dynamic that enhanced law's effective impact on aerial bombardment operations.

This dynamic positively affected law's application in two meaningful ways. First of all, because intelligence officers and targeteers effectively internalized the legal requirements applicable to these operations, there were many more "sets of eyes" that understood the basic requirements of proportionality and military necessity considering and balancing the military value of the targets with the potential civilian harm.

---

4    *See Id.* at 487–502.

This internalization of legal concerns by targeting and intelligence officers was already quite evident in the preparation of target lists for the 1996 "Desert Strike" airstrikes on Iraq. From a legal perspective, this beneficial dynamic has become even more pronounced in the use of airpower during the war on terror.[5]

Perhaps even more importantly, however, was the effect that this consensus among these supporting groups had on the aircrew performing these missions. In the aviation community, the vast majority of strike missions are flown by junior officers.[6] The individuals at the top of their influence hierarchy were tactically proficient mid-grade aviation officers.[7] While there was appropriate and necessary deference shown to more senior officers (aviators and non-aviators alike), when the junior officers wanted clarification on operational issues they turned to the tactically proficient mid-grade officers for answers.[8] The strong interaction between legal, intelligence, and targeting was particularly effective at bridging the understanding gap with this influential group of tactically proficient mid-grade officers, because the targeteers were former combatants assigned to a support role, unlike the legal and intelligence officers who were viewed as independent experts from other fields.

## Criticisms and Responses

The overall success that law achieved in embedding itself within the aerial bombardment planning process did not mean that the conduct in this area of combat was without its legal critics. In fact, the legality of "effects-based targeting" strategies was strongly questioned after the Persian Gulf War. And the scrutiny in this area became even more

---

5    *Id.* Also 1998 interview with LCOL Tony Montgomery, the senior JAG officer for the Desert Strike operations against Iraq in 1996; and 2008 interview with COL Gary Brown, the senior JAG at the Air Force operations center in Afghanistan.

6    In this context junior officers are defined as O-2s through junior O-4s or Air Force First Lieutenants, Captains and junior Majors, Navy Lieutenant(jg)'s, Lieutenants and junior Lieutenant Commanders.

7    Mid-grade officers are defined as senior O-4s and O-5s or Air Force senior Majors and Lieutenant Colonels, Navy senior Lieutenant Commanders and Commanders. These are the squadron commanders and senior flight leads or mission commanders. While rank is important, the perception of the tactical proficiency of the mid-grade officers which is generally based upon their combat experience and reputation had more to do with whether their opinions influenced junior officer interpretation of the ROE.

8    *See* footnote 1 *supra.*

intense as airpower's ability to limit the risk of American casualties made it the "force of choice" after the debacle in Somalia. The force used in response to events in Iraq in both 1996 and 1998 was a combination of airstrikes and cruise missile strikes. This same combination was used in Afghanistan and the Sudan after the U.S. Embassy bombings in Kenya and Tanzania in 1998. In addition to these very limited operations there was the far more extensive bombing campaign conducted by NATO against Serbia and Serb forces in Kosovo in 1999. The legality of all of these operations was challenged on IHL grounds, based on the claim that the harm done to civilians and civilian infrastructure was disproportionate to the military advantage gained by the strikes.

The military responded to these criticisms by developing different weapons, improving the accuracy of existing weapons and creating more sophisticated damage assessment models. For example, in response to the criticism that targeting electricity during the Persian Gulf War caused extensive civilian suffering both during and after the war because the generating facilities were so severely damaged, a new type of air-dropped weapon was developed. The carbon-fiber bomb which releases thousands of thin carbon filaments over electrical transmission lines and generating facilities short-circuits the electrical systems. This weapon was used extensively during NATO's 1999 Serbia/Kosovo campaign. It poses no risks to human beings and shuts down electrical power for hours (or at most a few days) rather than for weeks or months, as happened in Iraq after the generator halls were destroyed.

## Aviation and the War on Terror

The cycle of legal criticism and reaction that has characterized the use of aerial bombardment since the 1991 Persian Gulf War continued after 9/11. Operations in Afghanistan since late 2001 and Iraq since 2003 have received the same sort of scrutiny as the operations of the 1990s. While it was widely recognized that many of the instances of civilian casualties involved human error or technical malfunctions, legal critiques of some weapon types and targeting decisions persisted. Technology and weapon development remained at the center of the most contentious issues.

## CLUSTER MUNITIONS

In the early stages of the Coalition's operations in Afghanistan and Iraq, one significant legal criticism involved the use of cluster munitions. These anti-personnel weapons are air-dropped canisters that open up and spread submunitions (bomblets) over an area of several hundred square meters. The criticism of their use is two-fold. First of all, the fact that they are area-affect weapons means that, by their nature, they cannot be delivered with pinpoint accuracy. This makes their use on targets that are near civilians inappropriate. Secondly, cluster munitions with high "dud" rates result in large numbers of unexploded bomblets being littered across the target area. Like landmines, these can pose a grave danger to the civilian population in the months and even years after the conflict has ended.

While cluster munitions were used extensively during the early stages of the operations in both Iraq and Afghanistan, as these conflicts developed into lower intensity insurgencies, the use of such munitions subsided. Because they are area-affect weapons, it would be extremely difficult for them to pass a proportionality test when used against small numbers of widely dispersed insurgents, and as a result they have not been used since 2003–04.[9] Although they have not been used in over four years, and the prospects for their future use in the war on terror seem remote, the United States maintains that cluster munitions may be legally employed in certain circumstances. As a result, the United States (along with Russia, China, and Israel) has refused to join the recent international treaty, likely to enter into force in 2009, banning all cluster munitions.[10]

## TARGETING LEADERSHIP

Another aerial bombardment operation in the war on terror that has been criticized is the use of "decapitation" strikes and "targeted killings." While these two types of strikes are similar in that they both involve targeting individuals who occupy a leadership role, it is important to differentiate between the two because they raise different legal issues. So-called "targeted killings," a rather strange phrase considering that IHL expects all killings during wartime to be "targeted," are best exemplified by the 2002 strike which killed Qaed Salim Sinan al-Harethi in

---

9    Interview with COL Gary Brown.

10   Diplomatic Conference for the Adoption of a Convention on Cluster Munitions, *Convention on Cluster Munitions*, 30 May 2008, CCM/77, available at: http://www.unhcr.org/refworld/docid/4843e59c2.html [accessed 1 July 2009]; for a summary of the US position on cluster munitions *see Cluster Munitions: Background and Issues for Congress*, June 27, 2008, available at http://fpc.state.gov/documents/organization/107221.pdf [accessed 1 July 2009].

Yemen and the 2006 strike directed at Ayman al-Zawahiri in Pakistan. "Targeted killing" attacks occur in geographical areas that are not involved in an armed conflict. Like any other strike, they must pass a proportionality test. Unlike other strikes, these attacks also commonly raise other legal criticisms based upon state sovereignty issues and the body of law that should apply.

Both of these criticisms, however, are somewhat beyond the scope of this chapter. The questions involving state sovereignty, whether the attacking state must have permission of a neutral third country to conduct a strike on their territory, or under what circumstances such as "hot pursuit" such permission is unnecessary, must be answered by the national civilian leadership and their legal advisors. As a result, this is not a question that combatants are allowed to decide.

There is also a debate over which body of law applies. If the "war on terror" is viewed through the law enforcement paradigm, then international human rights law applies and its prohibition on extrajudicial executions would make these strikes illegal. If the conflict with transnational terror organizations, such as al Qaeda, is viewed as an armed conflict between the United States and a non-state actor, then international humanitarian law would apply, thereby permitting the targeting of properly identified "combatants." As mentioned in Chapter 1, an underlying assumption of this book and of the military forces engaged in the conflict is that the fight against transnational terror organizations is properly viewed as an armed conflict. Therefore this debate also does not reach the combatants' level.

In contrast, the legal issues posed by aerial "decapitation" strikes directly involve the creation of proportionality analyses, which is a primary function of military lawyers. These strikes involve the individual targeting of senior military or political leadership as part of an ongoing armed conflict. They include the 2001 attacks on the cave complexes in Tora Bora in Afghanistan and the strikes targeting senior Iraqi leadership during the 2003 operations in Iraq. The remoteness of the Tora Bora complexes meant that there was little need for proportionality analyses in the Afghan strikes. However, the Iraqi leaders were most often located in urban areas within reasonably close proximity to civilians, so that difficult and numerically specific proportionality analyses had to be undertaken. The "value" of removing figures like Saddam Hussein, his sons or other senior leadership had to be stated in terms of the acceptable number of civilians that might be expected to die in the attack. This analysis was based on the belief that eliminating these leaders would significantly shorten the conflict, thereby saving the lives of many more soldiers and civilians alike. Unfortunately these analyses fell victim to an unaccounted-for technological blind spot that undermined the accuracy of the attacks themselves, as well as the underlying proportionality analysis.

A critical assumption of these proportionality analyses was that the military value of the target is actually "gained", i.e., that the target is destroyed. The likelihood of mission failure was made part of the analysis and was based primarily upon the known accuracy of the weapon, given the proposed delivery mode,[11] because historically this was the largest source of error in the system. However, by 2003, the accuracy for some of these weapons was down to just a few meters, and an overlooked source of error became more important than the accuracy of the weapon itself. Many of the decapitation strikes based their target's location on cell phone signals that were reliably associated with the target. Unfortunately the accuracy of the cell phone signals was much lower than that of the weapons being used.[12] As a result, a number of strikes hit the targeted location only to miss their intended target because of the margin of error involved in pinpointing the cell phone signals. This increased incidence of mission failure caused by target location error meant that many of the decapitation strikes did not satisfy a proportionality analysis, and they were greatly curtailed.

## TECHNOLOGY, SIMPLICITY, AND CLARITY IMPROVE OUTCOMES

The criticism of "decapitation" strikes and the military's reaction to this criticism illustrate two important aspects of how the law of aerial bombardment has continued to develop during the war on terror. The first involves the continuing use of technology to improve the accuracy of

---

11    The CEP (circular error probable) is the standard measure of weapon accuracy that describes the distance from the intended aimpoint that 50 percent of the weapons will impact. Data on this accuracy is available for all types of weapons and all standard delivery modes. For reference the CEP of "dumb" bombs used during Vietnam was well over 100 meters. This was considered to be quite accurate for the aircraft and munitions being used and was achieved in part through low release altitudes in many attacks. By contrast, many precision-guided munitions have a CEP of around five meters or less, even when dropped from much higher altitudes.

12    HUMAN RIGHTS WATCH, OFF TARGET: THE CONDUCT OF THE WAR AND CIVILIAN CASUALTIES IN IRAQ fn. 48(2003) (stating that the GPS coordinates derived from cell phone intercepts could be off by as much as 100 meters).

proportionality analyses, while the second underscores the importance of simplicity, clarity, and certainty in the communications between legal officers and the aircrew that execute strike missions.

Technological advances during the war on terror have improved the accuracy of proportionality analyses in a number of ways. Not only have these advances improved the accuracy of existing weapons, developed new weapons that curtail the effect on the civilian population[13] and improved target location accuracy, they have also vastly increased the information available to strike planners. The widespread use of unmanned aerial vehicles (UAVs) such as the Predator and Global Hawk has provided strike planners with a wealth of information that was undreamed of twenty years ago.[14] The planners use this information for a variety of purposes, from assessing air defenses to improving delivery profiles and weapon selection to assessing target activity.

Because the cooperation between legal, intelligence, and targeting officers has continued to develop in a way that strengthens the law's role in the planning of aerial bombardment operations, this information is also used specifically to improve legal compliance with proportionality requirements. Intelligence and targeting have used this information to create increasingly sophisticated collateral damage estimation computer models. These models not only account for the weapon type, delivery method, and fuse settings, but also for observed patterns of civilian behavior. This modeling influences the timing of preplanned strikes to minimize both the likely civilian presence and the likelihood of mission failure. These efforts have resulted in the acknowledgement by Human

---

13    Such "technological advances" in weapons are not always as profound as the "carbon fiber" bomb described above. In Afghanistan, many bombs have had their heads filled with concrete to allow for greater penetration before detonation, thereby reducing the blast radius and fragmentation effect.

14    Critics of the Coalition's airstrikes in the Persian Gulf War, particularly the strike on the Al-Firdos intelligence bunker that also served as an air raid shelter for the family members of Iraq's Mukhabarat secret police, cited the failure of Coalition forces to conduct adequate prestrike reconnaissance that might have revealed the dual-use nature of the bunker. *See e.g.*, MIDDLE EAST WATCH, NEEDLESS DEATHS IN THE GULF WAR, 140–43 (1991). However, the reconnaissance assets available at that time were severely limited. Less than three percent of the total sorties flown during Desert Storm were dedicated reconnaissance sorties. Today long endurance UAVs ensure that preplanned attacks almost never take place without detailed prestrike reconnaissance, and in many cases they provide several days of continuous surveillance prior to an attack.

Rights Watch "that civilian casualties rarely occur during planned air-strikes on suspected Taliban targets."[15] Considering the weapons that are being used, and the uncertainties that remain in any combat environment, this is an exceptional achievement.

The other critical factor in law's successful application to aerial bombardment has been the recognition that simplicity and clarity are vital. Law is better served when aircrew are given concrete guidance. While correctly instructing aircrew on the legal standard that they are expected to uphold, that the harm to civilians must be "proportional" to the military advantage gained, is perhaps legally sufficient, in many ways it is not particularly helpful. While aircrew may benefit from receiving much more concrete Rules of Engagement ("ROE") guidance, JAGs tend to favor the exercise of judgment by those executing the mission. This represents an important point of tension in the legal regulation of aerial bombardment. Although the final judgment rests with the aircrew conducting the attack, curtailing or simplifying that judgment so that it will not be subject to the inevitable vagaries of split-second decision-making may be a legally sound choice for JAGs or senior officers to make when promulgating ROE. Even though humanitarians instinctively recoil from the prospect of assigning a value to a target that may be measured in human lives, making such assessments proves to be a valuable humanitarian task. Once agreement is reached that the proportional number of civilian casualties exceeds zero, this task begins.[16]

Critics will theorize that providing numbers or other concrete guidance removes a degree of judgment from the aircrew and may make them uncritical in their assessment of whether civilian casualties can be avoided altogether, thereby legitimating or in some ways pre-authorizing the

---

15    Human Rights Watch, "'Troops in Contact': Airstrikes and Civilian Deaths in Afghanistan" September 8, 2008. This is not to say that airstrikes no longer cause civilian casualties in Afghanistan. The report goes on to say that more needs to be done to reduce civilian casualties during rapid-response strikes that are carried out in support of ground troops under insurgent attack which has become a more significant problem as the number of ground forces in Afghanistan has increased.

16    A consensus has not necessarily been reached on this threshold issue. The military legal teams of several NATO members in Afghanistan would probably say that an attack that killed Osama bin Laden would not be proportional if it also caused a single civilian death. Interview with COL Gary Brown.

killing of civilians. In reality, giving aircrew concrete guidance proves valuable in preventing civilian casualties in two ways. First of all it provides simple and clear criteria that aid in relatively consistent and accurate split-second decision-making. Secondly, by pragmatically addressing the difficult choices inherent in combat, it reinforces law's credibility in the process.

Simplicity and clarity are critically important when providing standards for combatants. While the law ultimately relies on the judgment of combatants and the military lawyers that advise them, it is beneficial where possible to relieve combatants of the need to make such judgments in a time-compressed setting. If the proportional "value" of a target can be predetermined to be two and the aircrew can see four people that cannot be positively identified as "hostiles" in the target area, there is no room for judgment, and the weapons are not released. Without such simple and clear guidance, the individual judgment of each pilot would determine whether the attack should go ahead. Quite naturally, this judgment will be influenced by a number of factors that are legally irrelevant, such as the tone of the flight briefing (more or less aggressive), a personal antipathy toward the enemy, a concern about personal combat reputation or a number of other factors that should not enter into a proportionality analysis. When the mindset of combat aircrew is considered, the wisdom of providing simple and clear guidelines becomes even more apparent. Combat pilots are selected in part for their self-confidence, aggressiveness, and competitiveness. Air combat training necessarily reinforces the value of these attributes. Avoiding concrete guidance and thereby abdicating all proportionality determinations to individual pilots would likely result in far fewer attacks being aborted.

Perhaps even more important for the continued application of law to the combat environment is the positive effect that pragmatism has on the legal advisors' credibility. If legal officers consistently took the position that civilian casualties are never proportional to the military advantage gained, particularly where the advantage gained significantly improves the survivability of the combatants, then their credibility with combatants would be severely compromised. In the large number of cases in which the target does not warrant any civilian casualties, the significance for the aircrew of the number zero is reinforced by the fact that legal officers have displayed some pragmatic understanding of combat realities in other situations. This greatly improves the likelihood that attacks will be called off not only when civilian casualties are likely, but even when they are merely possible. The group refrain from legal, intelligence, and targeting officers that "we'll get them next time" rings far truer in the ears of combatants if there is a belief that when the target really matters, it can and will be struck.

## GROUND FORCES

### Artillery—Managing Predictable Uncertainty

Amongst ground forces, the legal oversight of artillery fire missions most closely resembles that described in the aviation section above. This is not surprising because the law governing aerial bombardment grew out of the Hague Conventions that regulated artillery and naval bombardment in the pre-WWII era.[17] Much like the regulation of aerial bombardment described above, the integration of targeting, intelligence, and legal has resulted in legal considerations being embedded in the decision-making processes of many non-legal officers. This is particularly true of pre-planned artillery fire missions which, like pre-planned airstrikes, almost always have the benefit of UAV reconnaissance. This real-time (or almost real-time) reconnaissance information often allows legal officers to recheck their proportionality assumptions just seconds before weapons are employed, and to call off the fire mission if the situation in the target area changes unexpectedly.

The indirect fire card pictured below (Figure 1) illustrates the considerations that enter into any decision to employ artillery. While it is not suggested that such a card is filled out before each artillery shell is fired, it is fair to say that each of the factors listed on the card is considered before firing begins.

---

17    *See* Convention Respecting the Laws and Customs of War on Land, with annex of regulations, Oct. 18, 1907, 36 Stat. 2277 (also known as Hague Convention IV), Articles 23–27; *see also* Convention Concerning Bombardment by Naval Forces in Time of War, Oct. 18, 1907, 36 Stat. 2351 (also known as Hague Convention IX), Articles 1–7.

Commanders are responsible for assessing proportionality before authorizing indirect fire into a populated area or protected place (NFA/RFA). Refer to ROE; seek legal advice; copy SJA, G5 and FSE.

**POPULATED AREA TARGETING RECORD**
(Military Necessity – Collateral Damage – Proportionality Assessment)

**I. MILITARY NECESSITY** – What are we shooting at and why?

1. DTG of mission: _____
2. Location – Grid Coordinates: _____
3. Enemy Target (WMD, CHEM, SCUD, ARTY, ARMOR, C2, LOG)
   a. Type and Unit: _____
   b. Importance to Mission: _____
4. Target Intel:
   a. How Observed: UAV, FIST, SOF, other: _____
   b. Unobserved: Q36, Q37, ELINT, other: _____
   c. Last Known DTG of Observation or Detection: _____
5. Other Concerns as applicable:
   a. US Casualties: Number: _____ Location: _____
   b. Receiving Enemy Fire: Unit: _____ Location: _____

**II. COLLATERAL DAMAGE** – Who or what is there now?

6. City: _____ Original Population: _____
7. Estimated Population Now in Target Area (if known): _____
8. Cultural, Economic, or Other Significance and Effects:
_____

**III. MUNITIONS SELECTION** – Mitigate civilian casualties and civilian property destruction
9. Available Delivery Systems Within Range:
   155, MLRS, ATACMS, AH64, CAS, other:_____
10. Munitions: DPICM, Precision-Guided Munitions (PGM),
    other:_____

**IV. COMMANDER'S AUTHORIZATION TO FIRE** – Proportionality analysis

11. Legal Advisor's Rank and Name: _____
12. Civil Affairs/G5 Advisor: _____
13. Is the anticipated loss of life and damage to civilian property acceptable in relation to the military advantage expected to be gained? _____ Yes/No _____
14. Commander or Representative's Rank, Name, and Position:
_____
15. Optional Comments: _____
16. DTG of Decision: _____

Figure 1[18]

As the conflicts in both Iraq and Afghanistan evolved into insurgencies relying primarily on guerilla tactics, the use of artillery in the war on

---

18   This card was developed by lawyers for the Third Infantry Division during Operation Iraqi Freedom. It was reprinted in Mike Newton, The Military Lawyer: Nuisance or Necessity? in CURRENT PROBLEMS OF INTERNATIONAL HUMANITARIAN LAW, International Institute of Humanitarian Law, (Proceedings of the 28th Round Table, San Remo, Sept. 2004) at 114, 122.

terror became more restricted. Its relative inaccuracy[19] means that it is difficult for it to be proportionally employed in urban or suburban environments. Therefore it is principally employed as counter-fire, responding to enemy mortar or rocket fire, in rural areas. Because counter-fire missions allow little time for reflection and no time to fill out cards, mentally or otherwise, the legal direction for counter-fire missions is given by developing predetermined rules for weapon employment. Counter-fire may be limited to smaller caliber weapons, or may be forbidden entirely in certain geographical areas because of the population density. In other areas where counter-fire is less restricted, the ROE create a predetermined decision matrix that is completed before responding with counter-fire. Because counter-fire is, by definition, employed in self defense, the "reasonably necessary" standard underlying this matrix is somewhat more relaxed than the formal proportionality analyses that are conducted for pre-planned fire missions. The decision matrix considers, among other things, the reliability of the target identification and verification information, the type of weapon that will be employed and the geographical area into which the fire will be directed. These factors determine the proper level of approval authority for employing counter-fire.

The interaction between legal officers and artillery units demonstrates a couple of methods that legal officers employ to effectively inject law into combat. For pre-planned artillery fire missions, this is done in much the same way as it is done in aviation. When presented with the challenge of predictable uncertainty posed by artillery's counter-fire role, officers apply the law by creating a pre-determined decision matrix, which ensures that the most potentially problematic (from a legal standpoint) decisions are made at increasingly high levels of responsibility. The mere fact that the final firing authority comes from a Colonel instead of a Captain does not guarantee that the decision is legally correct. What it does do is put the decision in the hands of an officer who has done a great deal more legal consultation and is more likely to have fully internalized the legal issues related to the firing decision.

### Infantry—Meeting the Challenges of Complexity

For legal officers advising infantry (including mechanized units) in the war on terror, the task of providing simple and clear legal direction is far

---

19     The CEP for a 155mm shell is approximately 100 meters, compared to <10 meters for precision-guided bombs. The exception to this are the Excalibur fin-stabilized, GPS-guided munitions that also have a CEP of <10 meters.

more difficult because these combatants, by their very nature, face much more complex compliance challenges than their counterparts in aviation. This is because the decision-making in aviation is binary. Either release the weapon or bring it home. Any nuances concerning the purpose of the strike or its intended lethality are dealt with by pre-selecting different weapons, different fuse settings, or different aimpoints. In contrast, the fluid situations that routinely confront infantry forces require that the combatants themselves select different weapons and determine their aimpoints and their intended lethality.

The legal complexity confronting infantry units is even greater in the war on terror because most of the combat has been, and for the foreseeable future will be, a series of low-intensity conflicts involving insurgent or guerilla activity that is fought in close proximity to the civilian population. In such circumstances, the questions can seem endless. What weapons should be employed? Airstrikes, artillery support, machine guns, grenades (which kind? fragmentation, concussion, stun, etc.) or rifles? Is the objective to capture or kill the target? At what point is the target so incapacitated as to not pose a threat, thereby requiring capture? In an environment in which women and teenagers have been suicide bombers, are the other people nearby threats, willing participants, hostages, or something in between? What else does the unit have to do before it can leave the area and return to the relative security of its base? The existence of so many complex decision trees that can neither be passed up the chain of command nor adequately resolved by referencing a simple number, a single rule or a pre-determined matrix presents difficulties for both the combatants and the legal officer attempting to advise them. Not only does this complexity undermine the goals of simplicity and clarity, it can also challenge the legal officer's ability to achieve buy-in from the ground forces.

Like aviation, the combatants' internalization of the ROE is driven by the attitudes toward the ROE requirements of those at the top of each combatant's influence hierarchy. As a combatant's role becomes more personal, that is it more likely results in face-to-face confrontation with the enemy, the importance of combat experience on the influence hierarchy increases. This is not to say that rank is not important, but junior combat officers' opinions on how an operation should be conducted are more strongly influenced by the inputs of combat-experienced enlisted personnel with good combat reputations, than by those of combat-inexperienced senior officers that have no combat reputation. For this junior group to buy in to the restrictions imposed by the ROE, it is necessary to demonstrate for them how the ROE improves the outcome of their missions.

Legal officers answer these complex challenges, and improve buy-in from critical influencers, with a combination of simplification and persuasion. Given the limitless number of potential scenarios that ground forces face, and the narrow "bandwidth" they have available for legal considerations, legal officers are always required to condense and simplify legal rules into easily understood, and easily recalled, principles. While legal officers might engage in an informational discussion on the concepts of proportionality and military necessity with combatants, the principles that will actually influence behavior in combat are much more basic. Numerical examples that relate to specific scenarios that are likely to occur might be discussed, but given the fluidity of most ground combat scenarios, legal considerations are most effectively injected into this environment through the repetition of broad principles and the use of thought exercises.

For example, "humane treatment" is a basic guiding principle for custody operations. While its repetition is one method of reinforcement, the internalization of this principle can be enhanced with a thought exercise, directed at senior NCOs and junior officers and including such questions as: "Would you find it acceptable if the people under your command were treated this way by the enemy if they were taken into custody?" Similarly, admonitions to be "reasonable" (i.e., proportional) in the use of force in close proximity to civilians are more effective if supported by another thought recommendation: "When you are choosing what force to employ, ask yourself if you could explain that choice to your grandmother." While neither of these examples accurately articulates the precise legal standard applicable to the situation, they are an effective way of influencing the actions of combatants in the field in a way that enhances legal compliance.

While legal officers always have to engage in some degree of simplification when working with combatants, there are many occasions on which the legal outcome is improved when the legal officers also employ a degree of persuasion. Persuasion may seem like an odd term to use in as rigidly hierarchical an organization as the military. After all, if a senior officer orders that certain ROE are to be followed, what choice do junior personnel have but to obey that order? However, as indicated above, failure to comply with ROE falls into the category of "things that can hurt your career," and combatants are far more focused on "things that can get you killed." This is not to say that such orders would ever be ignored by junior personnel. Rather, the combatants would merely put their own gloss on them. Persuasion is necessary to encourage the acceptance of the spirit of ROE that may require combatants to compromise their safety for reasons that do not provide them with any apparent corresponding benefit.

One example of such persuasion was used by legal officers in Iraq when questioned about the value of collecting evidence at the scene of a capture.[20] The ROE requiring such collection potentially increases the capturing forces' exposure to counterattack or ambush by extending their stay at the scene of the capture without offering any obvious benefit in return for that risk. When questioned about the value of these evidence collection requirements, the legal officers focused the combatants' attention on the operational realities of Iraq.

> How do we put the enemy out of action? The vast majority of the time it is done by capturing him. Under the current rules that are in place we cannot keep the people that you capture out of circulation unless you provide us with the evidentiary support that the ROE is requiring you to collect. So this mission may last longer, but if you follow the rules, you won't have to worry about these people again. If you don't follow the rules then you will have to conduct a whole new mission to capture them again in a month or so.[21]

Discussions like this contribute greatly to the buy-in of important influencers by directly addressing their chief personal metric of success: survival.

## Matching Mindset with Operational Objectives

Another very important tool that commanders have at their disposal for improving legal outcomes is properly matching the mindset of their forces with the operational objectives. This is particularly true in the low-intensity conflicts that continue to characterize the war on terror. While matching forces with objectives is a basic tenet of military operations,

---

20    Interviews with Capt. Jesse Greene. See an additional discussion of these evidence collection requirements below.

21    Interview with Capt. Greene. This is a summary, rather than a quotation, of the JAG's response to a push-back from ground troops on the evidence-gathering requirements.

and is widely recognized as improving the safety and operational effectiveness of combatants, the effect that it can have on legal outcomes may be underappreciated. An example from the United Kingdom's experience combating the IRA illustrates how a mismatch between the mindset of the forces utilized and the objectives sought can result in a legally undesirable outcome.

In 1995, the European Court of Human Rights heard the case of *McCann v. the United Kingdom*, in which the families of IRA members killed by the British military sued the United Kingdom for unlawful killings.[22] Although the claims were based upon an alleged violation of the European Human Rights Convention, not International Humanitarian Law, the legal issues discussed should resonate with legal officers involved in the war on terror.

In 1988, British intelligence had information indicating that three suspected IRA members had arrived in Gibraltar to conduct a car bomb attack on a British military installation there. After shadowing the suspects for a while, the British decided to apprehend them. They assigned the apprehension to Special Air Service (SAS)[23] forces. As the SAS moved in to apprehend the suspected IRA members, one of them allegedly reached for something, either a weapon or detonator, and the SAS forces killed them.[24]

The court did not fault the SAS for the killings. A car full of plastic explosives and four detonators were discovered as a result of items found on one of the bodies, so the intelligence about their intentions was correct. The court did not try to determine whether the IRA members intended to detonate the bomb as they were being apprehended. It held that the soldiers had a reasonable apprehension of harm to either themselves or others and so their actions were not improper. However, they did find the UK liable for wrongful killings and ordered the UK to pay compensation to the IRA members' families. The rationale for this decision was that the UK sent the SAS to apprehend the suspected terrorists. Because the Court found that the UK knew that a likely SAS response

---

22    *McCann and Others v. the United Kingdom*, application no. 18984/91 (ECHR 1995).

23    SAS are British special forces, somewhat comparable to U.S. Navy Seals or Delta Force.

24    *McCann, supra* note 22, at paras. 20–23, 60–62.

to a problem with the mission would be the killing of the IRA members, the court concluded that it was foreseeable that assigning the SAS to apprehend the suspects would result in three dead suspects rather than three live suspects in custody.[25]

Although it is not surprising that properly matching the mindset of the people assigned to conduct a mission with that mission's objective has a great deal to do with the mission's outcome, there is at least some evidence that ground forces in the war on terror have been placed in situations that make this concept a difficult one to apply. The form below (Figure 2) is a capture tag that is used by most of the U.S. forces in Afghanistan when taking an individual into custody.

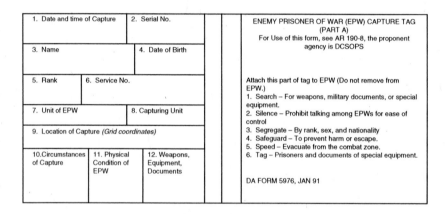

The capture tag contains the information required by Article 70 of the Third Geneva Convention[26] for the proper acknowledgement of custody by the detaining power, and the notification of the prisoner's relatives. It is an unremarkable document until it is compared with the two-page Coalition Provisional Authority Forces Apprehension Form (Figures 3 and 4) that the ROE require most units in Iraq to use when documenting a capture.

25   *Id.* at paras. 98–99, 180–184, 212–222.

26   It is modeled on the card found in Annex IV B to the Third Geneva Convention.

⭘ **COALITION PROVISIONAL AUTHORITY FORCES APPREHENSION FORM** ⭘
YELLOW FIELDS MUST BE FILLED IN, IF APPLICABLE, UPON APPREHENSION

**Offense against Civilian(s) [check one] If "Other" then describe:** _____

| | |
|---|---|
| ☐ Arson (I.P.C. 342) | ☐ Burglary or Housebreaking (I.P.C. 428) |
| ☐ Solicitation of Fornication/Prostitution (I.P.C. 399) | ☐ Extortion/Communicating Threats (I.P.C. 430) |
| ☐ Rape/Indecent/Sexual Assaults/Acts (I.P.C. 393-98, 402) | ☐ Theft (I.P.C. 439) |
| ☐ Murder (I.P.C. 405) | ☐ Destruction of Property (I.P.C. 477) |
| ☐ Aggravated Assault/Assault With Intent To Kill (I.P.C. 410) | ☐ Obstructing a Public Highway/Place (I.P.C. 487) |
| ☐ Maiming (I.P.C. 412) | ☐ Discharging Firearm/ Explosive in City/Town/Village (I.P.C. 495) |
| ☐ Simple Assault (I.P.C. 415) | ☐ Riot or Breach of Peace (I.P.C. 495(3)) |
| ☐ Kidnapping (I.P.C. 421) | ☐ Other |

**Offense against Coalition Forces [check one] If "Other" then describe:** _____

| | |
|---|---|
| ☐ Violation of Curfew | ☐ Trespass on Military Installation or Facility |
| ☐ Illegal Possession of Weapon | ☐ Photographing/Surveilling Military Installation or Facility |
| ☐ Assault/Attack on Coalition Forces | ☐ Obstructing Performance of Military Mission |
| ☐ Theft of Coalition Force Property | ☐ Other |

| Apprehending Unit: | Location Grid: | |
|---|---|---|
| Date of Incident: (D/M/Y)  /  /  to  /  / | Time of Incident: ___ hrs to | Date of Report: (D/M/Y)  /  /    Time of Report: ___ hrs |

| | |
|---|---|
| Detainee # _____ | Key Connected Person: ☐ Victim ☐ Witness |
| Last Name: | Last Name: |
| First Name:    Given Name: | First Name:    Given Name: |
| Hair Color:    Scars/Tattoos/Deformities: | Hair Color:    Scars/Tattoos/Deformities: |
| Eye-Color:   Weight: ___ lb   Height: ___ in | Eye-Color:   Weight: ___ lb   Height: ___ in |
| Address: | Address: |
| Place of Birth: | Place of Birth: |
| Ethn/Tribe/Sect:   Sex: ☐ M ☐ F   Phone#:   DOB D/M/Y:   ☐ Mobile ☐ Regular | Ethn/Tribe/Sect:   Sex: ☐ M ☐ F   Phone#:   DOB D/M/Y:   ☐ Mobile ☐ Regular |
| ☐ Passport ☐ Dr. license ☐ Other (specify)   Document #: | ☐ Passport ☐ Dr. license ☐ Other (specify)   Document #: |

Total Number of Persons Involved ___ (list names/identifying info on reverse under "Additional Helpful Information")

| ☐ Vehicle Information | Vehicle Number ___ of ___ Vehicle(s) | Owner: |
|---|---|---|
| Make: | Color:   VIN: | |
| Model: | Type:   Plate No.: | Number of People in Vehicle: |
| Year: | Names of People in Vehicle: | |
| Contraband/Weapons in Vehicle: | | |

| ☐ Property/Contraband   ☐ Weapon | Photo Taken of Suspect with Weapon/Contraband: Yes/ No |
|---|---|
| Type:   Model: | Color/Caliber: |
| Serial No.:   Quantity:   Make: | Receipt Provided to Owner: Yes/ No |
| Other Details:   Where Found: | Owner: |

| Name of Assisting Interpreter: | Email, Phone, or Contact Info: |
|---|---|

| Detaining Soldier's Name (Print):    Last, First MI | Supervising Officer's Name (Print):    Last, First MI |
|---|---|
| Signature: | Signature: |
| Email: | Email: |
| Unit Phone:   Date:  /  / | Unit Phone:   Date:  /  / |

○     COALITION PROVISIONAL AUTHORITY FORCES APPREHENSION FORM     ○

Why was this person detained?
_____
_____
_____
_____

Who witnessed this person being detained or the reason for detention? Give names, contact numbers, addresses.
_____
_____
_____
_____
_____
_____
_____

How was this person traveling (car, bus, on foot)?
_____
_____

Who was with this person?
_____
_____

What weapons was this person carrying?
_____
_____

What contraband was this person carrying?
_____
_____

What other weapons were seized?
_____
_____

What other information did you get from this person?
_____
_____

Additional Helpful Information:
_____
_____

The most troubling aspect of these forms is their striking similarity to a police report, and what that similarity implies about the (lack of) clarity of purpose that ground forces may carry into their missions. As discussed above, evidence collection to support continued detentions may be a necessary task in counterinsurgency/counterterrorism operations because it represents the best way to incapacitate insurgents/terrorists.

However, to the extent that such requirements represent a shift in mission objectives, it is both operationally and legally important to examine the mindset of the units being used for this task.

The *McCann* example illustrates one way in which a striking mismatch between mindset and objectives can go wrong, but even more subtle mismatches or changes have their costs in terms of operational readiness and less than desirable outcomes. When a broad range of forces are tasked with evidence collection a predictable result occurs. Those units that are more highly trained in personal combat generally do a less thorough job of evidence gathering than units whose expertise lies elsewhere.[27] If a broad range of forces continues to be used for such operations, two things can occur. The more "kinetic" forces may continue to produce less complete evidentiary reports, which will presumably lead to fewer long-term detentions, or those forces may get better at producing these reports because they spend more time working on them. Although this second result may seem positive, it comes at a price to operational readiness that should be considered.

Because fractions of a second matter in personal combat, and often represent the difference between winning and losing, between living and dying, forces that engage in such combat have constant training requirements.[28] The time required for such forces to learn to improve their evidence-collection procedures would likely come at a price in combat readiness. This price will not be quantifiable, and will likely be minimal if this proves to be a short-term change in the way forces are utilized. But if the changing nature of the conflict anticipates a need for long-term improvement in evidence gathering and report-writing, then a careful consideration of the type of unit assigned to these operations should be undertaken.

---

27  The apprehension forms produced by the "Stryker" Brigades conducting custody operations in Iraq have tended to be less thorough than those produced by field artillery or other less "kinetic" units. Interviews with Capt. Greene.

28  In air-to-air "personal" combat training (1 v 1 dogfighting), the pilot that had the received the most recent intense 1 v 1 training usually performed much better than his experience or aircraft type would have predicted. It was generally agreed that recent 1 v 1 training significantly improved the split-second recognition and reaction process that makes for a successful engagement. This is almost certainly true for ground forces engaged in house-to-house operations in a generally hostile environment.

## CONCLUSIONS

For IHL to be effective, it must be successfully translated from words on paper into core beliefs and principles that alter behavior on the battlefield. In prosecuting the war on terror the United States military has stayed true to its core belief that, in addition to obeying the laws of war, it has a duty to continually improve the civilian outcome of clashes between U.S. forces and the combatant groups it targets. Technology has been an important tool in pursuing this goal. By creating weapons that minimize the effects on civilians and civilian infrastructure, and by greatly improving the information flow on the battlefield, the military has consistently acted on the underlying belief that it has a legal obligation to use available technology to improve the civilian outcomes of war-making.

But an even more important tool in furthering this goal is the mindset of individual combatants, and their *belief* in the value of the restrictions placed upon them by the ROE. It is the first task of legal officers to communicate the core principles of IHL in a manner that increases the likelihood that combatants will *believe* in these restrictions and guidelines rather than just accept them. This is done most effectively by tailoring the message to the right audience, those at the top of the influence hierarchy, and enlisting the aid of other combat support specialties (such as intelligence and targeting) in addressing the target audience's chief concerns.

# INDEX

Abu Ghraib, interrogation and treatment of
detainees, 150–152
Accountability of commanders for
subordinates' misconduct, 187–208
accomplice liability and accessory
liability, 190
Additional Protocol I, 192
Additional Protocol II, 198–199
Akayesu, Jean Paul, 201
Balkans, 198
*Celebici* decision, 199–200
*de facto* command, 188, 200, 202
*de jure* command, 188, 200
derivative imputed liability, 191
direct liability, 189–190
historical perspectives on commander
responsibility for LOAC
violations, 192
imputed liability of commanders for war
crimes committed by soldiers.
*See* Command responsibility doctrine
International Criminal Court (ICC), 197
*mens rea* and *actus reus,* 191–192
Rome Statute, 197–198
strict vicarious liability, 190–191
transnational armed conflicts (TACs),
202–208
Tutsis, genocide, 201
unilateral application of command
responsibility doctrine, need for,
207–208
Yamashita, General, 193–194
*See also* Command responsibility doctrine
Addington, David, 141
Additional Protocols I and II, 50 n 29, 52, 82,
108, 115, 135, 155, 171, 173–174,
181–182
accountability of commanders for
subordinates' misconduct, 192,
195–199
direct or active participation of civilians in
hostilities, 78
ratification by U.S., 75 n 17, 77

Additional Protocols I and II (*cont.*)
revolving door effect, civilians participating
in conflict, 79
status of combatants, 88–89
status of detainees, determination, 88
Administrative Review Boards (ARBs), 108
Aerial bombardment operations. See
Aviation
Aimpoints, artillery, 226
Air Force, multi-service regulation,
designated as Army Regulation (AR)
190–8, 90–91
Air-land battles. See Aviation
Airpower. See Aviation
Akayesu, Jean Paul, 201
Al Maqaleh v. Gates, 117, 121
Al Qahtani, Mohammed, 144
Al-Harethi, Qaed Salim Sinan, 217
Alien occupation, fights against,
71 n 11, 75, 77 n 19
Al-Zawahiri, Ayman, 218
American citizen fighting for Taliban,
detention of, 103–104, 106, 116
American Civil War, Lieber Code, 38, 40, 82,
126–127, 131
"Anticipated" advantage of attack, 60
Antipersonnel weapons, 43, 216–217
API and APII. See Additional
Protocols I and II
Appearance of accused at trial, 183–184
"Applicable in armed conflicts," 2 n 2
Applicable law, 1–36
See also Law of Armed Conflict (LOAC);
Law of War
Approval authority, targeting of persons and
property, 62
AR 190–8
capture tag, use of, 230
detention of combatants, 90–92
interrogation and treatment of detainees,
133–135, 147, 152–153
Area-affect weapons, 217
Army Regulation (AR) 190–8. See AR 190-8

THE WAR ON TERROR AND THE LAWS OF WAR

**THE WAR ON TERROR AND THE LAWS OF WAR**

THE WAR ON TERROR AND THE LAWS OF WAR

THE WAR ON TERROR AND THE LAWS OF WAR